Urban Schooling
Theory and Practice

Leslie Bash
David Coulby
Crispin Jones

HOLT, RINEHART AND WINSTON
London · New York · Sydney · Toronto

Holt, Rinehart and Winston Ltd: 1 St Anne's Road.
Eastbourne, East Sussex BN21 3UN

W 32488 (1) /595.38)

British Library Cataloguing in Publication Data

Bash, Leslie
  Urban schooling: theory and practice.
  1. Education, Urban—Great Britain
  I. Title   II. Coulby, David   III. Jones, Crispin
  370.19′348′0941   LC5136.G7

ISBN 0–03–910609–8

Typeset by Inforum Ltd, Portsmouth
Printed in Great Britain by Biddles of Guildford Ltd.

Last digit is print number: 9 8 7 6 5 4 3 2 1

Contents

Introduction

This book is intended as an introduction to urban education in the UK. It suggests some theoretical approaches to the subject and attempts to apply them to some important issues. In this introduction we will briefly explain why these approaches and subjects were chosen and not others.

The first two chapters introduce the subject, first through a brief survey of the historical background and secondly through an overview of social theories which have been used to understand the processes of urbanisation and the conditions of urbanism. It is in Chapter 2 that the approaches of urban social theorists are examined. The authors consider these approaches offer a more critical insight into the institutions and processes of urban education than one based exclusively on history. In Chapter 3, a brief indication of the relevance of these approaches to the subject of urban schooling is outlined, before the important educational issues are examined in the succeeding chapters.

Important contemporary issues in urban education are considered in the subsequent chapters of the book: these include ideology and social control, education for a multicultural society, children perceived to have special needs, the relationship between school and work, and current positive developments in urban education. It could be asked why certain themes are omitted from this list. Surely, for instance, curricular issues are crucial to schooling in cities. While we entirely endorse this opinion, we do not consider it possible any longer to examine curriculur issues outside, for example, the context of multi-cultural education and the relationship between school and work. Hence, although the curriculum receives no separate treatment, it is considered in some detail in Chapters 4 and 6, as well as in Chapter 8. Other issues that might, in a more extended treatment, have provided main headings, such as bilingualism, disruptive behaviour or the con-trol of urban schools, are also similarly dealt with in the course of the chapters, each of which covers a wide range of issues.

One approach to urban education that is not examined in great detail in this book is that developed in comparative education. It would be possible to make comparisons between the difficulties and policies in educating children in cities in the various countries of the EEC, say, or between the UK and USA. The experience of the cities of Eastern Europe could also be examined. The rapid urbanisation of the cities of the Third World and the related difficulties in providing schooling would also be of central concern. At a more theoretical level a comparative approach would help to understand the patterns of international migration associated with rapid urbanisation and the new international division of labour. These elements could be related to patterns of growth and recession in the international capitalist economy. Comparativists have rarely approached urban education from this position. However, such an approach would offer a firm theoretical frame for understanding issues in multicultural education and the relationship between the performance of different groups in schools and their subsequent position in the urban labour market. The EEC's policy directive on mother-tongue teaching, for instance, or the US federal intervention in policies for educating bilingual children, might be illuminated by this type of theoretical understanding. The authors are currently attempting to develop such an international approach to urban education.

Urban education, as is explained in Chapter 3, consists of both a set of theoretical approaches and a range of specific (if not exclusive) issues. In this book we have sought to initiate an understanding of the current issues of school practice through theory. But theory itself needs to be reviewed through engagement with practice. This cannot be achieved simply through hit-and-run research into urban schools where pupils and teachers are subjects of investigation rather than collaborators in the process. Action research attempts to engage the subjects of research in the process of investigation, to feed back to them the results of the inquiry and to engage with them in discussion of what consequences should follow from it. These consequences may entail changes in practice but they must also involve the active reformulation of theory.

We would like to thank the editors (R. White and D. Brockington) and publishers (Routledge & Kegan Paul) of *Tales Out of School* for permission to print the quotations from pupils which enliven our text, and Angela Grusell for first drawing our attention to the poem quoted in Chapter 5. Our thanks are also due to all those pupils, teachers, students, colleagues and friends with whom we have discussed the subjects considered in the volume. We have all learnt much from the students who have followed the MA course in Education in Multicultural Urban Areas at the London Institute of Education. Our special thanks go to those students who generously agreed to discuss with us the contents of this book for which, of course, we accept total responsibility, including any errors or omissions. Dorothy Vernon typed the text with meticulousness and much patience for our revisions, insertions and diabolical handwriting. Helen Mackay and Juliet Wight-Boycott of Holt, Rinehart and Winston provided exemplary editorial advice and support during the conception and writing of this book. Our particular and final thanks are due to Angie, Jacquie and Rosalind for their support of our scribbling endeavours. We would like to dedicate this book to them.

1

Urban development and urban schooling in Britain

INTRODUCTION

> A town such as London, where a man may wander for hours together
> without reaching the beginning or the end, without meeting the slightest
> hint which could lead to the inference that there is open country within
> reach, is a strange thing.
>
> (Engels, 1892)

Travelling by road or rail through one of Britain's great industrial cities
gives the casual observer the feeling that they have always been there.
Vast sprawling areas of mean housing, Victorian and modern, stretch
to the horizon, relieved only by the outlines of factories and modern
office developments. In the centres, tall slabs of concrete tower over
the streets, dwarfing their inhabitants. But even here in the centre, the
gloss of modernity is seldom complete. Old churches hide in the
enormous shadows of the tower blocks; there is even the occasional old
house. In Coventry, as an example of civic pride in the past, the few old
houses that survived the bombing of the war and the equally dedicated
attrition of the planners, have been carefully dismantled and rebuilt
along one street of oak beams and boutiques. Such gestures merely
trivialise the continuity of our urban history. Equally noticeable in the
areas surrounding the historic cores of cities, are relics of the past that
remain amidst the cheerless redevelopments of recent years. Among
these relics the urban schools are often the most obvious, from the red
brick 'three deckers' of the old school boards to the cottage-style
primary schools of the progressive educationists of the first half of this
century.

Schooling and urbanism have indeed a long history. The first
movement of agricultural people into towns in the third millenium BC
was accompanied by the setting up of learning institutions which we
may call schools, designed to train people in the new tools of urban
government and control, namely organised religion and accounting,
practised through the new invention of writing. This was an education

for the new urban elite and it remained an elite activity for millennia, as the archaeological record demonstrates (Kramer, 1953).

Notwithstanding this, life for the majority of people remained rural and agrarian. Such schooling as was in existence was for the clerks — people who ran the bureaucracy of government. In England, for centuries this meant the schooling of the clergy and lawyers: a society whose principal focus was still the countryside. The main city of importance was London, the administrative heart of England. Even in 1760 no town outside of London, except Bristol and possibly Norwich, had a population of more than 50 000 people.

From that period on, the British industrial city grew increasingly quickly into a form that can still be recognised. Today, as a consequence, Britain is one of the most urbanised societies in the world with over 90 per cent of its population living in urban areas.

THE CONCEPT OF 'URBAN'

However, although we all have the commonsense definitions of types of settlement — for example, village, town, city, urban area, rural area — these commonsense assumptions often confuse rather than clarify, particularly the term 'urban'. What exactly is an urban area and how can it be distinguished from a rural area? If it is claimed that Britain is an urban society, how does that make sense to a teacher or child in Suffolk or Devon?

In attempting to make cross-national comparisons in this area, the researchers for the United Nations *Demographic Year Book* found that each country defined its own urban areas in a way that made comparisons extremely difficult. Certain patterns did however appear:

1. size of population;
2. density of population;
3. density of housing;
4. economic activity;
5. administrative, legal or governmental criteria.

Although often only one criterion was used, it was apparent that combinations of these factors were also common, although the statistical base often varied. The British definitions were administrative ones which, although appropriate for certain central and local government purposes, are not sufficient for the purpose of studying urban education. The built environment of cities in Britain no longer corresponds to lines drawn on a map, even if the lines are redrawn at infrequent intervals, as happened under local government reorganisation in the early 1970s.

A more acceptable provisional definition is the one adopted by Peter Hall and his colleagues (1973) where to the demographic and administrative criteria is added a *functional* one, that is, one which refers to the types of activity (both economic and social) that take place in these loosely defined urban areas. As Hall says, they are: 'essentially places with rather special sorts of interrelated activities, and these should be the main focus of our study, rather than the structures or shells, that happen to contain them at any time' (Hall *et al.*, 1973, p. 62). This definition has the virtue that it prevents the examination of the urban in a vacuum. Urban areas are located in the particular societies of which they are a part with all their historical, cultural and economic contexts.

This definition takes us a long way, but it was suggested as provisional in that it needs a firmer empirical base. The base most commonly accepted is one developed in the USA in the 1920s and adapted by Hall and his colleagues in their work, namely that of the Standard Metropolitan Labour Area (SMLA) (see Figure 1.1).

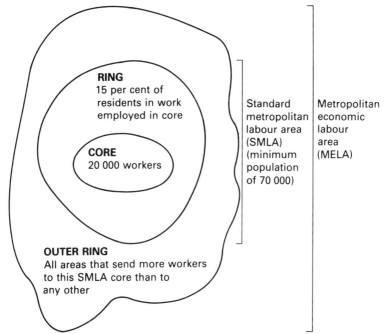

Figure 1.1 *Standard and metropolitan labour areas. Adapted from Hall, 1973.*

It consists of two main units, the Standard Metropolitan Labour Area (SMLA) and the Metropolitan Economic Labour Area (MELA). Very briefly, the SMLA consists of an area with a minimum population of 70 000 people divided into two areas:

1. the SMLA core, consisting of 'an administrative area or a number of contiguous areas with a density of five workers and over per acre, or a single administrative area with 20 000 or more workers' (Hall *et al.*, 1973, p. 128);
2. The SMLA ring, consisting of those administrative areas adjacent to the core that send to it 15 per cent or more of its economically active population.

A MELA consists of a SMLA core and ring and in addition has an outer ring of all administrative units (defined as local authorities) which send more commuters to that particular core than to any other.

SMLAs are urban areas, for it is the socioeconomic life and health of the heavily built-up cores that sustains them. Or rather *did* sustain them. For one of the interesting conclusions that has been drawn from analyses based on this concept is that the last thirty years has shown a massive population increase in the SMLA rings. At the same time the core population has declined — slowly at first, but at an ever-increasing rate in the 1970s and 1980s (Hall *et al.*, 1973).

In addition, the impact of the SMLA on its MELA is both considerable and growing, such that by 1971, according to Department of the Environment calculations based on the 1971 census, some 96.8 per cent of the British population lived within MELAs.

This conclusion is probably of less value than might be expected. If all Britain, more or less, is urban, what is urban education other than all British education? How does this assumption tie up with the somewhat loosely gathered together group of concerns, issues and problems called urban education? In fact it helps to clarify the situation by focusing attention upon education in the SMLA cores that consist mainly (certainly in terms of numbers) of the inner-city areas of our large towns, cities and conurbations. Some of the criteria adopted would be levels of educational attainment, socioeconomic status of pupil population, extent of cultural diversity, employment (or unemployment), destinations of school leavers and, in the light of the analysis briefly mentioned above, schools whose pupil rolls are in the main declining. These points will be taken up later in this chapter and are a major concern of the whole book. However, in order to gain a broader appreciation of the situation in these urban schools today it is important to trace two further elements: the growth of the British industrial city in the last 200 years or so, and the system of schooling that was evolved and developed, and in which we still work today.

THE GROWTH OF THE BRITISH INDUSTRIAL CITY

> The outstanding fact of modern society is the growth of great cities. Nowhere else have the enormous changes which the machine industry has made in our social life registered themselves with such obviousness as in the cities.
>
> (Burgess, 1925)

The so-called 'industrial revolution' in British society is a complex phenomenon. What is clear is that there was an unprecedented growth in the British population in the second half of the eighteenth century, from some 6 million to 9 million people by the turn of the century (Lawson and Silver, 1973, pp. 226–7). New technologies, enclosures and the wealth generated by the exploitation of African slaves on the sugar plantations of the Caribbean led to dramatic changes in the landscape of Britain. The first factories were established, like that of the Cash family in Coventry (of name-tape fame), where industrialists, through control over the new technologies of power generation, were able to concentrate production and thus control the workforce in a way hitherto denied them.

Indeed, we might argue that the development of urbanised factory production was closely linked with the need to discipline wage-labour by submitting workers to a direct means of surveillance. By concentrating workers in a distinct locale and emphasising the significance of *time* as a control mechanism, labour very quickly became seen not in terms of what was actually produced, or how it was produced, but rather as a commodity to be found in a factory and measured by the clock. (The implications of this radical change in productive forces for urban education are quite significant, especially when we examine the control of the behaviour of working-class children and the transfer from school to employment/unemployment. These themes will be explored in later chapters.)

At the same time, labour was not difficult to recruit. The De Ward Enclosure Acts, the Speenhamland system of poor relief, lower mortality and a higher birth rate all aided in the pauperisation of many agricultural workers and their drift towards the growing factory-dominated urban centres in Lancashire, the West Riding and the Midlands. In Wales, the new coal-mining areas in Glamorgan developed at the same time as the rural decline of much of southern and central Wales. In Scotland, the growth of urban centres in Dundee and in and around Glasgow completed the destruction of the Highlands initiated after the 1745 'Rebellion'.

These new urban centres were unplanned and in the main uncontrolled. Child labour was increasingly exploited for children could mind machines under adult supervision, and their labour was cheap. Low wages meant all the family had to work and the continuing influx from the rural areas kept wages down. Attempts by the workforce to improve their conditions were quickly stopped and legislation to prevent any form of trade-union activity was passed and brutally enforced. Such liberal protest as took place was, in the main, ineffective, particularly as events in France following the revolution made, in the eyes of the factory owners and other dominant groups in society, any protest potentially revolutionary.

The Napoleonic Wars speeded up the process of urbanisation and when the post-war slump ended in about 1820 the growth rate was tremendous. London had already a population of nearly a million by the turn of the century, but in the period 1821–30 other cities like Manchester, Leeds, Glasgow, Liverpool, Dundee, Birmingham and Bradford grew at rates from between 45 and 65 per cent. By 1851 many of these cities numbered half a million people or more, while London had grown to over 2.5 million. Indeed, by 1851, the year of the Great Exhibition, Britain was already, and in advance of the rest of the world, a heavily urbanised nation, with half the population living in towns or cities.

This city growth continued for the rest of the century, with London especially growing at a formidable rate. Districts around London like Leyton, Tottenham, West Ham and Willesden were the fastest growing areas in the country, to such an extent that London's population by 1911 was in the region of 5 million (Knox, 1982, p.9). Hackney, which had been a pleasant semi-rural area in the time of Defoe and Pepys, with a school equal in prestige to any in the country, was, by the turn of the century, a densely populated working-class area of an inner city, where many people lived lives of unimaginable hardship and squalor. We find powerful images of London's poverty in the writings of such figures as Henry Mayhew and Charles Dickens.

But by this time the British industrial city, in the form that grew up in Victorian times, was already, albeit imperceptibly, in decline. Britain's industrial strength was built on coal, iron, textiles, shipbuilding and other heavy manufacturing industries. The petrochemical revolution, which had galvanised the German, and to a lesser extent the US, economy in the last third of the nineteenth century, was not fully exploited in the UK. Only now is the scale and speed of Britain's relative decline obvious. Nowhere is this more apparent than in the large sprawling industrial urban centres that dominated Victorian Britain.

Thus, much of the character of Britain's inner-city areas was fixed by the turn of the nineteenth century. The comprehensive redevelopment of many inner-city areas that started after the 1914–18 war and gained pace after the 1939–45 war has changed the physical appearance but not the social structures located within this built landscape. Many of the hastily constructed and insanitary tenement blocks have been pulled down and replaced by modern-looking buildings. But the new high-rise blocks, or high-density low-rise buildings, were not so different from what went before. The old working-class areas of the city in the main are still working-class areas. The quality of life for the inhabitants still compares unfavourably with the quality of life found in the more affluent parts of the city. Paul Harrison's (1983) description of life in Hackney, much of it located in modern, purpose-built local authority housing, demonstrates that the realities of life in the poor areas of the modern British city differ only in degree from that portrayed by writers such as Booth and Rowntree. Few people starve, the children are no longer bare-footed, but many of the urban poor are still living at the very margins of our society. And as Coates and Silburn (1970) demonstrated, the children from these homes are physically smaller, more prone to ill health, and more frequently absent from school as a result. Infant mortality is still very high, indeed some British inner-city areas have neo-natal and infant mortality rates that are among the highest in Europe. If teachers in schools serving such areas talk about 'inadequate' homes or 'inadequate' parents this reveals more about the teachers' ignorance of the material circumstances of many of their children than about the children themselves.

In the previous section it was indicated that it was in the SMLA cores that one aspect of this decline, namely population loss, was to be found at its most extreme. For example, within the Inner London Education Authority (ILEA) which provides education within the SMLA core of the Greater London MELA, pupil population dropped by an average of 25 per cent between the 1971 and 1981 national censuses. Apart from the obvious consequences for schools of such a rapidly declining pupil population, figures like these raise several important questions, such as:

1. Who was moving out and why?
2. Who, if anybody, was moving in and why?
3. What predictions of future changes can be made?

In order better to approach these questions it is useful at this point to examine the stages by which British industrial cities evolved. What follows is based on the four-stage model of British urban development devised by Hall and his colleagues (1973), which was an attempt to describe the process of urban concentration and more recent dispersal.

In the first stage, Hall saw urban centres as consisting of an urban core, surrounded by a still mainly rural ring. This picture fits many of the Victorian and earlier cities although few urban areas today resemble this pattern.

At the second stage, which Hall sees as being typical of much English urban development in the period 1900–50, rapid urban transport systems saw major movements of population from the urban core to a new suburban ring located in what previously had been a rural area. Natural increase and in-migration maintained the population in the core so that the urban areas concerned grew absolutely. At the same time employment tended to become more centralised in the core, despite the decentralising trends in population figures.

In Hall's third stage, which he saw as happening in the larger urban areas from about 1951 and more generally since 1961, the inner core is rapidly redeveloped. This is accompanied by a shift to the suburbs of not just population, but also of employment, especially local service industries.

By the 1960s, Hall and his colleagues saw a fourth stage emerging, initially in London, but in the other large conurbations also. The process of decentralisation of jobs and people accelerates to and beyond the suburbs and will, they forecast, continue to cause a rapid and dramatic decline in both population and occupational opportunities in the centres of these huge metropolitan areas. The consequence is that the inner areas of cities, outside of their glittering commercial and financial centres, become vast tracts of unemployment, planning blight and physical decay.

Hall's gloomy prognostications have to a large extent been borne out by events subsequent to the research upon which his book is founded. However, three points need to be kept in mind while examining Hall's thesis. The first, which Hall himself drew attention to, is that urban areas are not all the same, following inexorable lines of urban development. What was true for London, he claimed, need not be true for Birmingham or Bristol. The second is the still unclear effect of neighbourhood revitalisation or *gentrification*. Gentrification is the process whereby more mobile and affluent groups in the urban areas are relocating themselves not in the suburbs or regions beyond (the 'exurbs') but are taking over areas of the inner city which had been middle class in earlier periods, usually Victorian and Georgian, displacing their current working-class populations. Economic stagnation, high transport costs and even an aesthetic distaste for suburban life are some of the reasons put forward for this process. Certainly it is an increasingly important factor in urban life in both the USA and Britain. The pattern is clear in London, but other cities like Birmingham, Manchester and Coventry reveal a similar, albeit smaller-scale, pattern of gentrification.

Finally, the full impact of new technologies in urban structures, specifically, electronic information, control and production systems based on microprocessors, has yet to be assessed. Writers like Braverman (1974) have indicated some of the possibilities, of which perhaps the most pertinent is the dramatic job losses entailed, particularly in the service industries that dominate so much urban life (see Chapter 7).

Most if not all of the cities that concern us are the products of over 150 years of capitalistic and civil endeavour. We mentioned earlier how the concentration of industrial production into urban areas gave the owners of the industries enormous financial benefits as well as greater control over the workforce. The economies of scale and of mass production relied upon a large workforce. In order to achieve efficient — that is to say, profitable — production, such a workforce had to be located near to the workplace. Attempts by the workforce to combine against the factory owners to ease their exploitation were fiercely resisted. Such resistance had the support of the state through the enactment of anti-trade-union legislation throughout the nineteenth and twentieth centuries.

However, although labour was cheap, machines could be even cheaper. The rash of inventions to save labour and to cut costs, which were such a feature of the last 200 years, had immense implications for urban growth. First of all, agriculture became less labour-intensive, and more profitable to farm owners, contributing to rural pauperisation and the movement of people to the cities in the hope of finding work. Secondly, the rapid growth of urban populations throughout most of the period enabled employers to keep wages down because there were nearly always fewer jobs available than there were potential workers. Thirdly, the massive expansion of Britain's power and prestige (by the end of the century half of the world's trade was under British control) meant that although fewer workers were needed to do many specific jobs, there was an increasing number of jobs to be done. However, Britain's command over the world's economy did not last and industries began to decline. Those that did manage to survive tried to replace costly human labour by machine labour. The jobs disappeared; the people, however, remained and have continued to move into and away from cities in the period under examination. Since this has important consequences for urban education, it merits closer attention.

PEOPLE, MIGRATION AND CITIES

> We no longer need to bring in workers from abroad because we can find sufficient labour from deprived urban communities.
> (A representative from Grand Metropolitan Hotels quoted in Friend and Metcalf, 1981)

The three questions raised earlier, namely who was moving into and out of the cores of these burgeoning urban areas and why, were raised for more than historic purposes. The third question, which addressed itself to the future, is best answered if there is some knowledge of the past, particularly, as in cities and their education systems, this past as reflected in existing structures and institutions. An essential part of this understanding is a knowledge of not just the process of migration but also of the people involved in that process.

Earlier in this chapter it was indicated that, for a variety of reasons, factory-based capitalist enterprises grew at a dramatic rate towards the end of the eighteenth century. As has been indicated, people, mainly poor agricultural workers, were pushed off the land by landowners adopting more profitable and less intensive agricultural methods. The new factory owners, in old established towns or on 'green field' sites, pulled in the dispossessed labourers and their families to the 'dark satanic mills'. With the break-up of long-standing rural ties and obligations, the legal suppression of any form of organised protest and the sheer weight of numbers, the dominant classes in the new cities were unable and probably unwilling to provide an environment at even a modest level of decency.

With the rapid growth of the Victorian city, stronger and more general patterns of migration emerged. The rich moved out, followed by the new industrial managers and what are now termed white-collar workers. In came the new migrants, sometimes into the houses that had been vacated by the affluent, although at a high rate of residential density, but more often into hastily erected tenements. From the rural areas of Scotland, Wales and England they came, sometimes with hope though often in despair. The jobs they took were the most menial, the least well paid and the least secure. A few managed to get a tenuous hold on the bottom rungs of the economic ladders, but most did not. The description of writers like Mayhew (1861), Engels (1892) and Booth (1896) and official government reports, as well as the writing of literary figures such as Blake and Dickens, reveal the degradation of urban life both for the new immigrants and their descendants.

Perhaps the clearest manifestation of the conditions of the urban poor are found in the mortality statistics of the time. The 1842 Report on the Sanitary Conditions of the Labouring Population of Great Britain stated that the average age at death of the urban poor was 17 in contrast with the 38 years of age of the rural poor (quoted in Knox, 1982, p.10).

The largest group, and possibly the most exploited, were the Irish. Political and economic conditions in Ireland, of which the potato famine of 1846 is perhaps the most extreme instance, forced hundreds of thousands of Irish people to leave and seek employment in Britain. Cities like London, Glasgow, Liverpool and Manchester owed much of their mid-century industrial growth to the work of such immigrants. Many more went elsewhere, particularly to the USA, where they also helped build up, in the literal sense, the economic infrastructure and wealth of the nation. Some British cities today have clearly identifiable Irish communities, still, in the main, at the bottom of the economic heap.

Other groups from abroad continued to arrive in British cities throughout the century, and the process still continues. Jews from central and eastern Europe around the turn of the century; people from the Caribbean, India, Pakistan, Bangladesh, East Africa in more recent times, particularly in the period 1950 to 1980. While their labour was welcomed by employers their physical presence was not. As they arrived they tended to settle in the inner-city areas, around the central business district or around the factories where they worked. Until comparatively recently, as the Hall analysis reveals, they increased both the population and the density of population in the core areas of the industrial cities. However, a process of decentralisation of both population and employment has affected the lives of the most recent arrivals (the black groups) most markedly.

The flight from the inner cities has occurred alongside a general fall in the birth rate, resulting in a significant change in the social make-up of such areas. Government-sponsored inner-city studies (DoE, 1977) that examined three inner-city areas in Liverpool, Birmingham and London (Lambeth) showed that as industry declined or was relocated elsewhere much of the skilled workforce left as well. Those who remained were the old, the unskilled, the unemployed, and the very young. Thus, the Lambeth study found the area to have, compared to inner London as a whole, a higher percentage of single-parent families, of households with young children and/or old people, and of families living below the poverty line. What is significant about such groups is that they have neither economic nor political power and tend to be safely ignored by those with both. Successive governments, both at local and national levels, despite their rhetoric, have done little to ameliorate their plight. This includes the schooling that is offered to them — a point taken up in Chapter 3.

The picture so far described is far more static than the reality. It is possible, however, to trace the intra-urban movement of groups, the 'ethnic succession' described by Park, Burgess and McKenzie (1967) in their analysis of Chicago (see Chapter 2). Here, as groups established themselves in their new city surroundings, they were put under housing and other economic pressures by new immigrants to the core, who pushed the established groups out into another area where they in turn were resisted and so on. Much internal conflict in North American cities has this as one of its foundations, and similar patterns have emerged in British cities in recent years. It is worth noting that such movements do not occur in an economic vacuum and that while certain groups are pressurised, others — those of high economic status — seldom are.

For education in the city, the discussion of the first two 'who' and 'why' questions posed earlier, raises interesting issues. For example, the linguistic, religious, racial and economic position of pupils attending schools in the core of cities has changed quite dramatically in short periods of time. Schools in the East End of London that were catering for a mainly Jewish population thirty or so years ago now cater for a mainly Bangladeshi population. In addition, it has always been difficult to predict changes in the population structure of the urban core (for example, the numbers in any particular age group). Consequently, the provision, even during the infrequent periods when there was some extra money set aside, was seldom made.

This brings us to the third question, that of predicting future changes. One of the dubious pleasures in writing this section is that we will probably predict wrongly, yet if we are only reasonably accurate we gain small comfort from being so, for the analysis that we have made points to a depressing future, certainly in the short and medium term.

It is likely that the decentralisation of both jobs and population will continue. Few job-creating enterprises, save those heavily subsidised by the state, are likely to be located within inner-city areas. An economic upturn is likely to benefit the MELA rings before the SMLA of the older large urban conurbations. In addition, the economic structure of the country is changing in ways that it is extremely difficult to predict. Unskilled and semi-skilled jobs are in decline owing to the current economic climate (see Chapter 7). But this only masks the deeper structural changes that are happening in Britain's industrial base. There has been an absolute loss of such jobs for many years now, and if and when the microprocessor revolution does produce new jobs they are unlikely to be for unskilled workers, the group of people increasingly being concentrated in the city. This group is not so much the 'reserve army of labour' of some contemporary analysis, but more prisoners of a war about which they never have been consulted and to which they have never been committed. Harrison's account of life in one particular inner-city area (Harrison, 1983) is a stark reminder of how unpleasant life had become for these 'prisoners of war' by the 1980s.

This jeremiad does, however, ignore certain vital factors. The most important one of these is that it implies a passive acceptance on the part of the victims. The historic and contemporary record, not least as found in schools, would deny this (a point to be examined in later chapters). To state that many of the young people in the inner city leave school as potential unskilled workers is more of a comment on the schools and the society they reflect than on the young people concerned. Finally, the seeming economic inevitability of industrial relocation and microprocessor-based technology of the type that seems to be developing is not inevitable. It can be changed. It is this belief that makes the careful analysis of schooling in such urban areas crucial, exciting and potentially liberating.

The cities of Renaissance Italy, the London of Dr Johnson, and the Edinburgh of Sir Walter Scott, brought into dominant British culture the idea that the city was a wondrous place, the pinnacle of human achievement. For the rich, and the so-called 'cultivated', this was, and probably still is, true. For the vast majority of urban dwellers the reality was, and still is, very different.

THE DEVELOPMENT OF MASS EDUCATION IN CITIES

> Witness the many riots and tumults which of late years have been often wantonly, and on the slightest and idlest pretences, but never on any justifiable grounds, broke out in this great metropolis, and in many other cities and towns and places of great trade, and among the lower class of people in general; from no other cause than for want of being better principled and taught.
>
> (William Wallington, 1765, quoted in Rothstein, 1966)

At the beginning of the chapter it was asserted that schooling and urbanisation appear to have developed alongside one another. This type of schooling, however, was in the main for the children of the urban elite rather than for the masses. The development of universal educational provision in Britain often takes as its starting date the year 1870 when locally elected school boards were set up and empowered to make schooling compulsory (though not free) for those between 5 and 13, under Forster's Education Act.

However, the basis of a mass urban education system was laid a long time before that when the churches were the only real providers of schooling for the urban poor. The first charity schools for the urban poor were established in the seventeenth century in London. As one historian put it, their establishment arose from 'the desire of the upper and middle classes to establish social discipline among the poor, who in contemporary opinion were peculiarly susceptible to the poison of rebellion and infidelity' (Jones, 1938, quoted in Rothstein, 1966, p.10). Such a view was not without its critics, particularly from those who saw no need to squander resources on groups who previously had received no schooling. Bernard de Mandeville, in his famous *Fable of the Bees* (1712), was an early exponent of this view, claiming that every hour spent in school by the children of the poor was 'so much time lost to society' and would, in addition, make such children used to an 'easy sort of life, [such that] the more unfit they will be when grown up for downright labour' (quoted in Rothstein, 1966, p.12).

In the years 1816–18 there was a parliamentary inquiry reporting on the education of 'the Lower Orders in the Metropolis and Beyond'. It indicated the deplorable material conditions in which many of the urban poor and their children existed but affirmed that the poor did want education for their children. In 1834 a leading educationist of the time asserted that the sheer numbers in need of education in East London was too vast for the churches to cope with. In addition, he asserted, 'Another great obstacle is the very low scale of intellectual power and of moral feeling in the lower orders' (quoted in Maclure, 1965, p.39).

This lack of 'intellectual power' and of 'moral feeling' dominated discussion about urban mass education for the next hundred or so years. It could be claimed that it is a view still held today by some people. The lack of 'moral feeling' was coupled with the continuing fear that without it the urban poor might become disaffected. Schooling therefore had a clear aim for many of those in the middle and upper classes who advocated its expansion. As Hannah More, a noted evangelical reformer, put it, the purpose of education for the poor was quite straightforward: 'to form the lower classes to habits of industry and virtue' (quoted in Gordon and Lawton, 1978, p.52). (These views are further discussed in Chapters 4 and 7.)

There was at the same time a liberal strand in educational thought that, although equally fearful of the unruly mob, saw mass education as a measure for the general improvement of society. An important Victorian educator, Sir James Kay-Shuttleworth, writing in 1839, saw education as protecting the urban poor from 'pernicious opinions' because of the 'useful knowledge' that it would impart (quoted in Simon, 1960, p.338). The views of the urban working class on the matter are more difficult to ascertain. Commentators such as the ones mentioned would emphasise the desire for education among the urban poor, often while simultaneously castigating them for their feckless lives. Radical groups like the Chartists demanded free elementary education for all and during the Victorian period prior to 1870 there were attempts to introduce free, secular and compulsory education through Parliament. The quarrels between the various religious denominations prevented this from happening, although by 1858, when the Newcastle Commission produced its report on the state of 'popular education' in England, it was established that the vast majority of working-class children did attend school at some time in their lives.

The concern of the professional educators before 1870 (and indeed after) was that the urban poor be educated to know their place. Gerald Grace's book *Teachers, Ideology and Control* (1978) presents a vivid picture of the way in which educators saw their role, not merely as gentling the urban masses, but persuading them to see social stability as being of more benefit to them than to any other class in society. If anything, these views became more clearly expressed after the 1870 Act when free compulsory elementary education became a reality. Schools were built all over the major urban areas, designed to impress the great unwashed with the spirit of enlightenment and disinterested high culture. Not only were the schools designed to impress the urban working class, so were their teachers. Themselves mainly recruited from the lower middle class or skilled working class, their training was designed to ensure that they had ideas neither above their station nor about their station. Grace describes how concerned certain elements of middle-class opinion were by the influence of socialism on the urban schools and their teachers. He quotes one writer's warning that socialists:

> already perceive what a splendid field the elementary schools afford for that particular propaganda. What better career can they offer to their sons and daughters than to enter the teaching profession and in a discreet way plan the socialist missionary (Grace, 1978, p.17).

If there was a political battleground, it was not so much in the schools as in the urban school boards. Many of the urban school boards were famous for their strong commitment to working-class education, and the elections for places on the board were often fiercely contested. In one election address in 1858, the East End radical clergyman, Headlam, claimed that schools might work:

> above all to make them [the pupils] discontented with the evil circumstances which surround them. There are those who say that we are educating children above their station. That is true; and if you return me I shall do my utmost to get them such knowledge and such discipline as will make them thoroughly discontented (quoted in Fishman, 1983, p.68).

The battleground in the schools was of a rather different nature. Gerald Grace's claim that the urban teacher was at the 'focal point of class antagonisms' (p.31) is demonstrated by the quotations he makes from the memoirs of teachers who worked in Victorian urban schools. The accounts of daily life in the classroom, of survival through violence, parallel the 'crisis literature' about US ghetto schools in the 1960s.

Thus by the turn of the century many of the issues that concern urban teachers and schooling systems in Britain today had been clearly set out. In brief these were:

1. A concern to teach the urban working-class child to accept his or her position in life and specific slot in the workplace.
2. A belief that urban schools for the working class were generally bad schools, with unintelligent children and uncaring parents.
3. A curriculum that discouraged independence of thought, encouraged nationalism (and by implication racism) and confirmed gender stereotypes (that is, a girl's future was as a mother rather than as a wage earner).

Yet, by the end of the nineteenth century, the rhetoric that emanated from commentators on the urban board schools suggested a rosier picture. The view was that such schools had had a 'humanising' effect upon the growing population of Britain's largest cities. The Fabian Beatrice Webb concluded that the influence of elementary schooling upon the behaviour of the London manual working class was 'one of the most remarkable chapters of social history' and that the educational revolution had fashioned a quiescent and industrious urban population. Furthermore, the weekly journal *The Spectator* claimed (1903) that 'the children of London today love their schools', while Charles Booth observed the symbolic effect of school buildings standing proudly above the dingy terraces carrying the flag of education.

Undoubtedly, these views reflected an elitist perspective on urban working-class education which in the case of the Fabians suggested a conflict between an ideology of mass 'liberal' education and a desire to control working-class behaviour. (Aspects of social control will be taken up in Chapter 4.) At the same time, however, it would be a mistake to assume that the goals and practices of urban schooling were entirely defined by the dominant groups.

Nineteenth-century cities were the sites of struggles by working-class communities to make their voices heard in the context of the education of their own children. A study of Attercliffe, in Sheffield, has suggested that the difficulties involved in the imposition of compulsory schooling, of enforcing attendance, were in large part a consequence of a working-class tradition of self-help and community-based education (Parsons, 1978). The development of mass urban educational provision around the turn of the century could be seen, to some degree, as a response to and a reflection of class solidarity and conflict. Indeed, one type of view that prevailed among the urban working class was that schooling could be the salvation, not only of individuals, but of the class as a whole (a view expounded by the leaders of the labour movement).

By 1900 the expansion of mass urban schooling was well under way. The dialectical relationship between education and urban development became apparent: on the one hand, education was seen by social reformers as ameliorating the urban condition, while, on the other, population changes in the cities created acute difficulties for educational planning. Resources were needed to satisfy the increased 'demand' for education, and while they were often found, their distribution was unequal both between and within urban areas. This was frequently aggravated by the migration of the wealthy to the suburbs — taking their money with them. Following the 1870 Act, London, as the largest urban area in the country, faced some of the greatest difficulties. The child population increased throughout the period of the London School Board (until its abolition, along with the others, in 1902) rising to 880 000 by 1900. With an 84 per cent attendance rate at board schools, school building expanded to meet a growing demand in the capital.

Why, then, in view of the acceleration of urban schooling provision at the turn of the century and the apparent increase in educational opportunity for the working class, do we judge the situation in such a harsh light? One answer is that the urban school system tended to reflect the dominant norms of the time — competition and division — as well as the residential segregation that characterised the process of urban growth. In addition, the creation of the school boards (later, the

local education authorities) together with professional staffs (education officers and inspectors) resulted in the establishment of
bureaucratic control over standards and resources, without any reference to popular demands. Moreover, the new school system masked
fundamental social inequalities by implying that children needed to
adapt to the urban environment — hence, the development of 'vocational' schooling: industrial (for boys), domestic (for girls). No wonder
that when urban schools failed in their stated aims and objectives a
pathological perspective was adopted in relation to the schools, the
communities they served, the pupils contained in them and their
parents. The basic socioeconomic structure was certainly not viewed as
the major source of difficulties faced in urban schools either in 1900 or
some fifty years or so later.

So, we should not be too surprised to find that in the recent past
(supposedly a more enlightened era than that of 1900) similar views
have held sway with regard to urban schools and their pupils. Two
important government reports on education in the 1960s demonstrate
this point well: the Newsom Report (1963) on the education of
children aged 13 to 16 of 'average and less than average ability', and
the Plowden Report (1967) on primary education.

The Newsom Report had an optimistic view about the future
awaiting the children it was concerned with:

> In spite of popular belief to the contrary, technological advance —
> especially the introduction of automatic processes — is not leading to
> widespread unemployment among skilled workers or to the destruction of
> the level of skill (para 11).

The report was concerned with ensuring that those skilled workers
were produced by the schools. A major worry, however, was the inner
city. In an early chapter, bluntly called 'Education in the Slums', an
almost Victorian perspective on such inner-city areas is adopted by the
writers of the report and the teachers they quote. They claim (para 58):
'We have been careful in this chapter to write of "schools in slums" not
of "slum schools".' Yet three pages later (para 67) they lapse into
talking about slum schools. Schools in the slums, however, were
defined as those having an unusually high concentration of social
problems (para 62). Later in the report a slightly less vague definition
is given: 'Problem Area, i.e. an area of bad housing with a high
concentration of social problems' (para 559). In other words, the
definition is never really made except in the 'commonsense' perceptions of the upper middle classes. Slum areas are those that this group
do not approve of, as is evidenced by comments such as 'Gardens are a
good reflector of the attitude and outlook of householders. Here [in

the 'slums'] it is obvious that few take any interest whatever in the appearance of the garden' (para 54). Given the importance of a neat garden for the urban poor, it is not surprising that the final section of this chapter concludes:

> We are clear, too, that an adequate education cannot be given to boys and girls if it has to be confined to the slums in which they live. They, above all others, need access to the countryside, the experience of living together in civilised and beautiful surroundings, and a chance to respond to the spirit of adventure (para 72).

Implicit in the discussion is that the vast majority of children living in slums are of what they defined as average or below-average ability. Consequently, what they needed, and what it was claimed they were interested in, reflected this view. Boys were interested in using their hands, girls were interested in those things relating to what many, perhaps most of them, would regard as their central vocational concern: marriage. To this vocational end they further recommended a strengthening of religious teaching in such schools, partly to enable boys and girls 'to find a firm basis for sexual morality based on chastity before marriage and fidelity within it' (para 164).

When the report goes into detail about the curriculum, a similar range of preoccupations is to be found. Rural studies are to be encouraged, no doubt eventually to rectify the deplorable state of slum gardens, and there is a continual concentration on gender stereotyping as a way of maintaining pupil interest. Thus 'Housecraft and needle-work easily justify their place in the curriculum to most girls' (para 389) whereas 'A boy is usually excited by the prospect of a science course . . . the girls may come to the science lesson with a less eager curiosity' (para 421). The point here is not so much whether the picture of young children's interests is accurate, more the fact that the report accepts and condones this view.

The bulk of the report could be said to be loosely progressive and well meaning but a strong *deficit* model of working-class people (i.e. that they are personally deficient in certain ways) (see Chapter 6) pervades the whole. This is coupled with an acceptance of the link between what they perceive as low ability and working-class children, particularly those who live in the inner city.

The Plowden Report on primary education was much more influential than the Newsom Report, yet re-examined some twenty years after publication it reveals, albeit in a more subtle way, a similar range of attitudes. Complex statistical surveys were undertaken to identify the factors leading to the formation of the 'culturally deprived' child. That the factors tended again to be based on deficit conceptions of urban working-class children reveals not only the shortcomings of the statistical methods used but also the preconceptions of both the statisticians and the members of the committee. Education in the slums is replaced by 'The Educational Needs of Deprived Areas' (para 136), but the picture of the children concerned is similar. The world of the school and the world of the home are seen to be in conflict but the implication is that it is mainly the home that is 'wrong' or 'deprived', not the school. The solution was Educational Priority Areas, 'to make schools in the most deprived areas as good as the best in the country' (para 174).

This scheme was adopted with some enthusiasm by urban education authorities. Complex indicators of deprivation were drawn up and many inner-city schools became designated EPA (Educational Priority Areas) schools, although the added resources were never particularly great. And, as Halsey's work revealed (1972), much of the actual practice had little impact on the children for whom it was designed, principally because the attitudes of teachers towards such children had not really changed (i.e. they were deprived, came from inadequate homes, and were lacking in ability to achieve in academic terms anyway).

Many of the succeeding chapters question the preconceptions of these reports and of their nineteenth-century predecessors. Before considering specific issues, however, it is illuminating to examine how theorists have understood the phenomena of urbanisation and urbanism and the role of education within the processes.

GUIDE TO FURTHER READING

There is now available a wealth of literature regarding the history of urban development in general, although rather less in the case of urban schooling in particular. At a basic, although by no means simplistic, level, Knox (1982), *Urban Social Geography*, as well as Lawson and Silver (1973), *A Social History of Education in England*, provide backgrounds to urban development and schooling respectively. Examples of nineteenth-century accounts of urban life, such as Engels (1969), *The Condition of the Working Class in England*, have been mentioned in the text while Harrison (1983), *Inside the Inner City*, is an in-depth, largely impressionistic study of contemporary life in one part of London. Reeder (ed.) (1977), *Urban Education in the Nineteenth Century*, is an example of the literature on the growth of schools for the urban working class. Grace (1978), *Teachers, Ideology and Control*, gives an excellent account of nineteenth-century urban schooling as part of a larger analysis.

2
Urban studies

INTRODUCTION

This chapter considers a wide range of studies on the nature of cities and looks at their implications for urban education. We have tried to select what we see as some of the more important contributions from a wealth of material. In discussing urbanisation and urbanism, we are not necessarily looking at the main focus of some important writers' works. Nevertheless, we have attempted to concentrate on cities in the hope that such a selective overview may provide a context for understanding urban education. We suggest that the nature of urban social life has important implications for the way in which urban schools function as organisations and relate to wider elements in cities. To this end we examine urban social studies — geographical, political, economic, cultural and sociological — consider their importance, and emphasise the way in which they relate to urban education.

The urban environment is often seen as the focus for the major ills of our society. The descriptive account of Hackney in East London, mentioned in Chapter 1 (Harrison, 1983), paints a vivid picture of poverty, unemployment, decaying industry, exploitation, poor housing, inadequate social services, frightened old people, struggling schools, violence, vandalism, theft and racism. The book centres around interviews and accounts from a large number of Hackney residents. For example, here is a tenants' leader talking about old people on a council estate:

> At Christmas we had a little party, the man at the top was supposed to come, but he didn't show up. We found out that his neighbour hadn't seen him for a week. We broke the door down and found him dead, he'd committed suicide. He'd been without heating for three weeks because his radiator was broken, and he'd been going down to the estate office every day in the snow. I'm not saying that's what killed him, but it certainly didn't help (pp. 273–4).

The book provides many such dramatic insights into what it is like to live in the inner city. As a complement to the theoretical writings examined later in this chapter, this is a direct and depressing picture that is all too familiar to many who live in urban areas. It is necessary to place people's accounts and perceptions of their own lives alongside more abstract and general theories about cities.

Another descriptive account, beguilingly entitled *Soft City* (Raban, 1975), again presents a version of the city that is easily recognisable to its inhabitants. The writing here is often more colourful and cheerful, as in the description of the gentrification of an Islington square:

> they settled avidly on the land, taking over its shops and pubs, getting up little campaigns to preserve this and demolish that, starting playgroups, and giving small intense dinner parties for other new pioneers. They took tutorials in local gossip from their chars, and talked knowledgeably about 'Ron' and 'Cliff' and 'Mrs. H.' and 'Big Ted', as if the square and its history were their birthright (pp. 189–90).

But behind the humour here there is the story of local people gradually being moved out of their homes under the pressure from the rich incomers:

> Some landlords locked tenants out of their lavatories; some hired thugs in pinstriped suits; some reported their own properties to the council as being unfit for habitation; many offered straight cash bribes (Raban, 1975, p. 188).

Such accounts as those of the novelists and writers mentioned in Chapter 1, describe forces of rich groups and poor groups, of contrasting cultures, of speculators and landlords, which the theoretical works we examine below attempt to analyse and understand. We would emphasise, however, that in such an analysis it is worth trying to keep in contact with the 'soft city', the city of experience, with its everyday contrasts between dirt and luxury, poverty and riches. Urban schools form a part of this pattern and it is necessary to ask whether they serve to change these divisions and contrasts or rather to perpetuate them.

In the following pages we suggest a number of different ways of looking at urban areas and that these different perspectives have different implications for our understanding of issues in urban education. Indeed, there is an argument that the urban social processes under examination are fundamental to society as a whole — especially in the so-called advanced industrial societies. In which case, those issues that have been identified as specific to urban education — multicultural education, school (un)employment transition, school and social order, etc. — should not be seen as necessarily confined to cities. The issue of multicultural education is as relevant in non-urban areas, where there are few members of racial minorities, as it is in the multi-racial communities of large cities; unemployed school leavers can be found, after all, in remote villages as well as in the large metropolitan areas.

On the other hand, we might be led in quite a different direction: that urban educational problems are frequently *regional* problems. These may be regions within cities that exhibit specific characteristics such as declining opportunities for work, lack of investment in industry and commerce and poor-quality housing. Other regions within cities, however, may be experiencing none of these problems. A tempting analogy here is with the different regions of the world. The 'North–South' divide suggests that the 'Third World' has experienced some of the hardships of underdevelopment that characterises poorer inner-city regions in the more affluent industrialised countries (though, perhaps, in a more extreme form). This is discussed further in Chapter 7. In either case schooling is seen to be the victim suffering from underinvestment, lack of amenities and low levels of academic attainment.

We have divided our selection of important urban theories, which, as stated above, came from a wide range of academic disciplines, into three categories: first, those associated with notions of community, functionalism and human ecology; secondly, those derived in broad terms from Marxist theory; thirdly, those connected with the work of Max Weber, which may be broadly termed Weberian. After examining each of these categories in turn we go on to consider the implications of these theories for an understanding of urban schooling. The theories are also referred to in the more detailed examination of urban education in the succeeding chapters.

COMMUNITY, FUNCTIONALISM AND HUMAN ECOLOGY

Many people regard the city as a community or as a series of communities. The notion of community is one that was explored by Tönnies towards the end of the last century. Tönnies makes a distinction between community (*Gemeinschaft*) and association (*Gesellschaft*). Community is characterised by family life in which people participate with all their sentiments; its controlling agent is the people; occupations centre on the household economy with its tasks of creation and conservation. Community may be typified in rural village life with its folk traditions in which people participate with their minds and hearts.

The rural community centres around agriculture based on regularly repeated tasks and co-operation guided by custom. At its widest, community may embrace home life, religion and the arts based on beliefs and collaborative work. By contrast, association is typified by city life, based on connection and people's intentions, where the main occupation is trade which involves deliberate calculations and contractual obligation. At a wider level association is typified by national life which is controlled by the state and legislation and where the predominant occupation is industry based on the profit motive, the role of labour and factory regulations.

For Tönnies the movement from community to association was an historical process generated by the development of urbanisation. Tönnies's theory conceptualised one of the enduring myths of Europeans: the contrast between idyllic rural life and urban corruption and alienation. This myth with its central concept of community remains influential on urban policy in many areas, not least education. The rigidity of Tönnies's distinction between community and association is moderated by his recognition that with the process of urbanisation, the values and institutions of association are likely to spread even into rural areas:

> The more general the conditions of *Gesellschaft* become in the nation or a group of nations, the more this entire 'country' or the entire 'world' begins to resemble one large city (Tönnies, 1955, p. 265).

Community and association, then, are concepts that may be understood apart from spatial and historical circumstances. They represent the two ways in which Tönnies thought society could be ordered. But how far is it possible to talk of an urban community? Surely cities are composed of many communities, each of which is defined according to criteria that are not essentially urban. People living in the same area of a city, even close neighbours, may have little or no contact of the type that Tönnies cherished. However, these people may have close and various contacts with people with whom they work or with others in various interest groups, religious, cultural or political. Likewise, contact with families may be maintained across or between urban areas, even when residence in the same locality is no longer considered possible or even desirable. Each person in a city may have an individual contact group or 'community' and these will develop, but they are unlikely to be based only on the accident of place of residence.

This concern for communities and the city was also a major preoccupation of the writers in the Chicago School. So named because of the work of sociologists at the University of Chicago in the 1920s, this school of thought was concerned with the nature of the urban social environment. It was felt that urban social life could be understood as constituting an *ecosystem*: an environment to which human beings adapted and in which they formed ties of interdependence. It was an approach that used a biological analogy — the natural environment where animals and plants contribute to its maintenance. Indeed, the Chicago *ecological* approach likened human social processes to the processes of 'competition, invasion, succession, and segregation' in plant and animal life. In the same way that plants and animals in a given natural environment form a web of interdependence (insects feeding off plants, animals feeding off insects, plants giving off oxygen to maintain atmosphere, and so on), so the inhabitants of an urban environment form a similar web: this is the process of symbiosis (Burgess *et al.*, in Park, Burgess and McKenzie, 1967, p. 145).

The consequence of the process outlined by the Chicago sociologists was that cities developed natural areas within them where certain forms of social life would flourish — rather like the natural environment where plants and animals would tend to have their own clearly defined territories. In the city, industrial zones, immigrant ghettoes, the red-light district, could all be seen as examples of 'natural' areas. They were not, however, the outcome solely of an ecological process, for this did not explain how such areas came to achieve a certain stability and, consequently, contribute to the stability of the city as a whole. We need, then, to examine how *social norms* are generated within these areas, that is, agreed rules of behaviour which may form the basis of some moral code. The existence of such norms is crucial for the maintenance of the city as a social entity. Indeed, in a wider sense, many would argue that society as a whole is based upon agreed norms of behaviour — a moral consensus.

The Chicago School was further concerned, then, with how social order was maintained in the city — a crucial question for those dealing with such views as urban conflict, crime and poverty. This is a question that has frequently been asked by social scientists. One answer has been that, collectively, human beings have found it necessary to devise methods by which the actions of individuals are constrained — usually through norms (which may be beliefs, conventions, laws) and frequently through organised social life (e.g. families, churches, schools, police forces, governments, and so on). Social order would seem, therefore, to be based on quite a complex network of relationships between people. Such terms as *interaction* and *system* suggest ways of looking at patterns of relationships: the former emphasising individuals who relate to one another, the latter focusing upon the interconnections within society as though it were a machine. As societies become increasingly complex so there is an increasing multitude of *sub-systems*, each specialising in a particular set of processes (e.g. the education sub-system deals with processes of ensuring children learn the appropriate norms of their society, and with the allocation of individuals to different kinds of occupations).

This approach is generally termed *functionalism*. It has the merits of showing how relatively permanent features of the social environment contribute to its maintenance, that is, are *functional*. At the same time, such features are shown to be functional because they also respond to human needs. This was quite significant for the Chicago School writers since they attempted to show how an urban structure, which arises in response to the needs of city inhabitants, in turn is imposed upon individuals as 'a crude external fact' (Park *et al.*, 1967, p. 4). But it is also functional to the maintenance of social order because this urban structure comprises a number of natural areas or *moral regions*, each performing the function of controlling the various 'passions, instincts, and appetites' (Park *et al.*, 1967, p. 43) of human beings. (Paradoxically, the red-light district of a city is seen as one of the more interesting moral regions in this respect!)

We sum up their position by noting that the city was, for them, a clearly demarcated entity both as a consequence of natural ecological processes and as a consequence of the generation of a normative structure. Consequently, the city was at one and the same time based on competition and consensus. The approach is neatly encapsulated in a diagrammatic representation — the Burgess model based upon a conception of Chicago itself during the 1920s which showed the process of urban expansion (see Figure 2.1).

The model depicts the expansion of the urban population through a number of zones shown as concentric circles. Terms such as *extension* and *succession* suggest that individuals move from one zone to the next and become resident just as organisms do in the natural environment. As individuals settle within the city they acquire roles in different natural economic and cultural groupings such as classes, ethnic groups and religious affiliations.

The ecological view of urban social life is one that purports to be 'scientific' and 'objective' — discovering the way in which the city operates. None the less, the Chicago School writers did consider this approach to have potential for social reform. If, after all, the 'facts' about cities were laid bare, then policy-makers could have a sounder basis for initiating change. If, for example, the approach yielded data that suggested that one of the natural areas of the city was characterised by social deprivation, housing decay or juvenile delinquency, then it would be possible to quantify such data and use them to justify programmes of reform.

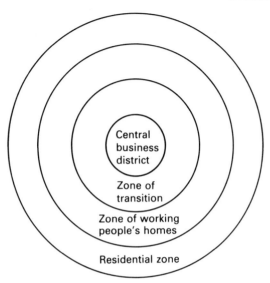

Figure 2.1 *The Burgess model of city structure. Adapted from Burgess, 1925.*

Within this same category of studies then, it is convenient to include those empirical sociological and geographical studies that either follow or have much in common with the Chicago School. Such investigations have sought to establish facts about the urban social environment through direct observation, interviews, and other forms of inquiry. They have tended to eschew overt theorising, being more concerned to discover 'hard data' that can frequently be quantified and, therefore, be of more use to the policy-maker.

Empirical social inquiry was a dominant tradition in British urban investigation until fairly recently — and is typified by the many surveys of life in cities carried out at around the turn of the century and referred to in Chapter 1. With its basis in liberal social reform, this kind of approach emphasised examination of the standards of living and the quality of life of those inhabiting urban environments. The result was that through detailed descriptions and quantification the extent to which poverty prevailed in towns and cities was highlighted. Early poverty surveys of London and York gave new perspectives on the character of these cities, influencing not only the later studies of communities within large cities (especially working-class and ethnic-minority communities), but also a subsequent group of writers concerned with the formulation of social policy (particularly significant in the rise of the 'Welfare State') (Blowers *et al.*, 1982, pp. 91–2). In North America we can find similar empirical work undertaken in urban areas. From the great industrial conurbations of the north-east to the smaller towns of the mid-west, urban researchers conducted studies of communities and neighbourhoods, and social groups such as street gangs in Chicago. Similarly, these types of inquiry, whether in rural or urban areas, are still referred to as community studies. However, Louis Wirth, a writer closely connected with the Chicago School, noted, like Tönnies, the tendency of urban values and life-styles to become universal rather than being geographically constrained.

In writing of 'Urbanism as a Way of Life' (1938), Wirth was at pains to point out that while cities were the dominant feature of industrialised societies, characterised by their population size, density and heterogeneity, city boundaries were, in fact, arbitrary lines. Modern societies were indeed permeated by the urban mode of life — villages as well as cities. Certainly urbanism reflects human action originally associated with the city, but it may well continue for quite different reasons and be taken up in rural areas; it is an indication of cultural change affecting an entire society. Critics of Wirth, most notably Gans (1977), have argued that cities reveal the perpetuation of rural values and social structures rather than the reverse.

Another important strand of analysis has been that most usually associated with geographical studies of the city, for geographers have long regarded cities as important entities and subjects of study. Many tend to understand cities as arising either in response to needs — the need for a concentrated population to serve industry and commerce, the need for centralisation of communications — or on the basis of certain favourable environmental conditions, such as the presence of a major river, easily defended against attack. The *human* geographer, above all, has viewed the city as 'an integral part of the landscape' and 'as the most significant human transformation of the natural environment' (Park *et al.*, 1967, p. 165). This transformation has frequently been seen as having an economic basis: indeed, certain geographers have attempted to classify towns and cities by grouping together those that perform similar economic functions, for example, capital cities, manufacturing towns and holiday resorts (Carter, 1981, p. 66). In this way, we gain a picture of a country that is neatly divided not only into rural and urban areas but also into different kinds of urban areas which can be clearly seen on the maps contained in school atlases.

Now this might be regarded as a rather static view of towns and cities. After all, urban areas do tend to change over time; London, for example, is hardly the same place as it was during the Middle Ages; nor, for that matter, is Sunderland the same place it was some fifty years ago. Urban areas have continued to exist and grow despite the disappearance of factors involved with their original development. Cities are now frequently *multifunctional*, that is, associated with more than one economic activity, owing to the interaction between industrial development and urban development. (In some cases, especially as a result of recession in the 1970s, there are urban areas that are now hardly associated with any kind of productive economic activity.)

However, it is not merely that the economic functions of cities have become diversified. It is also apparent that, socially, urban areas are now rather more complex than they once were. Big cities in advanced industrial societies are frequently characterised by what is called *cultural heterogenity*: different ways of life, different values and beliefs. There now appears to be a tendency to adopt a more abstract approach to the study of urban areas — one that emphasises the *urban or spatial organisation of a society*. According to this approach, cities cannot be understood as entities unless seen as part of a country's spatial organisation of social and economic activities, which in turn is determined by overall economic and political considerations.

The point is, then, that modern big cities reflect modern societies: they are the way in which such societies are spatially organised. In the past, traditional societies were not, in the main, organised on the basis of urban life — even though cities did exist as commercial and administrative centres (London being an obvious example). As described in Chapter 1, it was the Industrial Revolution that brought about the urbanised society with which we are familiar today, characterised by the great conurbations that, until recently, were the hub of Britain's economic dominance.

Many geographers, however, have tended to see space itself as the crucial determining factor, that is, space is something natural which places limitations on the way human beings organise themselves collectively as communities, as producers, and as consumers. More critically, others have talked of space as something that is *created*. Space is the outcome of social practice: it is what human beings do in the context of their social, political and economic organisation which creates relationships that have a spatial dimension. This is nowhere more apparent than in the built environment where houses, office blocks, shops, factories and highways are the outcomes of human decision-making and yet, because of their relative permanence, define the space available.

Many of the views of urban life described above, particularly perhaps that of Louis Wirth, carry with them a certain psychological model of the urban individual. Because of the complex structure of the city it appears that the individual can escape from the domination of the simple social group. The metropolis encourages individualism, which is further reinforced by the division of labour experienced at work (where the individual specialises in a particular function) and by a consumerist economy oriented towards the individual through, for instance, the large number of retail outlets and places of commercial entertainment.

One of the questions raised by the kinds of approaches outlined in this section is how far is the city *per se* a specific form of social life? Is the modern industrial city of the same order as the medieval city? Can we expect the same sorts of issues and difficulties in cities throughout the world and in different kinds of societies? These questions are of some significance for those concerned with urban education for the answers may well determine the analysis made of the issues. Our response to these questions is that it is ill-advised to consider the nature of urban life in isolation from the society as a whole. It is also, perhaps, mistaken to assume that industrial urbanisation is a direct development of pre- (or non-) industrial urbanisation (Giddens, 1981, p. 140). It is important, therefore, to take note of more critical writings which demand an analysis of urban phenomena in relation to the processes of modern capitalist societies.

MARXIST PERSPECTIVES

In the previous section we considered the ways in which urban space was created. The question arises as to whether all members of society are equally involved in creating space. Some writers suggest that the large financial and industrial concerns that developed during the course of the Industrial Revolution have had disproportionate power in this respect. The physical structure of cities according to this view is the outcome of investment decisions taken by the economically powerful. So, the decision to site a factory in a particular location is neither based upon a simple recognition of it being the most suitable piece of land, nor upon some consensus among the local population, but upon market forces and the profit motive (Harvey, 1973, pp. 397 and 311).

Urbanisation — the increasing preponderance of cities in a society — has not necessarily occurred as a response to actual human needs; rather, it is a consequence of this need for maximum profitability on the part of industry. This view fits in with a Marxist approach to the study of societies, that is, one that emphasises the significance of a ruling class where that class is composed of those who own and control finance and industry. The economically powerful 'dictate' the process of urbanisation not only directly through speculative investment but also indirectly through domination of the political process. From this perspective, then, the state too is seen as an instrument of the economic interests of the ruling class. It is the control of industry and commerce (often called the economic *base* or the means of production) that determines the pattern of society, its government and even its culture and way of thinking. These latter elements are sometimes referred to by Marxist writers as the *superstructure*. Around the mode of production there is a constant class struggle between those who own and control the means of production and those who have to sell their labour. For Marx, when the mode of production was capitalist, this struggle was between the bourgeoisie and the proletariat. Thus a major emphasis of Marxism has been on social conflict and the relationship between the economy and society. In this respect Marxism has become a profound influence on analysts of urban areas in the last two decades.

While Marxist writers in general have stressed the significance of class conflict (or struggle) and the all-pervading character of the capitalist system, in other respects there has been a tendency towards a divergence of thinking. There are those who have given primacy to class struggle, emphasising the radical nature of conflict, arguing that it is the process of becoming conscious of oppression, and exploitation, that is the key to social change. Implicit in this school of thought is that political organisation at a number of levels will arise out of this growing awareness. On the other hand, there is a different kind of approach within the Marxist tradition that tends to play down the importance of human beings as conscious actors: instead, there is a stress on the nature of capitalism as a system and its 'inevitable' consequences.

Sometimes the emphasis is on the ways in which the capitalist economy determines social life, while more recent approaches have dwelt upon what has been called *ideological* domination, that is, the ways in which people are constrained and guided in their behaviour by propaganda and more subtle forms of persuasion that emanate ultimately from class interests. Ideological domination operates in the interests of those who, ultimately, hold economic power.

A well-known Marxist contribution to the analysis of urban areas has been that of Manuel Castells (Castells, 1977; 1978; 1980). His more recent writing has indicated a movement away from a classic Marxist position and an increasing concern for researching *urban social movements* (groups of people in protest or conflict over specific urban issues) at the expense of an understanding of the formation of the city as a whole (Castells, 1983). But his earlier writing had attempted to understand the tension between the *structures* (economic, social, ideological, political) of the capitalist city and attempts by various groups to modify them. Hence the development of his interest in urban social movements, which he perceives to be the new form of class struggle rather than the traditional Marxist emphasis on conflict at the workplace. In the later Castells these social movements include such diverse phenomena as a rent strike in Glasgow or the organisation of gay groups in San Francisco.

In his earlier, and more influential, work, however, Castells had concentrated on cities as mechanisms for the *reproduction* of labour power. Essentially, the city has the prime function in a capitalist society of reproducing the workforce. In order to ensure the survival of the capitalist system it is necessary to have an appropriate labour force ready and willing to work within it. Since workers retire, become ill, or die, it is important to renew continually the pool of available labour, as well as to make sure that the existing workers are kept reasonably healthy. As we will indicate in subsequent chapters (especially Chapter 7), education plays a crucial role in this reproduction of the workforce.

Among the mechanisms generated by the capitalist system to reproduce the urban workforce are what Castells has called *collective consumption*. As he says, urban organisation is 'the expression of the process of collective treatment of the daily consumption patterns of households' (Castells, 1978, p. 16). The notion of collective consumption refers to items of consumption, publicly provided, and where market considerations are largely absent. Major examples of collective consumption observed in advanced capitalist countries include: education, housing, transport, health care, social welfare. (Perhaps one should note that the situation varies from one society to another, e.g. urban transport may be heavily subsidised in one country but not in others.) In short, collective consumption constitutes an *indirect wage*: it provides an indispensable element in the income of urban people. It is in the large urban areas that collective consumption can be seen in its most concentrated form — and it is in these urban areas, in the context of collective consumption, that new forms of social inequality have begun to appear. Capitalist interests shed some of their necessary expenses on to the state through collective consumption. This is the *statisation* of necessary provision for the continuation of capitalism (i.e. the passing of expenditure from private capitalism on to the state).

One consequence of such inequality, where some have better access to items of collective consumption than others, is that there will be conflict which, unlike the classic class struggle at the site of production, takes place elsewhere. Such conflict will be seen in the development of urban social movements where broad-based alliances of people from different strata arise in response to cutbacks in this indirect wage — an event more likely as crisis becomes more apparent in the advanced capitalist countries. Since the state is largely responsible for the provision of items of collective consumption, it tends to become the target for urban protest. Conflict is therefore diverted away from a struggle against capitalism into a struggle against the state. However, since each urban social movement is likely to be conflicting with the state over different (and even potentially oppositional) issues, they will probably be weakened by their fractures and divisions.

WEBERIAN PERSPECTIVES

Max Weber opposed Marx's insistence on the economy as the determining element in society. He suggested that cultural and political elements must be considered as being of at least similar importance. Thus, for instance, religious beliefs could help shape the form of economic practices themselves. In his book *The City* (Weber, 1958), he likewise insists on the importance of cities as centres of power as well as of wealth. Groups were able to become dominant in societies through 'ownership of the means of warfare', often centralising their control, historically, in fortified cities. To talk of a Weberian perspective is then, broadly, to include those theorists who have insisted on the centrality of culture and religion and of power structures and bureaucracies.

Many social scientists have assumed that urbanisation has produced a distinct culture — and, possibly, a distinct type of human being: the urban person. Some have suggested that it is the very presence of a large heterogeneous population that determines the pattern of social relationships in urban areas; it is this that to their mind results in the impersonal character of cities, the isolation of individuals, the lack of 'community'. Urbanism is manifested in the way in which the built environment is taken for granted and permeates our thoughts and actions. Urbanism is reflected in the patterns of communications that prevail in urban areas — the use of telephones, urban transport systems, the compartmentalised contact with a range of people on limited specific issues. Urbanism is 'fast' living characterised by transitory, fleeting relationships between people. It is a culture that transcends the specific type of economic conditions that accompanied the onset of urbanisation and indeed has spread to non-urban areas.

The point at issue is that the significance of cities in modern societies is felt not only through the domination of industry and commerce but also through the acceptance of a culture of urbanism. Urban dwellers are limited in their actions not only by the 'created' space in which they find themselves but also by the fact that they accept this space as something natural. It also means that urban dwellers live in an *exploitative* system — excessive house prices and rents, high consumer goods prices, etc. — while taking the system for granted.

Just as Weberian writers have included a cultural dimension in the analysis of cities, so too they have criticised Marxist views as too deterministic and too confined to economics. The forces that shape cities, they have insisted, are not confined to those of industrial capitalism. Perhaps greater attention should be paid to political processes, where what goes on in modern cities is the outcome of a precarious balance of power between competing groups in the urban community.

The emphasis here is on the democratic character of advanced industrial societies (with, of course, some exceptions). *Pluralistic* views of modern democracy suggest that there are a number of conflicting groups, each with a particular set of interests, attempting to wield power and influence. Since these groups are more or less equal in power (according to this view) the decision-making process will reflect some kind of 'general will', that is, it will take account of the demands of the community as a whole. If this is applied to the way in which cities are governed we might conclude that the problems of urban life will be solved if the process of democracy is allowed to take its course. Presumably, since democracy is not a perfect system, some injustices will occur — there will be inadequate housing in some areas, lack of recreational amenities in others, and poor educational facilities in yet others. In looking at these injustices it will be important to consider the relative power positions of various groups and to look at those mechanisms, particularly bureaucracies, which control access to relatively scarce urban resources. The people within bureaucracies who control access to urban resources — housing managers, for example, or educational psychologists — are often referred to as *social gatekeepers*.

Weberians, with their emphasis upon bureaucratic rules and social gatekeepers, are likely to view issues in social policy terms. Here the change in the values, norms and goals of *urban managers* is of the utmost priority. Thus, Rex and Moore conceive of urban change in terms of changes of values. The social scientist in laying bare social processes, can pose alternative goals and alternative institutional arrangements (Rex and Moore, 1967, p. 258). However, their analysis of conflict over housing in the Sparkbrook area of Birmingham did not suggest that such alternatives would gain support easily since there were 'built-in' reasons for urban conflict (p. 271). Pahl is even less optimistic, since he suggests that present goals of urban managers are entrenched to such a degree that capitalism will continue to be served at the expense of social needs (Pahl, 1975).

Pahl's argument here would seem to have much in common with the latest conclusions of Castells. Castells postulates the rise of urban social movements — the outcome of the politicisation of the consumptive process as a result of increasing state intervention. Thus, even though on the one hand Castells implied a vicious circle of reproduction, there is, on the other, especially in his later works, the possibility of real urban (cum social) change as a consequence of political organisation around the articulation of popular demands. Such demands will inevitably arise, although not necessarily be articulated, in the context of increasing conflicts within the urban system. So, while the state, through the provision of mass schooling, attempts to ensure the reproduction of the labour force, cutbacks in education (the consequence of a crisis of capitalism) will result in disaffection among not only the working class but also among other classes which appear to have benefited from publicly provided education. According to Castells, around such issues urban social movements, as popular broad-based anti-capitalist organisations, can be built.

TWO DIFFICULTIES WITH URBAN THEORETICAL PERSPECTIVES

The overview given above has been necessarily brief. (For a more detailed treatment, see the works cited in the Guide to Further Reading at the end of this chapter.) We have not attempted to subject the theories mentioned above to detailed scrutiny. However, even from our brief treatment there would seem to be at least two difficulties with the theories outlined above. First, there seems to be a great deal of overlap between urban social science and social science *per se*. Secondly, gender differences appear to play little part in any of the theories mentioned. Since these two points may be important to our subsequent discussions of urban schooling we will give them some brief consideration here.

By now, the reader will have gathered that not only does 'urban social science' incorporate within it a divergence of perspectives, frequently reflecting quite distinct sets of assumptions, but that it also appears to cover such a wide range of disciplines and subject-matter that urban social science might simply be called social science. A central issue of debate concerns the validity of the 'urban' concept as a theoretical construct. Is it possible for urban phenomena to be treated in a similar manner to, say, political or educational phenomena? In other words, is the urban concept of the same order as other concepts which have become categories for social scientific investigation? At first glance, the answer to the question appears to be that the urban is not comparable to other categories: the urban after all does not allude to a specific dimension of human relationships. That sub-discipline of social science that might be categorised as political science or political sociology for example, attempts to deal with aspects of decision-making, and sociology of education has as its subject-matter teacher–learner relationships, cultural transmission, and the institutionalised process of schooling.

However, urban social science would appear to incorporate a subject-matter which could equally be the province of established disciplines or sub-disciplines. An emphasis on the importance of space, *spatiality*, it might be argued, is the key notion of urban social science. On the other hand, many of the substantive concerns of urban social science appear to relegate spatiality to a relatively minor position. However, space may be a defining feature of urban economics in that it has a direct bearing upon investment processes, or it may be concerned with the effects of moral density on patterns of social relationships. Saunders argues with regard to urban sociology that if it is to be regarded as having significance for advanced industrial societies, it should abandon spatiality and instead be redefined as a new kind of political sociology which is concerned with questions of 'social consumption, competitive struggles and local politics' (Saunders, 1981, p. 278). Urban sociology, therefore, has little to do with cities as such — even though, in practice, the city provides the focus for research in the field.

The idea of urban social studies not being connected to cities seems, at least superficially, to be absurd. Perhaps the crux of the matter is that it is relatively unimportant whether it can be established that urban social science exists as a coherent discipline which may be justified on theoretical grounds. Pahl has argued that urban sociology can certainly be said to exist where there are self-styled urban sociologists with a common language and a culture (Pahl, 1975, p. 200), although more centrally its significance lies in its orientation towards a specific set of human dilemmas. This set of dilemmas concerns the distribution of resources and facilities, and the framework of urban social studies is, therefore, 'the pattern of constraints which operate differentially in given localities' upon access to resources and facilities (p. 204). These constraints are both spatial (in terms of the time/cost/ distance) and social (in terms of distribution of power in relation to bureaucratic rules and social gatekeepers).

The role of women has been largely ignored by (male) theorists in almost all areas of study. It needs to be included within urban social theory in at least two ways. First, urbanism may in fact be a very different way of life for women than for men. Secondly, in analysing conflicts between groups — whether defined in Marxist or Weberian terms — it is essential to bear in mind that women may be a separate and largely ignored group and that previously located groups may actually be fragmented on the basis of gender. The first point is easy to understand: the lifestyles, contacts and experiences of, say, a middle-class woman bringing up children at home, a woman who works as an office cleaner and a Bengali woman living as part of an extended family differ not only between themselves but from the men with whom they come into contact.

The second point indicates that previously tight categorisations of urban groups need to be broken down to take account of gender. In the three examples mentioned above it is likely that the women suffer different degrees of exploitation, isolation and ideological dominance from men who would normally be categorised as belonging to the same group or class.

As was mentioned at the beginning of this section, this chapter has, of necessity, been more of an overview than a detailed examination of a vast amount of theoretical endeavour that has tried to make sense of the urban. It is this very range of explanation that has made urban education a potentially fruitful field for exploitation and at the same time a most frustrating one. The next chapter suggests ways in which some of these urban theories may be related to educational issues.

GUIDE TO FURTHER READING

Novels and films provide one way of perceiving the 'soft city'. Raban (1975), *The Soft City*, provides a penetrating and amusing insight into urban life. Harrison (1983), *Inside the Inner City: Life Under the Cutting Edge*, is a disturbing and realistic account of the conditions within Britain's cities and why nothing is done to change them.

A text that provides a detailed literature review of the theories mentioned in this chapter and of many more is Saunders (1981), *Social*

Theory and the Urban Question. However, his view that urban social theory is not related to cities may strike the reader as a little perverse. For a more geographical and empirical view, see Knox (1982), *Urban Social Geography: An Introduction*.

3
Urban education

URBAN PERSPECTIVES AND URBAN SCHOOLING

This chapter attempts to consolidate both the historical overview of Chapter 1 and the social theories of Chapter 2 into a systematic view of urban education. It would be possible to develop an approach to urban education based rigidly on one of the theoretical perspectives outlined in Chapter 2. The danger with this might be that the analysis would remain remote from the practical business of teaching in urban schools. We have chosen then, in the rest of the book, to use a theoretical perspective on urban schooling to illuminate practice rather to constrain our analysis of it. The next section of this chapter indicates more specifically how the different approaches to urban studies might be linked to different approaches to urban schooling. The experience of urban schools in the USA is then considered before attempting an overview of urban education in the UK.

The urban perspectives that have been outlined have begun to have some impact upon attempts to theorise about urban education. At the broadest possible level of generality the theories can be categorised as *consensus* (the functionalist, community and Chicago School writers) or *conflict* (those deriving from Marx and Weber).

Consensus perspectives tend to be those that view the city as a functional entity, as both a harmonious albeit competitive community, and as exhibiting a specific culture — urbanism. In terms of schooling one variant of this type of perspective suggests that there has been a breakdown of moral ties and social solidarity. The 'crisis' of urban schools is seen as a reflection of this break-up, with the most serious consequences being the undermining of order, hierarchy, teacher and pupil roles. The related responses emphasise a reassertion of a traditional mode of schooling (social control, strong leadership, 'good teaching', 'standards', received culture). Another variant of the consensus type of perspective, on the other hand, tends to stress the functional inefficiency of schools and the deficiencies of technical expertise on the part of teachers, that is, the maladies of city schools reflect a technical breakdown in the urban system. The response suggested is that of better management, curricular change and 'community' schools. Here, there is a recognition that, though there is a need to re-establish consensus, it may well require the urban school system to become more adaptive.

The ecological/functionalist perspective provides a view of 'urban' phenomena that might lead us to suspect that the structure of schooling in cities is the consequence of a 'natural' process. The free play of market forces and the healthy competition between groups and between individuals — within an integrated structure — is evident in the different character of different schools, each related to a different section of the urban community. Thus the zone of transition, as suggested by the Burgess model of the city, is characterised by 'so-called "slums" and "bad lands" with their submerged regions of poverty, degradation, and disease' (Burgess, in Stewart, 1972, p. 123). It is, in ecological or functionalist terms, a consequence of the natural process of urban development which gives 'form and character' to the city (p. 124).

The schools located within the zone of transition, by the same token, will reflect the urban process identified through the ecological/ functionalist approach. It is possible to make the kind of observations noted in the Plowden Report (1967) concerning the state of schools in 'Educational Priority Areas', such as cramped conditions and the 'ingrained grime of generations', within the ecological framework. These schools would be considered to be products of 'natural' forces and therefore part of the network of a particular moral region and of the city as a whole.

Although this approach may seem to have much in common with *laissez-faire* economics, where a stable system may be seen to be the result of the interplay of 'free' market forces, this is not to say that the Chicago School writers were advocates of unfettered capitalism. Their analysis of early twentieth-century industrial urban society was coupled with a wish to lay bare the hardships of city life with a view to amelioration. Nevertheless their perspectives do not appear to lead consistently to a consideration of urban reform.

Conflict perspectives, by contrast, indicate a view of the city as an arena for struggle — either on the part of individuals, groups or both. Sometimes such conflict is viewed as endemic to cities in advanced industrial societies. Perceived trends towards bureaucratisation and the seemingly inexorable march of technology are linked with the increasing dominance of hierarchical authority. This is consistent with a Weberian perspective which sees schools as essentially custodial and authoritarian, where cultural and personal domination prevail and pupil resistance is a consequence. Related remedies appeal to relativistic notions of knowledge within which it is accepted that no approach has universal validity, and to non-hierarchical concepts of teacher–pupil relationships. The Marxist variant of the conflict perspective suggests that since the city is the location of class struggle and of the dominance of industrial capital, schools will inevitably be seen as agencies for the reproduction of the social relations of capitalist production. Both teachers and pupils in urban schools are perceived as victims of the system (either in economic terms or in terms of ideological domination), and the consequent response must be seen as the creation of a movement of resistance, of critical awareness, and of the advocation of radical social change (see Chapter 4).

In the case of Weber the work of Rex and Moore provides a good illustration (Rex and Moore, 1967). The endemic conflicts of the city result in a multiplicity of groups with differential power and status seen in relation to access to urban resources. (In particular, their emphasis was on the position of non-white minority groups in one particular English city, Birmingham.) The development of a 'housing class' system (while separate from a general class system based on capital–labour conflict) has clear implications for access to schooling. The unequal distribution of educational facilities can then be viewed in relation to differential power within the urban community, especially where power can be further used to manipulate that distribution. The physical state of urban schools, the resources available for teaching, the kind of staff employed and the population served, may all be considered to be the outcomes of conflict within the city as viewed from a Weberian perspective.

Pahl's approach also moved further away from an ecological/functionalist perspective and thus points to a more critical analysis of urban schooling, both in terms of conceptualising difficulties and advocating remedies. Bureaucratic 'social gatekeepers' are as relevant to access to educational resources as they are to any other aspect of the city. Access to schools is influenced not only by location and residence (that is, position in the housing class system) but also by the decisions of local government, education officials and headteachers. The gerrymandering of public housing can ensure the perpetuation of 'sink' schools; the politically powerful can exert disproportionate influence upon local government bureaucrats in relation to school closures and amalgamations.

Current Marxist urban sociology offers a yet more radical critique for analysts of urban schooling. For unlike the Weberians, who view democratic control of the bureaucracy as a way of minimising injustice, the Marxists suggest that urban educational processes (including access and the kind of education offered) are the consequences of a particular kind of social system. Whatever the differences in approach between different Marxist theorists there is a fair measure of agreement on the issue of urban schools being linked with an inequitable socioeconomic system. Marxist approaches, however, suggest the importance of change. But while one variant appears to view change as possible only at the macro level (that is, revolution), an alternative variant emphasises the significance of human agency for (limited) change at the micro level.

While those following the former variant may have distanced themselves from the day-to-day issues facing urban schools, there are others who, in claiming to be part of the Marxist tradition, offer a more positive approach for educational practice. Arguably, there is an overlap with a broader radical tradition which has, for some time, penetrated urban education. What is rejected here is the simplistic notion of the inevitable reproduction of a class society through schooling under capitalism and the conclusion that little can be done to change the nature of schools until the inevitable revolution comes. In its place the role of the teacher or administrator, as active within a collective process, becomes more significant. This is not to say that the rather more romanticised libertarian view of teachers as initiators of fundamental educational change is accepted. The independent 'free' school as an oasis of educational liberty in a desert of capitalist slavery is as unrealistic as it is elitist.

Yet, this does not mean that teachers in urban schools cannot respond positively to a situation where there exists impoverished facilities, an inadequate curriculum and racism. Radical urban theory suggests that teachers cannot isolate themselves from the social context of schooling; on the contrary, they are in a position to involve themselves in the struggle for change — at a number of different levels. Teachers in UK cities are in a relatively powerful position in respect both of institutional change and changes in values. However, teachers as a body cannot radically affect the provision of financial resources for schooling; only as part of a broader community of interests is it possible for them to fight for such a change.

Of course, this raises the thorny issue of the professional integrity of the teacher. Surely, it is argued, the teacher in an urban school has no business in using his/her position as a professional in an avowedly political manner. The teacher, after all, is employed to teach — to impart knowledge and skills; he/she is not employed to stir up trouble.

Yet, if nothing else, current perspectives in urban theory highlight the political nature of the functioning of social institutions, not least the urban school system. If we accept that the situation of urban schools is already somewhat politicised — certainly in so far as many such schools are having to confront youth unemployment and racism on a large scale — then we may also have to accept that teachers cannot play the role of neutral professional. In short, the teacher cannot be absolved from collaboration in an inequitable education system unless he/she is prepared to question, and to demand fundamental change.

This review of the manner in which urban theory might illuminate approaches to urban education will be referred to at the end of this chapter, in an attempt to describe more clearly the relationship between the various strands of urban theory and schooling practice. However, at this point it is valuable to examine how the concept of 'urban education' has developed over the last few decades, and how this development, seemingly haphazard and atheoretical, has in fact been strongly influenced by consensus models. A major reason for this orientation is that although city education has been a concern for a long period of time, the specific articulation of this concern as one of *urban education* is, as has been said, of recent introduction and, equally importantly, originated in the USA, where functionalist perspectives had a strong following throughout the educational community. This history is worth briefly exploring, as it provides a setting within which urban education today can be located and analysed.

URBAN EDUCATION IN THE USA

The American journal *Urban Education* was founded in 1964. There is still no equivalent in Britain. The conceptualisation of urban education as a category to delineate a whole cluster of educational issues arose as a result of an increasing concern over the seeming disintegration of certain key urban education systems in the USA. The reasons for this are complex and can only be summarised here. Desegregation of the schooling system, the whole civil rights movement, the start of the capital flight, white flight and economic decline of many major industrial cities led to a growth in educational concern for the children within inner-city schools. A plethora of terms were coined to describe such children: 'deprived', 'disadvantaged', 'deficient', 'discriminated against'. And, perhaps, most importantly given the context, the children were mainly black. The inner cities in the 1960s were becoming increasingly black as their white inhabitants moved out to the more salubrious suburbs ('white flight'). As they moved out, blacks, and later Hispanics, moved in. Most were poor; those who did become more affluent followed their white predecessors in the flight to the suburbs. In 1965 large swathes of such inner-city areas were destroyed in a hot summer of riots.

These events concentrated the minds of educationists and other social-policy-makers. The urban poor were, in a sense, rediscovered. A war on poverty was initiated under President Johnson with education as a major component. It is a cruel irony that many of the intended beneficiaries of such a war were soon to end up in Vietnam in a war of a very different sort. The cost of that war and the impact that it had on the USA diverted attention yet again from the educational needs of the inner city. Yet, during that brief period of concentration, urban education as a named area of study flourished. Its conceptual base was weak, namely that urban education was concerned with the issues raised by education in urban areas. The specificity of the urban was not really examined. Instead, a range of issues that were seen to be at their most manifest in urban areas were investigated. Principal among these issues were underachievement and school desegregation. The former issue spawned a vast literature and also, in the US context, a whole range of remedial educational policies. These in turn, notably the compensatory education programmes such as Head Start, have had effects on British urban education. Interestingly, the issue of racial mix in urban schools has never really been an issue in British schools, save for a brief flirtation with bussing by some English LEAs in the early 1960s, most notably Ealing.

From the debate on underachievement, a conceptual division of theory which is still of value emerged, namely *deficit* and *difference* models of children. In examining underachievement, much of the earlier theory located the issue in deficiencies in either children and/or their home and cultural background. The educational solution was to remedy the deficiency by means of compensatory programmes. An example of this would be linguistic deficiency. It was claimed that black American children spoke a form of English that was unsuitable for the sort of learning that took place in schools. The solution was to teach them standard American English. This and other similar solutions to the claimed deficiencies in children and their backgrounds were soon under attack. In the case of language, for example, Labov (1969) and other researchers demonstrated that black American English was not deficient and was not incapable of abstract thought.

Difference models, of which Labov's work is an example, argued that it was difference between the world of the school and the world of many urban children that caused the lack of achievement. Why these differences existed was to become another fruitful field for inquiry, as will be seen in subsequent chapters.

It is important to note that this is not a simple conservative/radical dichotomy, with difference theories being inherently radical and deficit theories being inherently conservative. American researchers found abundant evidence that the material conditions from which many urban children came did cause real deficiencies, most notably in terms of health. Consequently, it was argued by some, radical changes in these material conditions were an essential prerequisite for a more equal schooling system. In a similar fashion, Jensen (1969) argued that black children were not deficient in terms of their intelligence but were actually different due to genetic factors. It should be noted here that however scientifically 'neutral' Jensen claimed his research to be, it was taken up by many as evidence of the inherent inferiority of black children. (For a fuller account of this debate, see Chapter 6.)

In the main, by focusing attention on deficiencies, real or imagined, in the child and his/her background, US writers on urban education allowed schools to continue holding the view that their practice was basically satisfactory. The widely held view of the incapacity of the urban poor to benefit from education was, as a consequence, allowed to retain its hold over teachers' perceptions of the children in front of them.

As the urban educational journals reveal, concentration was placed upon the minutiae of urban educational systems. Much of the work undertaken was valuable, for example, analyses of teacher burnout in urban schools, improving levels of attainment, and linking school and work. But by becoming an issue-based area of inquiry without a strong conceptual urban frame, it has done little to help provide an understanding of why urban schools continue to throw up educational difficulties in a seemingly never-ending stream. The American sociologist C. Wright Mills had criticised the approach that typified the vast majority of this type of urban educational literature before it was even written:

> The emphasis upon fragmenting practical problems tends to atomise social objectives. The studies so informed are not integrated into designs comprehensive enough to serve collective action, granted the power and intent to realise such action (Wright Mills, 1943, quoted in Beck *et al.*, 1976, p. 96).

URBAN EDUCATION IN BRITAIN

The writings on urban education and the policies that emanated from them in the USA quite quickly crossed the Atlantic. In Chapter 1 the Plowden and Newsom reports were seen as being significant indications of the state of mainstream liberal educational opinion in the mid-1960s and early 1970s. From Newsom's education in 'the slums', Plowden had moved, influenced by work from the USA, to a discussion of educational disadvantage and its effects on urban schools. At the same time, British academics were looking at issues central to the debate on urban schooling, and propounding theories that complemented contemporary work in the USA. In terms of policy, the most influential work was that done in Educational Priority Areas recorded in the five-volume report published from 1972 onwards (Halsey, 1972). In the first volume, Halsey, the project leader, was quite clearly deeply influenced by the US experience. What the project reports do reveal, however, is that despite a concentration of resources, the teachers in the urban schools involved still tended to regard the educational difficulties they encountered as residing in the children and their environment rather than in the school. It was a point of view put forward most forcefully by a government minister, Sir Keith Joseph, in 1972, when he claimed that, 'inadequate people tend to be inadequate parents and that inadequate parents tend to rear inadequate children' (Joseph, 1972, quoted in Braham, 1977, p. 25). Such propositions, firmly based on deficit models, need to be examined a little more closely, particularly as their appeal is so powerful on the surface. They have within them two elements, empirical and normative, which need to be distinguished. Thus, there is an empirical element in that such statements claim that 'inadequate' people lack certain definable and measurable attributes. In addition, there is also an overt normative element, that is, that these people *ought* to have such attributes.

Urban education, as such, was still not on the agenda of teacher training, specific academic inquiry or local authority policy and practice. However, in the mid-1960s, the Open University produced a course on urban education and Gerald Grace at King's College, London, introduced a higher degree course in urban education. The Open University course was widely used in teacher training courses and during the 1970s courses in urban education proliferated in the teacher-training institutions, particularly in new BEd courses. Despite this growth, the actual subject of study still remained remarkably diffuse and atheoretical. Was urban education merely an examination of some current educational issues found in all schools, albeit concentrated in urban schools, or was the urban environment within which schooling took place a unique context throwing up unique issues? This lack of a firm theoretical underpinning made urban education appear to be yet another educational fad, to be replaced at the appropriate time by courses on computers in education or multi-cultural education. This is not to say that such new courses are not significant or without importance, but without a clear perception of what the 'urban' component actually entails, they seldom rise above a ragbag analysis of a series of apparently unrelated educational issues.

WHAT IS URBAN EDUCATION?

This conceptual confusion over urban education was matched by a similar debate that was occurring within other social sciences. As Chapter 2 indicates, there was a growth in urban studies within a variety of academic disciplines, most notably in sociology and geography. The early writings of Castells and Harvey (Castells, 1977, 1978; Harvey, 1973) stimulated a whole range of inquiry into the specificity of the urban which is only now beginning to influence, to any significant degree, the way in which urban education is conceptualised. These issues were discussed in the last chapter. What is important to repeat here is that such modes of analysis are essential if urban education is to be coherent and related to policy and practice.

Although much of this more rigorous analysis of the 1970s was written from a Marxist perspective, it has not remained so. There has been a two-way movement. Writers like Castells, as was indicated in the last chapter, whose work was firmly within the Marxist tradition, have in their more recent writings moved to a position that might be called Weberian (Castells, 1983). Other writers, such as Pahl, have modified their earlier *managerialist* positions (i.e. a stress on the role that urban managers play in urban life) to take into greater account the insights into economic and political relations within cities formulated by Castells and his followers. The danger is, however, as was pointed out in the last chapter, that a stress on political and economic relations can lead to a lack of specific focus on the actual physical urban environment. In other words, just as much of the American writing lacked specificity as regards the urban, so do some of the more radical investigations.

So, given these recent formulations, how should urban education be conceptualised? This is an important question, because it is one of the assumptions of this book first that the range of issues that affect urban schools are interrelated, and secondly that the sociospatial location of such issues within the urban environment adds a further dimension to them. This sociospatial location is crucial to an understanding of urban educational issues.

Given this position, the study of urban education can help us to gain a clearer understanding of some of the issues that face teachers in urban schools. The remaining chapters of this book attempt to do this in relation to four specific issues, namely order and control, cultural diversity, special educational needs and the relationship between school and work. These issues obviously appear to have a current importance; they have in fact been a source of constant preoccupation of urban teachers since mass education within cities commenced, as was indicated in Chapter 1. In addition, an analysis of them throws light on other areas of schooling, most notably the curriculum and the structure and organisation of urban schools, which is more revealing of these topics than if they were simply taken as the starting point for analysis.

There are other fruitful linkages resulting from this approach. Urban areas are the lynch-pins of our society. Much of the wealth of society is generated and controlled from within them. As a consequence of this concentration, the division of labour is both complex and visibly unequal. The urban riots of 1981, disturbances arising out of the activities of racialist political parties, claims about the extraordinary high levels of disturbance in urban children and the disproportionate rates of youth unemployment, all catch the headlines but are often portrayed as both exceptional and unrelated, both to one another and to schooling. By stressing the sociospatial element in analysing urban education it can be demonstrated that such phenomena are inter-related and that a policy for urban schools that does not make such links is likely to be unsuccessful. These linkages are worth examining so that the more detailed accounts in subsequent chapters can be better related one to another.

MAJOR ISSUES IN URBAN EDUCATION

In the previous section it was asserted that the sociospatial location of the urban environment made more visible the inequalities and tensions within modern British society. Urban schools are likely to be a reflection of these inequalities and tensions. For the majority of children urban schooling becomes a process by which they are trained for, and accept (however unwillingly), their future position in the lower rankings of the urban and national social order. In an effort to explain this apparent failure of the urban schooling system, those professionally involved in education have, in the main, enthusiastically adopted deficit models of the children whom they teach: the 'they do it because they're . . .' syndrome. In the urban schools of Britain today, four major deficit model responses may be found. These are that the children fail because they lack discipline and self-control, they are black, they are stupid or that they are in some way work-shy. The sociospatial structure of cities facilitates the categorisation of large numbers of children within these deficit perceptions. These four deficit positions are critically examined in the next four chapters.

URBAN EDUCATION: DIFFERING PERSPECTIVES

At the start of the chapter two major strands were identified, the consensual and the conflictual. From these a series of positions could be taken, based principally on sociological writings. At this point we would like to broaden these terms, not only to help in the understanding of policy and practice as was indicated above, but also to indicate the political implications of the various positions previously identified.

One classification that has the virtue of being both simple and helpful here is that of defining the issues and subsequent policy and practice in terms of conservative, liberal and radical perspectives (Grace, 1978). A disadvantage of this division is that the words have been used to describe current British political parties. It is important to note that this is not the purpose for using these terms; indeed the perspectives that we outline could not be attached readily to any particular party. Furthermore, the distinctions between perspectives are not clear-cut but merge one into the other. What such a division does do, however, is stress the political dimension involved in any study of urban education.

Conservative perceptions, like the other two, would accept that the urban environment is an unequal one. It accepts that many children do not achieve at satisfactory levels in urban schools and that this state of affairs is to be deplored. There is a concern that working-class 'talent' is not being exploited as it might and that the majority of urban children who are not talented are not given an education that readily suits them for their future position in life. Deficit models, as explanations for lack of success in the school system, are strongly held. Children do not achieve because they come from inadequate backgrounds or, in some cases, because they are 'naturally' not very intelligent.

It is our contention that much policy and practice is predicated on such views. This does not mean that there is a deliberate design to inhibit and depress children's progress. Far from it. There is a real concern for educational standards, however defined, and a belief that teachers face an uphill struggle against impossible odds, among which must be numbered recalcitrant children. However, the equally strong belief in merit and, by implication, a form of meritocracy, means that every effort should be made to ensure that all children should have an equal chance to attain those positions in society where rewards are greatest. Aligned with this view is that which asserts that if the competition is seen to be fair those who fail will readily accept their position. Resistance, or worse, riot, is seen as the result of an education that falsely raises aspirations, or which explicitly encourages dissatisfaction.

Liberal perspectives are more difficult to characterise as they are, in a sense, the spectrum of views between the conservative and radical. At one end, the advocacy of gradualistic incrementalism is at the forefront, at the other, the view that urban society is unjust but that measures can be taken, within the confines of the existing social system, to make it more fair and equitable. Concepts based on ideas of disadvantage and deprivation are acknowledged. Views on institutional malfunctioning and an inequitable distribution of urban resources and opportunities are widely held. The consequence of this is that remediative action is often seen in terms of improving the administration of distribution to make it more effective. An example of this would be steps to ensure that all children entitled to free school meals and other welfare benefits actually take up those benefits. Thus although the city is seen as inherently an unjust social structure, there is the belief that the system is, theoretically at least, capable of reforming itself.

Radical perspectives argue that the urban system is not only inherently unjust but that the school system in the main sustains the injustice. Thus, reform of the school system is dependent upon reform of the urban system. Key concepts would be ones such as poverty and inequality and in general there would be the view that the schooling system by itself can do little to affect the greater inequalities within the urban system. Marxist perspectives would argue for the primacy of class conflict based upon relationships to the means of production but there are a range of other radical perspectives which, while not denying the importance of such economic arrangements, would challenge their determining role. All radical perspectives would challenge dominant views about the existing hierarchical relations within urban systems and insist that for any system of real social justice to emerge, fundamental structures of society would have to be changed. However, it is important to note that neither are all radical perspectives revolutionary, nor are they necessarily Marxist in orientation.

As with all general categorisations, exceptions to this rather crude tripartite division can be found. However, a few general conclusions can be drawn. In terms of urban education, much policy and practice is rooted in liberal and conservative perspectives. In terms of recent academic writing on the subject the balance between the three is somewhat reversed, with radical theorising being of considerable influence. However, at some levels there do appear to have been modest shifts in emphasis. Several urban LEAs' policy statements have been more radical than has been seen for many years, and the academic writers concerned with examining urbanisation and urbanism have tempered the more overt radicalism of the 1970s. Whether this means a closer relation of theory to practice is difficult to say. What is clear is that urban education is one of the most exciting areas of educational inquiry to be involved in at the present time.

A further point is that any categorisation runs the risk of solidifying what is in fact a rapidly changing situation. Its principal virtue is that it reveals that within an urban educational system at any one time there will be a diversity of views, not only between groups, but also perhaps within the same individual. Furthermore, the analysis of these positions does two things. It places the study of urban education on a firmer theoretical basis than can be contrived by a mere hotch-potch issue-based analysis. Secondly, and consequent upon this, the analysis of educational issues within the urban context can be more precisely undertaken. The subsequent chapters of this book in acknowledging the strength of this categorisation, attempt to develop the analysis of urban educational issues within a broad radical perspective.

GUIDE TO FURTHER READING

Of the vast US literature on urban education, perhaps the most readily available is the third edition of Miller (1978), *Social Foundations of*

Education. Earlier editions had a more radical perspective when the work was jointly written with Roger Woock. (He declined to be further involved with a book that he now sees as managerialist.)

In terms of the British literature, the two Open University courses on urban education, *Urban Education*, E351 (1973) and *Education and the Urban Environment*, E361 (1977) show the influence of the US literature on British thinking. As this book went to press, Grace (1984) (ed.), *Education and the City*, was published. The introductory chapter by Grace is an excellent summation of the position of urban education in Britain today.

4
Social control, ideology and resistance

> *Get order.* Drop everything else, if necessary, until order is secured. Stretch your authority to the breaking point if you can do nothing else. Pile penalty upon penalty for misdemeanours, and let the 'sting' of each penalty be double that of its predecessor. Tire out the recalcitrants if you can gain your end in no other way.
>
> (W.C. Bagley, quoted in Waller, 1932)

URBAN SCHOOLING AND SOCIAL CONTROL

We arrive now at what constitutes the major cluster of issues for many intending and practising teachers in urban schools. These issues seem to revolve around one theme: how to establish and maintain order and control. For those following courses of initial teacher education the question of discipline in the classroom arises sooner or later, followed by a sense of dissatisfaction when few positive answers are forthcoming. For those already working as teachers in urban schools the question of discipline is frequently dealt with through reference to the authority structure of schools, and in so far as disorder is perceived to have grown in recent times it is because the authority structure is no longer effective. Nigel Wright has shown how we are led to believe that disorder rules the school system:

> As I write, the *Daily Mirror* has a double-page spread about it, saying that the '3 R's' have been joined by a fourth — Rebellion — in the schools, and describing some sensational (if unattributed) examples: schools burnt to the ground, teachers chased screaming from the classroom (Wright, 1977, p. 111).

The sensational images of violence in urban schools, however, mask a much more fundamental set of concerns. Many teachers express anxieties about their role. The custodian of educational values, knowledge and understanding is frequently in conflict with — and subordinate to — the custodian of children. Pushing back the frontiers of knowledge has given way to keeping the kids off the street.

There are, of course, those who experience no such conflict of values: teaching is simply a way of earning a living where the ideals are no loftier than those that prevail in the prison service. At the other extreme, the lone, dedicated professional — untroubled by the system — propagates the gospel of education with all the zeal of a nineteenth-century missionary. For most, however, the conflicts remain unresolved. The desire to treat children humanely and an attempt to understand their demands, their goals and their ambitions is tempered by the need for a personal sense of security and acceptance by other teachers.

So it is easier to say that urban life is difficult, essentially 'because they're naughty'. Along with most people, we would accept that children may, from time to time, be naughty. Most parents — even those who have sound, caring relationships with their children — will know that kids can be horrors! What is more, most parents will respond in such a manner that their children will appreciate that their behaviour is unacceptable. This, however, is a far cry from a situation — in the popular image of urban schools — where naughtiness or indiscipline is regarded as an endemic, structural feature.

Perhaps it would be helpful at this stage to make a distinction between socialisation and social control. Many teachers, particularly in nursery and infant schools, have similar roles to parents in terms of socialisation. It is necessary for an infant teacher to establish a friendly and calm working environment, for the children to learn skills of co-operating with one another, of listening to each other and to the teacher and of behaving in the school buildings and playgrounds in such a way as not to cause any damage to themselves, to other people or to property. Developing these skills, attitudes and facilities may be taken as a valid and necessary process of socialisation. This is not to say that they are not also part of social control but it is hard to imagine a society that could thrive without even this minimal form of control. On the other hand, many school disciplines and practices may be seen to serve little other purpose apart from social control — wearing uniform, standing up when teachers enter a room, waiting silently in rows, saying 'miss' and 'sir' and so on. (The issue of rules and disciplines is returned to in Chapter 6.)

> Spontaneously, man was not inclined to submit to political authority, to respect a moral discipline, to dedicate himself, to be self-sacrificing. . . . It is society itself which, to the degree that it is firmly established, has drawn from within itself those great moral forces in the face of which man has felt his inferiority. . . . To the egoistic and asocial being that has just been born it must, as rapidly as possible, add another, capable of leading a moral and social life. Such is the work of education.
>
> (Durkheim, 1956)

The 'crisis' of urban education is, for many, the issue of social order. The regulation of human social behaviour has been a central concern of rulers, philosophers and teachers for many centuries. While some have held to a view that social rules and political regulation are a necessary evil to restrain the selfish impulses of the individual, others have considered that sets of social rules — norms — are a fundamental aspect of human life. This latter case, it is argued, is evidenced by long-enduring social institutions, such as the family, which provide standards of behaviour for the individual. Whichever is the case, social order is held to be fundamental to the satisfactory maintenance of collective life. *Socialisation* — the process of induction into the ways of life of a society — has been held to be the key to the integration of the individual into the social order. The family, the church and the education system have been held up as good examples of institutions that perform this induction process. Education above all was seen by Emile Durkheim as having as its prime function the development in the child of:

> a certain number of physical, intellectual and moral states which are demanded of him by both the political society as a whole and the special milieu for which he is specifically destined (Durkheim, 1956, p. 71).

On the other hand, when the school and the other agencies fail to perform this particular function others are supposed to step in to ensure that inadequately socialised individuals are subject to some kind of control. In modern Britain and elsewhere the police and other law-enforcement agencies are paramount in the area of *social control*. However, agencies of socialisation can also act as agencies of social control: a school can punish, a church can excommunicate, parents can withdraw their love. In other words, individuals can either acquire a sense of what is 'right' or 'wrong' or they can be coerced into behaving in an acceptable manner. Such coercion, though, as we shall see, can often be quite subtle in its operation.

Those who are subject to social control may well devise means to combat its consequences. The 'deviant' behaviour popularly perceived as a characteristic of urban working-class youth might be a way of resisting the demands of those in authority (those with power) upon young people — particularly in relation to established values. The 'disruptive' behaviour of some pupils in urban working-class secondary schools or the subcultural styles adopted by certain groups of young people can often be seen as threatening to those whose manifest responsibility is to maintain social order.

The expanding cities of middle and late nineteenth-century Britain were increasingly seen as the terrain for roaming gangs of working-class children. Delinquent acts and crime in general were the characteristics expected of a youth population that lacked the moral standards of the urban bourgeoisie. The 'problem of adolescence' was perceived in working-class terms (while the frequently destructive behaviour of Oxbridge undergraduates was defined as 'high spirits') and, as some writers have pointed out, it was to combat this 'problem' that voluntary youth organisations established themselves. The Boy Scouts, Boys Brigade, youth clubs and settlements were based on the city: their message was essentially moralistic in tone and they had the backing of organised religion. Indeed the church and similar organisations were — and still are — in the forefront of the movement to 'protect' and 'rescue' the youth of the country.

More pertinently, these organisations, which were outside the formal state sector, were in the business of defining what they saw as a particularly problematic stage of childhood — that of adolescence. The adolescent was viewed essentially as an immature adult who physically had attained adulthood, but mentally was unable to control *his* (note the masculine emphasis) drives and desires. In the context of the big city, the adolescent was not merely at risk himself in the metropolis; much more, he was — in association with others — a threat to the social order and the fabric of the community. It was therefore vitally important for all concerned to control the behaviour of urban youth.

The urban 'delinquent' is not merely a nineteenth-century invention of the frightened English middle class; s/he was, and remains, an international phenomenon. The phenomenon is reflected not only in the writings of social scientists, historians and other 'objective' observers of the scene, but is also apparent in popular cultural forms. From the novels of writers such as Dickens through to recent films and television programmes, urban working-class children are portrayed as troublesome and dangerous. It was not that such children were necessarily seen as defiant rebels against the existing social order; rather that they were amoral 'anarchists'. The notion of the 'Blackboard Jungle' was extracted from the American 1950s film of that name and became part of the general mythology of urban schooling: the inner-city teacher besieged by wild animals. However, even if we separate the fiction from the fact, teachers are still faced with the difficulty of how to respond in situations characterised by overt and covert pupil resistance.

What therefore we shall seek to examine here are some of the important issues associated with the control of the behaviour of young people in urban schools and the ways in which youth subcultures might be seen as responses to the imposition of authority, particularly in the context of economic recession and the deepening crisis of the inner city. A crucial question is, what kind of response is appropriate for the teacher in the urban school to make? It is especially pertinent in view of the gap between the cultural background and experience of the average teacher and that of the typical urban working-class adolescent.

Social control, at first glance, would appear to be characterised by the actual or threatened use of force against those who deviate from the norm. This is, of course, only one of a range of sanctions that could conceivably be employed. Psychological manipulation has long been used to keep individuals in line, whether it is the priest suggesting to the congregation the possibility of eternal damnation or the soap powder manufacturers implying that failure to use their brand is tantamount to child and husband neglect. We can indeed see that there are different kinds of mechanisms of control: force (threatened or actual), usually employed against those in prison; promise of remunerative reward (as in the case of employers in relation to employees); the threat of normative sanctions (as in the case of the church).

In practice, most groups/organisations, including nation-states, employ diverse techniques of social control. Indeed, it is only the state and its constituent agencies that possess the legitimate means of control through violence (and even then, it is argued, only as a last resort). Furthermore, these techniques become well established over a period of time with the consequence that they remain in existence whether or not there is a need for them. In other words, social mechanisms exist not so much as a reaction to various acts of 'deviance' but rather as structured aspects of particular organisations or states. Thus, the British police are now seen as a traditional, fundamental part of society; as a state agency of social control, they have developed their own norms and values regarding the way they should operate. 'Discipline' is frequently regarded as basic to the organisation of the school; unless a school possesses a clearly defined set of sanctions based upon a recognised hierarchical authority structure it is seen to lack credibility as a proper educational institution.

An important question we might then consider is whether 'deviant' behaviour is a response to control rather than the reverse. Mechanisms of social control, after all, pre-exist instances of deviance. Given a number of other preceding events, criminal activity may indeed be a direct consequence of law-enforcement procedures. It is, perhaps, more realistic to see social control as part of a complex process of interaction; it is not especially helpful to consider it simply as fulfilling a function of society. In short, control is essential to the very fabric of the social, or rather: 'the social *is* control. . . . Social control is not some dark opposite to liberation and freedom, it is simply the ubiquitous condition of women and men (and children)' (Davies, 1976, p. 7).

> I remember in my last year at primary school the teacher tended to arrange the desks so that the people doing best were near the front, going back to the ones who weren't doing very well, which I thought was a bit bad. It made you think you had to get on to the next desk and you got all upset about it. I was in the middle.
> (Ley Alberici, quoted in White and Brockington, 1983)

In the case of schools, social control is exercised in a subtle and pervasive manner. It is not merely enshrined in the sets of rules and regulations that govern the behaviour of children; it is built into the very structure of the educational process. The curriculum and the way it is organised is an important instrument of control. It is through the curriculum that some 'forms' of knowledge are made available to a minority of children, while the rest are condemned to diluted versions or 'low-status' forms (home economics, woodwork, technical drawing). The differentiated curriculum and the process of 'setting' intertwine to produce a system of control in schools whereby pupils either come to know their place in the hierarchy or else are encouraged to conform to a norm of educational mobility. For example, those who have been selected to study a foreign language will come to have a clear notion of their relatively high 'academic' standing, while those in the bottom set for maths might be rewarded with promotion to a higher set in exchange for greater effort. On the other hand, it is not unusual for a teacher taking a class for the first time to encounter the response: 'You can't expect much from us, we're the bottom set, we're the thicks.'

At the primary school level, Sharp and Green (1975) have provided interesting insights into the subtle operation of social control within institutions where a philosophy of 'progressivism' is openly professed. Their research centred upon a working-class housing estate primary school where the prevailing educational thinking was that of an acceptable 'progressive/child-centred' approach. It was the kind of approach that was reflected in the prescriptions of the Plowden Report (1967) and which found favour with the headmaster of the school. In practice, such a philosophy meant the 'free day' or the 'integrated curriculum' whereby children:

tended to be given wide discretion to choose between many activities, and
in so far as they appeared to choose to do things . . . the child-centred
approach was assumed to be in operation (Sharp and Green, 1975, p. 216).

What these authors have suggested, as a result of their research, is that
despite a disavowal of the overt socialisation function of schooling
(favouring a commitment to 'child-centred progressivism'), the
teachers exercised a subtle form of control over the children. This was
done through taken-for-granted norms based on notions of social
deprivation and social pathology. Here, the pupils' identities were
redefined and restructured according to a social hierarchy. Thus, those
considered to be intelligent were placed at the top of the hierarchy and
were deemed to be destined for success, while those labelled as dull,
underprivileged and deprived were placed at the bottom and were
deemed to be in need of remedial, compensatory treatment. Sharp and
Green further suggest that, paradoxically, the very actions of (progressive) primary school teachers functioned to maintain the social order.
It is in this way that social control is seen as a political mechanism,
unlike socialisation which is essentially a normative process. The
selection of curriculum content according to the perceived individual
needs of children can ultimately come to serve a political function: that
of ensuring that those who are likely to 'run things' in society are given
advanced notice of their capacity to do so. Likewise, those who are
likely to end up as 'social problems' will be rehearsed for their future
role through being placed in a subordinate position within the hierarchy of knowledge and ignorance within the school.

Although some of the perspectives adopted in Sharp and Green's
research have been questioned, we none the less accept that the
primary school can be a significant arena for the exercise of social
control in a quite covert and implicit manner. Moreover, we are made
aware that teachers are often the 'unwilling victims of a structure that
undermines the moral concerns they profess' (p. 227). At the same
time it is interesting to note that teachers do not seem to experience
any real conflict between their beliefs and their actions (however
structurally determined); as far as they are concerned, they are
continuing to act as liberal, progressive, and highly committed professionals.

SCHOOLING AND IDEOLOGY

It is probably apparent by now that in practice the exercise of social control and the process of socialisation are not always distinct. It is not easy to know whether behaviour is the consequence of having internalised particular norms and values or whether it is the consequence of the exercise of control. Many, of course, would reject the notion of socialisation altogether and simply view things in terms of control. If we take this line we might, along with Louis Althusser, consider social control as being either *repressive* (based on coercion) or *ideological*. Ideology is one of the most elusive concepts to be found in the social sciences. It is frequently used to deride those views that are considered to be undesirable or politically suspect. Whatever the precise meaning given to the term *ideology*, it would appear to denote a collection of beliefs, organised in a more or less systematic way, having the function of sustaining or promoting a particular view of the world which is in harmony with the holder's social class. This kind of definition might well include religion as ideology, although in the main the political sphere is considered more important. For example, capitalism has been portrayed as involving an ideology which sees the world in terms of individuals competing with each other for the ownership and control of resources. While capitalism functions to sustain and prescribe such a view, socialism on the other hand is an ideology that seeks to change it and prescribe an alternative view — co-operation, equality of access to resources, control over one's own labour and product.

In general, an ideological view of the world is frequently counterposed to an 'objective' view. If ideology pertains to a one-sided view of reality then it necessarily suffers from distortion. We are suggesting that the norms and values that are transmitted to the young and that are reinforced through the processes of social control are also characteristic of a specific ideology.

So, in urban society, the police, religious organisations, the courts, the mass media, all transmit an ideological — distorted — view of the world which masquerades as an objective, rational judgement. Young people are 'told' to conform to modes of behaviour that sustain the existing social order — moreover, a social order that is made to seem a natural order. It is 'natural' to conform to the demands of the economic system — to work hard, to buy the latest fashions, to marry and have children. By the same token it is 'natural' to accept the prevailing norms and values of the school system: a hierarchy of authority and knowledge, the competitive ethic, the importance of gaining 'O' and 'A' level passes.

It is a contention of this book that while many of the difficulties faced by teachers in urban schools are directly related to economic aspects of society (the control of capital, the demand of labour, technological change), the role of ideology is fundamental. This is not to say that the economic and the ideological are unrelated, but rather that the ideological aspects of schooling can and do operate in a relatively autonomous manner.

Althusser has emphasised the pre-eminent role of schooling in generating and reproducing an ideology of submission among the workforce. He sees the inculcation of this ideology as being as essential to the reproduction of the workforce under capitalism as is the development of necessary skills. In the past this ideology has been transmitted through institutions such as the church and the family. The development of the modern state has been accompanied by the emergence of two sets of state apparatuses. In the first place there are the repressive state apparatuses, primarily the armed forces and the police. Secondly, there are the *ideological state apparatuses* which, for Althusser, include the churches, the education system, the family, the legal system, the political system, trade unions, communications and media, and cultural institutions such as those concerned with the arts and sport. He sees schooling as now pre-eminent among these:

> I believe that the ideological State apparatus which has been installed in the *dominant* position in mature capitalist social formations . . . is the *educational state apparatus* (Althusser, in Cosin (ed.), 1972, p. 258).

Despite the apparent commitment of the schooling system to ideals such as freedom, they virtually serve to inculcate in children and young people an unquestioning allegiance to the accepted social order. They teach that the system is just and that each person's position within it is justly apportioned.

Althusser is deterministic and universal in his description of the role of schooling. He presumes that most teachers are unaware of their role in reproducing the system. He makes a few patronising references to those teachers who teach against 'the ideology, the system and the practices in which they are trapped. They are a kind of hero' [sic] (p. 216). In Althusser's view, then, teachers have very little autonomy within the structures of the ideological state apparatus. (This view is contested in Chapter 8.)

Not only might this be dubbed a pessimistic scenario but also a somewhat distorted interpretation of what actually happens in schools. Althusser's argument does seem to suggest that we are faced with imposing structures that inevitably bear down and crush those who dare to offer an alternative view of things. Indeed, according to this perspective, we are crushed before we even begin to articulate such alternative views. Althusser's structures seem to have no place for individual or group resistance. They are static. There is no sense of them actually being formed through the struggle between domination and resistance. Hence, there is no sense of them being open to change by human agency.

So, what are the implications for teachers, pupils and other actors in the urban school system? Are they merely cultural dupes whose thoughts, feelings and attitudes, and actions, are structurally determined by the state apparatus (DES, LEAs, MSC)? Should we discard notions of freedom and autonomy as fictions reflecting a good deal of wishful thinking? These are not rhetorical questions but real dilemmas, not easily solved by the process of reflective thought. The demands of practical living, the need for taken-for-granted routines, and the desire for non-conflictual situations, all militate against autonomy. However much freedom is valued as a principle, in practice many teachers are reluctant to enter the struggle.

In Chapter 7, we shall examine the way in which the dominant groups within the economy have affected and are continuing to affect the organisation and curricula of schools in sustaining and reproducing the social relations of work. Here, however, we shall attempt to show how schooling conditions the ideological expectations of both teachers and pupils. It would be a mistake, however, to assume that there is some kind of smooth cultural reproduction, as writers who have been influenced by Durkheim have tended to suggest. What is apparent, especially in urban schools where the gap between the dominant ideology and the experience of pupils is frequently at its widest, is that the precise opposite has often been the result. What we need to do now is to examine the practices of the urban classroom and reflect upon the difficulties involved in attempting to sustain traditional patterns of teacher domination and curriculum structure.

So, as Apple has noted:

> if you want to understand ideology at work in schools, look as much at the concreta of day to day curricular and pedagogic life as you would at the statements made by the spokespersons of the State or industry (Apple, 1982, p. 249).

Ideology, therefore, does not simply refer to the explicitly stated beliefs held by particular social classes, religions or other groups, which express their consciousness of the world. More significantly, it is a fundamental aspect of all social practice, of what we do, both collectively and individually, as a result of living in a society that is hierarchically ordered. There might well be different views as to what constitutes the basis of social hierarchy; those who have adopted a Weberian position suggest high status or bureaucratically held position as the basis for political domination in society, while Marxists view ownership of the means of production as the basis of economic *and* political domination (see Chapter 2). Whichever view is held, we can probably agree that the dominant group(s) seek to maintain and legitimate their position through ideology, and that the dominant ideology eventually becomes incorporated into the entire fabric of social practice. What is considered to be normal with regard to family life, work and leisure is, on deeper analysis, influenced — unawares — by the prevailing ideology. As far as schooling is concerned a study of ideology might examine how:

> the structure of the education system and the nature of everyday practices in schools are directly or indirectly related to the ways in which dominant groups in society attempt to secure acceptance and conformity to their beliefs, attitudes and interests (Barton *et al.*, 1980, p. 2).

CONTROL AND CONFLICT IN URBAN CLASSROOMS

> You can't put up your hand and say, 'Sir, this lesson's very boring'. . . . Everybody else is telling you what's best for you and what ain't but you're never taught to question anything. . . . If you do question anything, there's something wrong with you: you're insolent, you're naughty, you're a thug.
> (Mandy Smith, quoted in White and Brockington, 1983)

That classrooms in urban schools (especially inner-city secondary schools) are frequently characterised by conflict between the pupils and the teaching staff is not in itself a revelation. There is, however, some debate concerning the social significance of such conflict. One commonly accepted view is that of individual pathology. Here, the emphasis is on the 'culturally deprived' child from a poverty-stricken background, who having acquired anti-educational values is likely to exhibit behaviour that is unacceptable. The resulting conflict is defined in terms of unruliness which, while being explained according to notions of deprivation or disadvantage, must be dealt with as an individual breach of school discipline. From a liberal position, breaches of school discipline are more likely to necessitate interventions in terms of pastoral care, therapy or compensatory education rather than in terms of punishment.

This liberal view of teacher/pupil conflict, which locates it within the context of inadequate socialisation, contrasts with a more traditional view: that which suggests that misbehaviour in the classroom is a wilful act against authority. From this standpoint, classroom conflict reflects a situation of domination (on the part of teachers) and subordination (on the part of pupils). In the traditional view there is a recognition of the classroom as a place for the exercise of power: those in authority (the teachers) see themselves as being under constant attack by others (pupils) who may wish to challenge the power held by individual teachers, or even to deny the legitimacy of teacher authority altogether. The urban secondary school teacher who regards his/her day's work as 'going into battle' is not uncommon. The recognition of the classroom as a place of conflict typifies the traditional view of the urban school as well as more radical views. In the case of the former, however, the prevailing ideology emphasises teacher domination and pupil subordination. Teachers are socialised into a pattern of norms and values that underpin their position as holders of legitimate power in the classroom. The staffrooms of schools frequently act as agencies of reinforcement, giving mutual support in respect of traditional norms. New recruits to the profession, fresh from college, armed with the latest liberal notions of child development and pastoral care, are subjected to traditional pressures: 'you can forget all that education theory, the main task is to keep them under control'. This kind of approach is given a further boost by those teachers' organisations that place an emphasis on traditional discipline as the foundation of good schooling.

In this context it is worth noting that teachers are also quite firmly controlled in schools. The hierarchical promotion pattern of teachers tends to encourage conformity (we would not say servility) over originality or a critical approach. It is necessary not only to be an effective teacher but also to convince headteachers and heads of departments that this is so. What teachers wear, the way they speak, the newspapers they read, the political activities they are involved with, their gender, race and social orientation are all likely to influence their promotion chances. Newspaper 'scandals' indicate that the sex lives of teachers are deviously related in the view of journalists (and presumably of the public) to their professional competence to an extent that only applies otherwise to politicians. It certainly does not apply to journalists. Even the pupils can be a controlling influence on teachers after making it clear that curriculum and pedagogy should fulfil expectations that have developed through previous experiences of schooling.

In practice, many teachers in urban schools have found that the only way that they could survive in the classroom was to adopt a traditional mode of operation. Until the 1960s there were few alternative approaches available; the activities of progressive schools were considered to be irrelevant for mainstream education, catering as they frequently did for a largely middle-class population in rural surroundings. However, during the last twenty years, some education theorists and some teachers have begun to recognise the classroom situation as an arena for conflict between different interest groups. Teachers' interests, according to this approach, are clearly different from those of many pupils. At one level, this may be an aspect of crude Marxist analysis — middle-class teachers, representing the interests of the ruling class in society, in continual conflict with an urban working-class school population. At another level, it suggests a *relativistic* view of school knowledge whereby what teachers regard as good education is rejected by the pupils as irrelevant, having their own view as to what is legitimate knowledge.

Given this latter approach, domination and subordination are the outcome of a struggle for power. It is difficult for most teachers to accept that there might be this kind of struggle and almost impossible to accept an outcome that would deny them their authority. A minority of teachers in urban schools have adopted a radical approach, recognising the legitimacy of pupils' experiences and the cultural values associated with them. Here it is possible to apply an *interactionist* perspective to classroom situations where potential conflict is seen to be transformed through the process of negotiation. Whether such give and take between teachers and pupils is ultimately a face-saving exercise on the part of teachers is a matter of debate; it may well be that it becomes a device for enabling teachers to retain their authority (at least on the surface). Elsewhere, however, some teachers have decided that it is in fact legitimate for pupils to assume a position of power — at least in ideological terms. Not only do such teachers *not* view their role as one of socialisation, they also consciously act against the school as an agency of social control. One well-known example is that of Chris Searle, who, in the 1970s was prominent in what Grace has called 'the historic tradition of "resistance from within" ' (Grace, 1978, p. 101). Despite the fact that Searle found his position as a school teacher undermined by the prevailing official order his struggle indicates that it is possible for individuals to resist domination.

On the other hand, in a case where a large number of teachers in a school (including the headteacher) decided to challenge the accepted educational norms, the result was defeat. The case of William Tyndale Junior School in Islington, North London, provides an example of the kinds of contradictions encountered when a group of radical teachers attempt to put into practice what they see as a progressive pedagogy in an urban setting. The resulting confusion among those committed to radical reforms in schools only served to underline the difficulties associated with any attempt by teachers to challenge accepted notions of education. The structures of education may make it more possible for challenges to come from pupils than from teachers. However, as we indicate in the final chapter, there is space in schools for teachers to make radical and innovatory initiatives.

PUPIL RESISTANCE

So far, we have tended to examine issues of control, domination and subordination from a teacher-oriented perspective. It might be possible now to look at the issues from the angle of the pupils. It is wise, in this case, to consider the classroom as simply one part of the experience of children: the cultural life of urban schoolchildren is significant in its totality. The street life of working-class children in big cities has been well documented and in recent years much has been written regarding youth subcultures. From these sources we are able to recognise the complex nature of urban working-class culture as interpreted by the young. Large cities in Western industrial societies have tended to generate a variety of responses to the demands of capitalism and to the commands of authority. What is seen as an act of deviance when taken individually may be perceived as resistance when it is part of a collective or repeated action.

Resistance to institutionalised control can take a number of forms: it may be highly politicised and, therefore, 'rational' in both purpose and method. Political youth movements have traditionally had their strength in big cities and have, from time to time, recruited schoolchildren to their cause. On the whole, however, young children and adolescents have remained relatively immune to the more usual kinds of politicisation. For the most part, resistance has tended to be overtly 'non-political' in character; rather, it has taken the form of action rooted in expressive subcultures.

> The problem with a lot of kids today is that they haven't worked out who they are; they just want to belong to a visible group. They think they have an identity because they belong to a group. When I was at school, I felt more secure within a group. Nobody would ever challenge me, ask me, 'Who are *you*?'
> (Tory Crimes, quoted in White and Brockington, 1983)

The phenomenon of youth subcultures is largely a postwar one, and one that has been subjected to both intensive and extensive examination by social scientists and the mass media. Indeed, adolescence, which may be taken as the key concept of many of the standard works in the field, is itself a postwar phenomenon, a reflection of the lengthening of compulsory schooling. The expressive aspect of youth subcultures is seen in the variety of styles and rituals connected with music, dress, speech and relations with other groups. The complexity of subcultures (Teds, Skinheads, Rudies, and so on) reflects particular periods in the social history of Britain.

Youth subcultures — as cultures of the street — are an urban phenomenon, although they have apparently permeated the non-urban environment. At the same time, their influence has been felt inside schools where they can offer some kind of *normative protection* in the face of academic failure. By normative protection is meant that the individual can be buttressed against one set of norms through membership of a group that is characterised by a 'deviant' set of norms. So, for example, a punk possesses a particular set of values which may give him/her a sense of self-esteem when faced with being labelled as an educational failure, or, as Willis has pointed out, the working-class 'lads' of a Midland urban secondary school adhere to a 'delinquent' subculture in order to counter the demands of a school system which will inevitably confine them to particular inferior work roles.

Of course, teachers in urban schools have recognised the existence of collective forms of resistance in the classroom; not only are there individual 'disruptive' pupils, there are also groups of 'trouble-makers' who seem to generate collective strategies of opposition to those who wield authority. Many teachers can identify groups who are comparable to Willis's 'lads', regarding them as urban guerrillas within the school seeking to challenge its very foundations. In this case, subcultures are viewed as *counter-cultures*: they are in active opposition. School staffrooms buzz with conversations concerning such oppositional groups: What can be done about them? How can their activities be contained? What is the world coming to? Likewise, pupils interact with one another, reinforcing each other's negative feelings about school, devising tactics and strategies (frequently in an informal manner) to deal with the demands of school.

Perhaps the major component of subcultural resistance in schools is that of *myth*. Arguably, myths have played an important part in the lives of children: from those myths that are associated with early childhood, through to those associated with male adolescence, such as sexual prowess and physical strength. Modern anthropology has supplied us with the notion that myths are an essential aspect of people's lives. Myths can help explain events, even though they may do so in a distorted form; they help sustain and contribute to cultures of all kinds. In referring to events that are supposed to have taken place a long time ago, myths are regarded as valuable because they can be applied to current events — they are, in a sense, timeless. It is fairly easy to identify the kinds of myths related to youth subcultures which refer to teachers and schooling, work and authority, on the one hand, and to the lives of young people on the other. If schooling is accepted as a perpetual imposition upon the young which, for the most part, has to be resisted, it is because this view of schooling is enshrined in myth — and is one that is particularly pertinent to the urban working class.

So, what we have been arguing here is that resistance to authority structures is unlikely to be explained by reference to a simple model of individual deviance. We must, first of all, take into account the influence of social-control mechanisms upon the actions of young people, followed by an examination of the collective basis of 'deviant' behaviour together with the subcultural correlates of such behaviour. One further point to be made is that the *ideological* aspects of social control are paralleled by the *mythological* components of resistance. Myths then are 'ideological' positions that children develop to resist schools, teachers and adults. They may be repeated in different areas and at different times.

Finally, strategies of resistance as manifested in the 'deviant' behaviour of the young are not hermetically sealed from the wider working class and ethnic minority cultures. Indeed, it has been suggested that the counter-cultures of urban schools, far from breeding a population of rebels, in fact function to sustain the *status quo*. Delinquent young people in urban schools will tend to become conformist workers on the factory floor. To a large degree, this is a consequence of subcultural norms and values at the level of school becoming transformed into acceptable norms and values within the factory. Writers such as Willis have argued that the sexist and racist norms that characterise the culture of 'the lads' and similar groups, and which are regarded as contrary to the ethos of the school, become the basis for behaviour acceptable for factory workers.

SUBCULTURES, RESISTANCE, AND THE URBAN CRISIS

The year 1981 will be remembered as the one that English inner cities exploded. Leaving aside press sensationalism and the instant opinion voiced with regard to the 'disorders', there is no doubt that the actions of young people in places such as Brixton and Liverpool 8 suggested a serious malaise affecting the centres of Britain's largest cities. The surface manifestations of rampaging youth, riots and looting masked a much deeper and chronic phenomenon: the decline of the inner city both in terms of population and in employment opportunities. While the 'recession' of the 1970s and 1980s made headlines in the short run, it was the long-term 'structural' changes in industry and commerce, begun at the start of the century, that had eaten away Britain's urban cores. The flight of capital to the suburban fringe and beyond (even to other countries) meant that the inner-city working-class population was becoming increasingly redundant. (This aspect is examined at length in Chapter 7.)

The result was an inner city characterised by a declining working class, often ethnically diverse, unable to sell its labour, and with a young age structure. (Although, in addition, the elderly also comprise a significant section of the inner-city population, being relatively immobile and on low fixed incomes.) The lack of investment in the urban core and the failure to exploit human resources provide the material backcloth to the urban crisis as perceived by politicians, social scientists, journalists and others. The cultural correlate has been the development of forms of behaviour often judged to be antisocial, running counter to dominant norms and values. The term *alienation* has frequently been applied to the situation of manual workers in repetitive manufacturing jobs — suggesting powerlessness, little intrinsic meaning in the work and no control over the process or the product. Of late, it has found new meaning in relation to unemployed youth and school leavers; here, referring to alienation from the taken-for-granted world of regular employment, the associated values of thrift and hard work, and the general way of life of their elders.

As Robins and Cohen have pointed out, the relative affluence of the postwar era has enabled urban working-class youth to obtain 'freedom from school, from the parental nags . . . a wage of their own to do that they like with' (Robins and Cohen, 1978, pp. 8–9). On the other hand, they also add that the experience of inner-city youth is increasingly that of a different kind of freedom — that of enforced leisure, not bought, but imposed through the changing structure of employment opportunities (p. 11).

In short, it is becoming more and more difficult to explain the actions of urban working-class youth within a general context of full employment. The transition from school to work can no longer be taken as a given fact. Subcultural tendencies within schools might survive on the basis of scorn for the conformists and the academics, as well as for authority, but in the face of probable unemployment the pay-off of hard cash in return for hard graft is not on the horizon.

By the same token, the difficulties for the urban school as an agency of social control become magnified. The one possible way of obtaining compliance of urban working-class youth, so it was thought, was to suggest to them that they only had to suffer school until they were 16, during which time they might acquire some knowledge and a few skills that would be useful when they went out to work. When school can no longer be justified to young people on instrumental grounds it is difficult to see what other ideology can be employed to achieve adherence to the value of schooling. Little wonder that in the 1980s, an era of cuts in the teaching force and general retrenchment in education, there was a return to authoritarian modes of control (notwithstanding the pressure to abolish corporal punishment in schools). As unemployment becomes increasingly the norm for urban working-class school leavers, so the school becomes even more of a custodial institution. There is then the question of how the pupils themselves will respond. An HMI report on a Liverpool secondary school noted that 'a worryingly large proportion of students rejected or at best passively acquiesced in what the school provided' (*Times Educational Supplement*, 22 July 1983). In terms of young people actively constructing a positive subcultural response, we might conclude that 'there is no "subcultural solution" to working-class youth unemployment, educational disadvantage, compulsory miseducation' (Hall and Jefferson (eds), 1976, p. 47).

The imaginary solutions to the situation of contemporary urban working-class youth enshrined in current subcultural styles are likely to become even more transparent. Whether more young people are likely to respond in a *retreatist* fashion to an ever-deepening urban crisis is a matter for debate. (By retreatist is meant dissociation from both the goals of the 'community at large' and the means of achieving them.) Individualistic escapes such as chronic hard drug abuse have for some time offered a way out of urban life; so, for that matter, have suicide and insanity. But despite subcultural aspects to these escapes they hardly qualify as acceptable alternative lifestyles on the part of significant sections of urban youth. Adherence to ethnically based subcultures (such as Rastafarianism), while they may be seen as forms of collective retreat, none the less have a more firmly rooted set of values and more stable historical foundations. Other subcultures (Hippies, Mods, Rockers, Skinheads, Punks) have tended to be based on superficialities of style rather than adherence to any clearly defined set of values — and have had, to a greater or lesser extent, some kind of relationship with the dominant culture.

In a retreatist world dominated by a kind of passive cynicism there is ample room for the state to provide a cultural setting for young people in which chauvinistic values become fashionable. The early 1980s saw the British state involved in military action in Northern Ireland and the Falkland Islands. The latter was surrounded by a jingoistic campaign of such proportions that few voices were heard in criticism. Young people were caught up in the patriotic fervour and this combined with declining employment and opportunities led to an increase in recruitment to the armed forces. It may well be that the more overt expressive youth subcultures as we have known them are on the decline and that resistance to prevailing modes of domination could even cease to exist. There is certainly little evidence to suggest that an era of acute and chronic economic decline automatically brings about organised opposition — of any kind. With the disappearance of the youth wage for many young city-dwellers and the substitution of supplementary benefit or training scheme allowances, they are rapidly joining the old and the infirm as recipients of low fixed incomes. In short, the power previously held by young people is gradually being eroded — the power to win space in a world defined by bureaucracy and big business.

There was considerable argument concerning the disturbances in Brixton, Toxteth, Moss Side, St Paul's and elsewhere in 1980–1. Were they simply the outcome of frustration and the enforced freedom of unemployment? Or could they be interpreted as organised subcultural responses to racism and urban deprivation? Or were these events the result of outside 'agitation' and the exploitation of grievances by unscrupulous ultra-left political groups? But the fact that those involved in the 'disturbances' were both black and white and were not identifiable as belonging to particular subcultural groups suggested that this aspect had little part to play in the events. This does not, of course, mean that agencies of social control and authority figures do not continue to find 'folk devils' among the young; the media constantly help to sustain control ideologies by providing images of deviant youth that are wildly at variance with reality. (The folk devil — the contemporary figure of fear — has been created alongside what has been called 'moral panic': a kind of collective hysteria related to a heightened sense of what is right and wrong behaviour.) The suspicion that the mass media, particularly the popular press and television, have an important role to play in the creation of youth subcultures and their 'deviant' behaviour has appeared to be well founded. In their portrayal of sensational images of youth (violent Skinheads, cannabis-smoking Hippies) the media have encouraged the adoption and expression of appropriate action. This, in turn, rebounds upon young people themselves — frequently taking on board those very images, feeding them back into their own behaviour (sometimes called *deviancy amplification*). In other words, 'give a dog a bad name' and it is more than likely to conform to one's worst expectations.

If what we have said so far suggests that urban working-class youth have little hope of developing relevant strategies of resistance in the midst of declining work opportunities and an increasingly repressive dominant culture, then we have probably overstated the case. While not descending into crude generalisation, it is possible to note a certain amount of resilience among the young. Even in the most deprived areas of Britain's largest cities young people have learnt to cope with life on a day-to-day basis: participation in the 'informal' economy, even simply 'doing nothing' which can be seen as representing 'the largest and most complex youth culture' (Corrigan, in Hall and Jefferson (eds), 1976, p. 103). 'Doing nothing' is the street culture *par excellence*: it incorporates such activities as 'hanging around', 'talking', 'fighting' and, at least, is an attempt on the part of young people themselves to combat the boredom induced by an adult world which has forgotten the real needs of inner-city youth.

Moreover, we might follow Willis (1983) in suggesting that the young do not merely resist in a negative manner, but produce cultures of resistance; such cultural production is born out of the very conflicts that characterise social relations. Willis puts a dynamic back into reproduction theory that seemed to be absent from other writings. Society is viewed less as constituting formidable, static structures of domination against which various forms of resistance arise. It is more realistic to view the structures of society as 'produced through struggle'; the 'system' does not exist separately from the lives of the young (or of anybody else for that matter) (Willis, 1983). We are all part of the 'system', attempting to win space, power and a bigger share of the resources. In so far as urban youth generate subcultural styles they are part of the dynamic structure of a society which is undergoing continual change, while, at the same time, those in positions of economic and political power endeavour to maintain some stability.

However, a note of caution needs to be entered at this stage. We might well be criticised for having placed undue emphasis upon explicit forms of resistance and struggle on the part of urban working-class young people; that youth subcultures constitute rational, critical, collective responses to the system. But what of the others? Do we write off the majority of young people in urban schools as mere conformists — as tacit supporters of the *status quo*?

The so-called conformists, Willis's 'ear'oles' and others, are probably the most problematic category in schools. The appearance of conformity to established norms, not challenging the authority of teachers, not participating in counter/subcultural activities, hides, possibly, a more fundamental threat. As Fuller suggests, the conformists are often either indifferent or instrumental in their actions, rather than oppositional.

In which case, such resistance is passive rather than active. Moreover, conformity is a strategy readily adopted by female pupils — the hitherto invisible group in studies of deviance. In so far as girls are perceived to conform to the norms of schooling such conformity does not simply reflect the reproduction of gender relations, that is, passivity in relation to subcultural masculinity, but rather they are 'too busy resisting other aspects of their life that resistance to schooling has a lower priority for them' (Fuller, 1983, p. 190).

Elsewhere it has been noted that the appearance of conformity frequently masks a much deeper resistance to the dominant culture. Dumont and Wax (1971) were able to observe the activity of 'playing school' among Cherokee schoolchildren in the USA, in which the children insulated themselves from cultural penetration by treating school as a kind of game to be played, where the rules were adhered to, while at the same time reserving real cultural involvement for the Cherokee community (Dumont and Wax, in Cosin *et al.* (eds), 1971).

In sum, therefore, we should not necessarily equate silence with acquiescence. There is an important difference between behaving 'well' — accepting the maxim 'don't cause trouble' — and accepting the dominant value system. In the case of urban schools, most young people perceive education as something that is imposed, not as something in which they willingly participate because it answers a set of felt needs. It becomes difficult to gauge the extent to which a gulf exists between the world of the pupils and the world of the teachers when the emphasis is simply upon observable behaviour. While subcultural dissent, truancy and violence in the classroom are visible they may not be the most significant aspects of resistance and struggle. For as Willis (1977) points out, participation in subcultural activity does not mean challenging the system; rather, it helps to make life bearable for some young people until they assume their allotted places in the socioeconomic hierarchy. The 'conformists' often submerge their anger and discontent only for it to be realised later in life as social mobility or political activism.

THEORETICAL PERSPECTIVES

So far, we have attempted to examine the nature of social control, the function of ideology and the modes of resistance among urban youth to the imposition of authority. What we have yet to do is to place our analysis into some kind of urban theoretical context. An important question therefore is: how do we relate the various phenomena noted in urban schools to the perspectives discussed earlier in this book?

The ecological approach of the Chicago theorists no doubt would suggest that big cities incorporate downtown areas characterised by violence and subcultural activity. So long as it is confined to such areas the rest of the urban population can sleep soundly. Social control mechanisms would ensure that the balanced character of the city is maintained. Indeed, many of those involved in educational policy implementation readily accept the existence of 'problem' schools in 'problem' areas of cities. There is a sense in which inner-city schools are seen as functioning to maintain the rest of the education system. While teachers have to face issues of social control in the urban cores, others working elsewhere in the system can rest satisfied that all is well; resistance is less frequently encountered in the shires. The system is therefore working satisfactorily, and in so far as urban schools are characterised by conflict and dissent they serve to remind the rest of the country of the potential threats to society. There is nothing like a William Tyndale affair or a case of school vandalism to incite the media to burst into fits of righteous indignation and, thus, reinforce the established moral consensus.

This conservative view of 'disorder' in urban schools, though it might be accepted by those who feel that no action is called for other than the strengthening of the forces of law and order, seems to be somewhat at variance with those urban theoretical approaches predicated upon political/economic conflict. In this respect, liberal and radical perspectives may offer more plausible insights into the phenomena we have attempted to describe.

Here, urban space is regarded as having quite special social, economic and political significance. The logic of capitalism suggests that the demands of inner-city dwellers become increasingly subordinated to the demands of industry and commerce. Space is created for office blocks, not for a more human environment in which it is possible to live in a harmonious and co-operative manner. Where urban youth are confronted by the repressive state apparatus we also find the most deprived of urban environments. As Harrison indicates, it is in blight-ed areas such as Hackney which continue to descend on a downward spiral that the child 'encounters the police at an early age, and is hectored, lectured, labelled and sometimes arrested' (Harrison, 1983, p. 316). The cutbacks affecting collective consumption, as described by Castells, further ensure that certain sections of the urban population feel that they have no stake in the system.

It is not surprising, therefore, that urban schools remain arenas for conflict and struggle. In such schools mechanisms of social control sometimes succeed in establishing calm while ideological imposition frequently prevents conflict from manifesting itself as outright opposition. None the less, it may be possible to make connections between the behaviour of young people in inner cities and the effects of a changing capitalist economic structure. From a radical standpoint, disaffected urban youth represent the refracted demands of a deprived section of the community. Bearing in mind what Castells has had to say, however, it is hard to see urban social movements coalescing around youth subcultures, still less the making of common cause between those who operate the urban school system and those who resist it.

On the other hand, liberal perspectives linked to Weberian urban theory, in emphasising power as an independent variable, would suggest that the resistance of urban youth is very much the outcome of a crisis of authority legitimation. When those who wield power cease to have their positions legitimated, recognised and accepted as authority, alternative power structures arise which offer a challenge. Youth subcultures, according to such a view, are a direct outcome of this legitimation crisis. In short, such perspectives would suggest that the difficulties of social control and resistance faced in urban schools are not so much connected with a crisis of capitalism as with a crisis of political authority.

TEACHERS AND PUPILS – WORLDS APART?

Are we inevitably faced with an urban school system characterised by an endemic conflict of values and a clash of ideologies? Are urban school teachers to consider themselves no more than state functionaries — as guardians of the *status quo*? If the answer to these questions is 'yes' (and we suggest differently in Chapter 8), then there may well be a limit to what schools can do as instruments of radical change. Yet there are, in urban classrooms, real urgent practical difficulties that face teachers and pupils concerning how to ensure that school is something less than a wasting of time. At one level, it might be suggested that young people should develop a new kind of social awareness, replacing the often inward-looking parochial nature of youth sub- (or counter-) cultures. Such social awareness is not something that can be imposed from the outside — from youth workers, radical activists and the like. It does, however, demand that young people are not treated in the stereotypical manner characteristic of the media, that they are not used as scapegoats for the urban crisis.

It may also demand a sensitivity on the part of teachers to the needs of pupils in urban schools, without either trying to take on board the latest subcultural styles and incorporating them into the curriculum or using crude and oppressive techniques of domination. Either of these methods is a form of social control which may cut very little ice with urban school pupils. At a commonsense level what is frequently demanded of school teachers by young people are qualities such as patience, humour and straight dealing. These qualities can only show in teachers if they perceive themselves not necessarily as remedying the crisis of urban education — but, at least, as part of the struggle against an inequitable system.

At the same time, of course, teachers cannot ignore the structural constraints that necessarily shape their actions. As Sharp and Green point out, the beliefs a human being has about a situation 'may not necessarily be compatible with the structure of possibilities inherent in the facts' (Sharp and Green, 1975, p. 28). Quite profound changes are occurring in the upper secondary school curriculum, where the 1970s call for uniformity seems to be bearing fruit in the 1980s. 'Vocational preparation' and the teaching of 'basic skills' appear likely to replace any vestige of liberal education for the majority of young people; the possibility of gaining insights into the working of society will be further away than ever. The task facing teachers who do not see themselves as mere agents of the state, but as concerned professionals with a commitment to the liberating potential of education, is undoubtedly enormous. We discuss possibilities for action on the part of urban school teachers in Chapter 8.

GUIDE TO FURTHER READING

The literature in this area is fairly extensive, ranging from essentially theoretical studies of ideology and social control through to substantive publications concerning the lives of young people in cities. A basic approach to the study of social control is to be found in Davies (1976), *Social Control and Education*, while Sharp and Green (1975), *Education and Social Control*, looks at the issue in the context of primary-school practice. Both Apple (1979), *Ideology and Curriculum*, and Barton *et al.* (eds) (1980), *Schooling, Ideology and the Curriculum*, deal extensively with the ideological character of the educational process, while Karabel and Halsey (eds) (1977), *Power and Ideology in Education*, contains important readings in the area.

Resistance in the context of youth subcultures is examined in Hall and Jefferson (eds) (1976), *Resistance Through Rituals*, while there are a number of studies looking at specific urban instances of existence: Patrick (1973), *A Glasgow Gang Observed*; Pryce (1979), *Endless Pressure*; Robins and Cohen (1978), *Knuckle Sandwich*; and Willis (1977), *Learning to Labour*.

5
Education and urban cultural diversity

One of the major preoccupations of people who work in urban schooling systems is that of cultural diversity. In this chapter the issues raised by this are considered in more detail. In the first section a series of questions about the historical continuities in cities in terms of diversity are explored. The second section looks at the context in contemporary cities, particularly at the way in which various ethnic and racial minorities are disadvantaged and discriminated against. In the third section the recent responses of urban schooling systems to this diversity are discussed, with special attention being paid to two key issues, racism in education and differential educational performance. The final section, by looking at recent reports on what is happening in urban schools, sketches out some provisional suggestions for more effective policies in this area.

THE HISTORICAL SETTING

As Chapter 1 indicated, British cities are places of considerable cultural diversity. The degree and nature of this diversity differs from urban area to urban area and within the same urban area over time. To give some idea of this diversity, Figure 5.1 reveals the linguistic diversity in five urban areas in England. It shows, as one might expect, not only the range of languages spoken by schoolchildren, but also the marked differences between urban areas, even between those that are geographically close together, as in the case of the two London boroughs of Haringey and Waltham Forest. Other indicators of

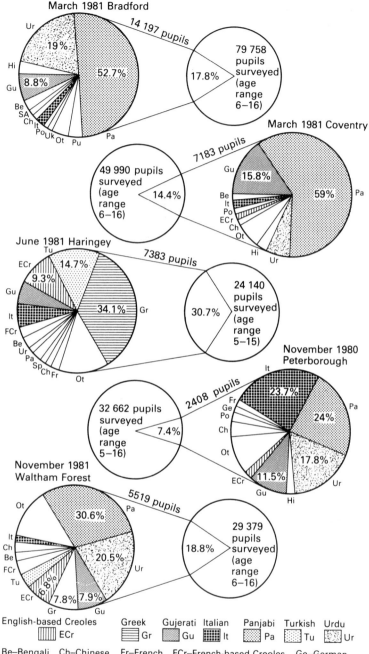

Figure 5.1 *Main languages reported as spoken in five urban LEAs. From the Linguistic Minorities Project, 1983a. Reproduced with permission.*

diversity, such as religion, race and ethnicity would show a similar range of variety. As for changes over time *within* an area, the Spitalfields area of East London has over the last few hundred or so years seen successive groups of immigrants moving in, settling and then, in the main, moving out. Of some of the earlier groups, such as the Protestant Huguenots who fled from religious persecution in France in the seventeenth century, and the Flemish weavers, also religious refugees, little remains except street and other locality names, such as Fournier Street, Leydon Street and Weavers Fields. More recent groups, such as the Jews who arrived in the period 1880–1914, also fleeing from persecution, are a more obvious presence, although they too have mainly moved from the area, leaving some small industries behind and a number of synagogues, the latter no longer as used as before. In the period after the war, people from the Caribbean and, most significantly at the time of writing, people from Bangladesh, have moved into the area. This ethnic succession is nowhere better revealed than in a building at the corner of Fournier Street and Brick Lane, the main north–south road in the district. Originally a Christian church, it has successively been a centre for the Christian Conversion of the Jews movement, a synagogue and is now a mosque.

Just as urban diversity is not a recent phenomenon in British cities, so is the negative approach to such diversity. Concern over the social stability of the city consequent upon such in-migration has been expressed for a considerable period of time. Queen Elizabeth I published an edict forbidding further settlement of 'blackamoors' within London (Milner, 1975), and James Galt, in his novels written at the end of the eighteenth century, bemoaned the moral degeneration found in the rapidly expanding cotton towns in the Glasgow region, caused by immigration from the rural areas around these new towns.

It was, however, the massive expansion of the Victorian industrial city that caused concern and worry to be expressed more widely. Most of this concern was about the dangers, real and potential, that commentators felt such in-migration and rapid expansion had led to, or could lead to. As Stuart Hall puts it, the Victorian middle classes had a nightmare:

> . . . the descent of the 'industrious poor' into the abyss, the spectre of the 'unruly mob', the 'dangerous classes', rising up to murder decent Englishmen in their beds, claiming with sticks and staves what they were clearly not going to win by franchise and ballots (Hall, 1977, p. 50).

We still do not know enough about the perspective from the 'other side of the tracks' although we can gain some indication from the writings of Dickens and Mayhew. The urban working class, however, was not the undifferentiated mass that many of its middle- and upper-class critics perceived it as. Perhaps the most significant section of it in Victorian cities, in terms of the analysis presented in this chapter, was the Irish. As Lees puts it: 'For a society that had received no large-scale immigration since the Norman conquest, this influx of Irish amounted to an urban invasion' (Lees, 1979, p. 15).

Although Irish immigration has been constant since about 1815, the period after the 1846 Irish famine, coupled with the burgeoning and labour-intensive industrial boom in England, led to a more rapid influx. Half a million Irish people had settled in England and Wales by 1851, four-fifths of them living in large cities like Manchester, Liverpool and London. Even more revealing are the figures relating to Irish- and English-origin Roman Catholics. In the Lancashire towns of Preston, Wigan, Liverpool and Manchester in 1791, of the 10 000 Catholics, 30 per cent were Irish. By 1850 there were 120 000 and 80 per cent were Irish or of Irish descent (Hall, 1983). Given the importance attached to providing a Catholic education by the Catholic hierarchy, this rapid increase had obvious implications for the provision of schools in urban areas. The issues that such provision give rise to are still important and controversial and will be looked at later.

The Irish communities were a major source of easily available (and easily laid off) labour. Originally working on railway and canal construction as the famous 'navigators' (hence the word 'navvies'), by the middle of the century they were to be found in many of the least pleasant and worst-paid jobs in urban areas. As a result of being located in the worst parts of the cities many people associated such dereliction and dilapidation with the Irish and eventually saw the Irish as the cause of such squalor. Engels, in his classic study of Manchester, although not making that type of analysis, did claim that one could immediately recognise the Irish 'race' by their physical appearance. Given these circumstances, it is not surprising that many Irish people met with great hostility in the cities. In Scotland 'racial' and religious riots about the Irish presence were common in cities in the nineteenth century, to the extent that the 'game' called 'Hunt the Barney', where solitary Irish people, usually men, were hunted down, attacked and occasionally killed, became a reasonably common activity (Foot, 1965). It is a grim reminder that the contemporary crime of 'Paki-bashing' has a long and ignoble history. The negative and the hostile stereotypes of Irish people have persisted, albeit in a somewhat watered-down form, to this day. It took the 1968 Race Relations Act to stop signs like 'No Irish' on pub doors and advertisements for accommodation in many inner-city areas. And even today many non-Irish people see little offence in telling so-called Irish jokes.

The more extreme manifestations of hostility towards the Irish declined with the arrival, towards the end of the century, of Jewish refugees from Europe. Like the Irish and other groups before them they settled mainly in the inner areas of the large cities. The East End of London, near to the docks where they had first landed in England, was the scene of their largest and most publicised settlement. Hostility towards them was open and forcefully expressed. As one MP said at the time:

> It is only a matter of time before the population becomes entirely foreign. . . . The rates are burdened with the education of thousands of children of foreign parents. . . . The working classes know that new buildings are erected not for them but for strangers from abroad . . . they see the schools crowded with foreign children and the very posters and advertisements on the walls in a foreign tongue (quoted in Foot, 1965, p. 80).

The passage has a curious contemporary ring to it. The references to housing and education could readily be replicated today. It is also interesting that there is a deliberate attempt to differentiate between the 'working classes', presumably non-Jewish, and the 'foreigners', presumably Jewish, but also working class. A question that this raises is, in whose interest was the creation of such a division between foreigners and non-foreigners, especially as they were all working class? In other words, who benefited then, and who benefits now, from the maintenance of such divisions? It is clearly not in the interests of the working class, whatever their origins, to be internally divided. Such divisions might, for instance, impede the formation of effective trade unions. It can further serve to direct antagonism against 'the blacks' rather than against the oppressive structures that serve to exploit all working-class groups.

The language used with regard to the Jews is also interesting and has a contemporary relevance. Then, as now, descriptive terms are used in an attempt to maintain the in-coming group's 'otherness'. Thus, the Jewish people were referred to not just as 'foreigners', but more frequently as 'aliens'. The Aliens Act of 1905 was a piece of legislation designed to restrict Jewish in-migration, just as the Immigration Acts since the Second World War have been designed to keep out black people. The word 'immigrant' is still used to refer, not to white Australians and South Africans resident in Britain, but to black people, that is, those from the Caribbean, Africa and Asia. Few of the people thus described, however, are immigrants. Indeed in cities like Cardiff, Liverpool and London, certain groups of the black population are likely to have lived in the city for several generations but may well be called 'immigrants' by members of the white community. It is a crucial abuse of language as it serves to maintain the 'out group' status of the group so described.

So far we have made the following assertions:

1. Cities in Britain have been culturally diverse for a very long time.
2. The nature of city growth has meant that differences in religion, language, lifestyles, race and ethnicity are an integral part of the urban system, and this includes the educational system.
3. For the owners and organisers of the means of production the immigration to the cities has provided a source of cheap and easily exploited labour. At the same time other elements within the dominant group and sections of the working class have seen the growth of diversity as a threat to the social fabric.
4. Prejudice and discrimination against immigrant groups appears to have been the norm, particularly if members of such groups were readily identifiable.
5. Working-class interests and solidarity have often been eroded by a white working-class view of immigrants that sees them not as working-class allies but as alien enemies. The unity between the two groups has rarely been articulated or encouraged.
6. The variety of historical responses to diversity are mirrored in contemporary responses. For example, racism has been a long-standing feature of white British society.

Some of these assertions appear contradictory. For example, in 1968 the CBI was one of the few organisations to oppose immigration controls as its members saw the value in having a readily available pool of cheap labour. Yet, many members of the CBI practised discrimination in their employment and recruitment practices. But the two views do not really contradict one another; it should be remembered that one function of the immigrant groups was to provide a reserve army of labour and that such an army had the effect of generally lowering wages in the areas that they worked in. In addition, the cyclical nature of the British economy since the war, with its booms and slumps, meant that in slumps it was easier tacitly to encourage the view among certain sections of the working class that it was the presence of immigrants that prevented them from getting jobs rather than to expose the inefficiencies in management and the place of such economic cycles within the workings of a capitalist economic system.

DIVERSITY IN CONTEMPORARY URBAN AREAS

In the first section of this chapter it was asserted that cultural diversity is a long-standing feature of British urban areas and that hostility towards such diversity is of an equally long standing. The persistence of such hostility is a major concern for public policy-makers, particularly those in urban areas where many minority groups are concentrated. Of course it is important to make clear that like many of the other issues raised in this book it is not exclusively an urban phenomenon: racism is found throughout British society, in rural as well as urban areas. The educational consequences of this will be examined in the next section. It would be wrong, however, to separate too distinctly the concern of policy-makers from the racism of other groups. Policy-makers have also fallen into the trap mentioned with regard to the Irish earlier: of seeing immigrant groups as the causes of their own poor physical environment and disadvantaged socioeconomic position. This is a form of blaming the victim. (A more psychological, but equally pernicious, form of such blame is to see such groups as having deviant family patterns or being locked into a culture of poverty.)

A classic educational example of this concern/hostility confusion is to be found in the statement made to the House of Commons in 1963 by Sir Edward Boyle, the then Minister of Education, after visiting primary schools in Southall, London. He said:

> I must regretfully tell the House that one school must be regarded now as irretrievably an immigrant school. The important thing to do is prevent this happening elsewhere (quoted in Jones and Kimberley, 1981, p. 137).

The language appears on the surface to be moderate, and concerned, but words like 'regretfully', 'irretrievably' and 'prevent' imply otherwise. Note also the continuing use of euphemisms to describe certain visible categories of people. Just as 'aliens' meant Jews, now 'immigrant' means black. As Sam Greenlee said:

> The chief change
> I've noted
> among ·
> White folks is
> now they talkin
> bout us in code (Greenlee, 1975, p. 24).

Sir Edward Boyle was commenting on the issues raised for urban school systems by one of the more recent waves of immigration into the urban areas of Great Britain, namely that of people from the Caribbean, Africa and the Indian subcontinent. Although, as indicated earlier, black people had been members of British society for many hundreds of years, this more recent movement of people quickly brought the issue of cultural diversity and social policy to the forefront of public debate and, in particular, educational debate. Their descendants, the new black British, have raised questions about the urban schooling system, as well as general public policy which are in fact not new, but merely newly stated.

> If you teach in an inner-city school which has a large proportion of black children, do you know you have an extra amount of money? They give you a special allowance. Yes, teachers get special allowances for teaching in those schools, because they are called dustbin schools. And because they are labelled in that way, they teach them in the same way. They think of them in that way and nothing ever comes out of it.
>
> (A black parent quoted in AFFOR, 1982)

Given the nature of the reception that many immigrant groups have received on settling in Britain, why did they come in the first place? Most usually, the process of migration is described in terms of push and pull factors. Thus, in the period since 1945, the push factors would have included poverty and unemployment in the countries from which emigration took place. In addition, for some of the groups, violent political changes, such as the expulsion of Asian-origin people from East Africa and the invasion (or liberation, according to how you see it) of Northern Cyprus by Turkey, has led to unwilling emigration. Pull factors are equally important, however, as they partly explain why people have travelled half way around the world to arrive at a small island off the mainland of Europe. The legacy of Empire is one crucial reason of course and will be looked at shortly. The primary pull factor, however, was a demand for labour in postwar Britain, particularly unskilled, undemanding and cheap labour. That this factor was crucial for many groups has been shown (Peach, 1968): immigration from the Caribbean rose and fell in line with the performance of the British economy. Minor recessions led to a decline in immigration, minor booms led to an increase. This pattern persisted until fear of immigration controls (eventually realised in 1962) pushed the rate up irrespective of the British economy, with people emigrating in comparatively large numbers compared to previous rates, getting in before controls were established. By moving to Britain, rather than to France or Germany, where there were equally severe shortages of labour, these people demonstrated one of the last, and perhaps most powerful — even ironic — ties of colonialism. Legal commitments to Commonwealth countries have remained, although legislation through successive Immigration Acts has sought to renege on such obligations. Thus fear of further groups claiming rights of settlement because they were British, such as the people living in Hong Kong, has led to wholesale changes in the laws concerning British nationality. This is now determined by descent, 'blood', rather than by residence or previous legal commitment subsequent upon decolonisation. Thus it was discovered in 1983 that the 1981 Nationality Act had removed British citizenship from the Falkland Islanders over whom the same government as had introduced the Act had just gone to war, to protect their rights to be 'British'.

The postwar immigration and nationality Acts were a negative response to the fact that the new Commonwealth immigrants had rights of settlement and initially were free to come and work as they chose. In the early years, the acute and prolonged shortage of labour in Britain made public policy-makers ignore or overlook the long-term consequences. This labour shortage was incidentally made worse by the continual steady emigration of white British people to the 'old' or white Commonwealth or such 'new' Commonwealth countries as Kenya or Southern Rhodesia which seemed at that time to be firmly white-dominated. Also women, who during the war had been encouraged to enter the waged workplace, were now encouraged with equal enthusiasm to stay at home and look after their children. Even so, employers would often only take on new black immigrant workers when all attempts to recruit white labour had failed (Daniels, 1968). If black labour was recruited, it was often non-unionised and was therefore often persuaded to work for less money than would have been acceptable to the white working-class labour force.

Several consequences have stemmed from this initial positioning in the labour market. First, because many of the black immigrants were in poor jobs, many people began to associate all black people with a low socioeconomic standing. Secondly, and as a consequence of the first point, many black workers came to be assigned to such poor jobs and status because they were black, irrespective of their educational or other qualifications, and irrespective of whether they were immigrants or not. Thus a British-born black graduate could and still may be regarded as an immigrant, not qualified and suitable only for the most menial of jobs. In comparing the job levels of a sample of white and black male graduates it was found that 79 per cent of the white men were in professional or management positions, whereas only 31 per cent of the black graduate sample were. No white graduates in the sample were in manual work, but 21 per cent of the black graduates were (Smith, 1977). Smith concluded from this and other investigations that discrimination is based on a general colour prejudice, which does not distinguish much between people belonging to different racial groups, having different religions, speaking different languages and coming from different countries. They are all lumped together as 'coloured' people.

The third and most significant consequence is that the British-born children of black immigrants meet with the same discrimination and show every sign of being made into a permanent underclass, a classic reserve army of labour. There is support for this view in the unemployment statistics, which show a disproportionate increase in the number of young black people without work. For example, unemployment among young blacks rose by 45 per cent between 1974 and 1977, before the economic recession gathered momentum, compared to an increase of 30 per cent in the population as a whole (Runnymede Trust, 1980). Since then, as Figures 5.2 and 5.3 show, the gap between blacks and whites has widened even further, compounded by the fact that many young blacks are so disillusioned that they do not even bother to sign on (Select Committee on Race Relations and Immigration, 1977; Navitt, 1979). And with official unemployment rates for young black males approaching 55 per cent in some urban areas, the real picture is even more serious. As Lord Scarman commented:

> There can be no doubt that it [unemployment] was a major factor in the complex pattern of conditions which lies at the root of the disorders in Brixton and elsewhere (Home Office, 1981, p. 107).

The lack of employment possibilities, with little prospect of any upturn, particularly in the inner-city areas where many of these young people live, has obvious links with the education that is provided in the schools. As a recent Home Affairs Committee of Parliament noted:

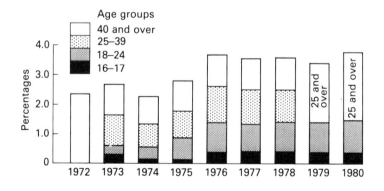

Figure 5.2 *Unemployment among minority groups as a percentage of total unemployed. From the Runnymede Trust, 1980. Reproduced with permission.*

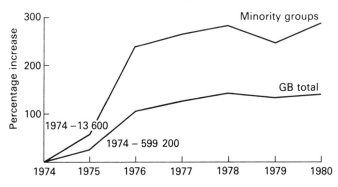

Figure 5.3 *Percentage increase in unemployment since 1974 of minority groups and total workforce in Great Britain. From the Runnymede Trust, 1980. Reproduced with permission.*

> Disadvantage in education and employment are the two most crucial facets of racial disadvantage. They are closely connected. Without a decent education and the qualifications which such education alone can provide, a school-leaver is unlikely to find the sort of job to which he aspires, or indeed any job. Conversely, pupils who learn from older friends of the degree of difficulty encountered in finding employment may well be discouraged from striving to achieve at school. In other words, there is no point in getting ethnic minority education right if we do not at the same time sort out racial disadvantage in employment and vice versa (Home Affairs Committee, 1981).

As this comment indicates, city schools have not, in the main, 'got ethnic minority education right'. What exactly 'right' is, is part of the problem. For despite the increased concern for this area of educational policy, revealed most clearly by the recent setting up of a government inquiry (the Swann Committee), it is still an area of great confusion for British educationalists, at both the practical and theoretical level. Much of this confusion is due to the lack of a sustained and coherent body of thought on what exactly is involved in education for a culturally diverse society. In addition, the widespread racial discrimination and prejudice found in British society makes it an educational issue of more than usual political sensitivity.

THE URBAN SCHOOL AND CULTURAL DIVERSITY

Race, ethnicity and culture

When educators talk about multicultural education, multi-ethnic education, multi-racial education and anti-racist education, what exactly are they talking about? In a similar manner, words like assimilation, integration and pluralism are used in ways that seem contradictory and confusing. Two points need to be made about this. First, the words can be given precise meanings but they will be the authors' meanings and subject to criticism like anybody else's. Secondly, words in this area quickly accrete political overtones and are used as part of the verbal warfare between groups within education.

One way to tackle this issue is to look at these definitional terms, using a further concept, namely diversity. The starting point is that all urban areas in Britain are diverse in terms of their populations. Such diversity can be seen in terms of class, gender, religion, language, historical origins, skin colour, etc. Urban areas contain groups of people who may differ from one another in terms of certain cultural attributes, most notably language and religion. In addition, British society, along with most others, uses arbitrary skin colour differences as a further basis for distinguishing between groups. Race, as this factor is called, bears little relationship to such scientific studies as do concern themselves with the division of the human population into identifiable biological categories based on genotypes, the study of genetic similarities and differences. The term *race* as popularly used is based on an earlier type of analysis, based on phenotypes, that is, grouping human populations on the basis of external physical characteristics, be they skin colour, height, skull size or whatever. While genotype research may have scientific value, phenotype research is generally discredited within the scientific community, being based on outmoded nineteenth-century theories of human population types. Indeed, continued use of such a discredited theory can only be described as racist and anti-scientific. Even research based on genotypes has to be carefully justified, given the political sensitivity of the area. As Washburn states:

> I think we should require people who propose a classification of races to state in the first place why they wish to divide the human species and to give in detail the important reasons for subdividing our species (quoted in Tierney, 1982, p. 3).

Despite comments like these, and the weight of scientific opinion, we still classify people by skin colour. Race, then, is an important social construct (see below) and consequently can be employed in an analysis of diversity. However, given the variety of forms that diversity can take, what aspects of it are especially relevant to the debate on education for a multicultural urban society? Moreover, in a society that is being increasingly urbanised, does the concept have a special relevance for any group(s) and how can such groups be usefully defined for the purpose of further analysis?

As was just mentioned, in the educational literature there is much use of terms such as multicultural, multi-ethnic and multi-racial, often used as synonyms one for the other. It is however useful at this point to distinguish between cultural, ethnic and racial groups. The following description is based on the work of Van Den Berghe (1967).

A *racial* group is one that is perceived by others, and/or by members of the group to be different from other groups, using phenotypical criteria — notably skin colour. In other words, it is a socially defined category, although, as discussed above, many people erroneously believe such criteria have an objective scientific basis. The term black is now often used by minority groups to designate solidarity among the peoples of Caribbean, African and Asian origins who are oppressed in white British society. As an educational concept, multi-racial education or, more appropriately, education for a multi-racial society, would have as its prime focus the specific issues that arise from the race relations between black and white groups in society.

An *ethnic* group is one where the criteria are mutable, in theory at least, rather than fixed — as is the case with the physical criteria used with reference to racial groups. Here the criteria could be aspects of culture like those connected with language or religion. Usually, such attributes are related in name to a putative 'country of origin', for example groups like the Irish and the Cypriots. This relationship to a country of origin has led to some people resisting the use of the term, as it encourages the idea that such groups are not part of British society but have a primary allegiance elsewhere. More worryingly, there is fear of the implication that these countries of origin have ultimate responsibility for these people. Given the current debate about nationality in Britain such fears are easily understood.

A *cultural* group is perhaps the most difficult of all to define, given the plethora of definitions of the word *culture*. For our purposes here it may be defined along the lines that anthropologists have been using, namely, it is the total social matrix within which a human group operates and which maintains such a group through time. Thus it could include language, religion, forms of social interaction, diet, dress, the history and location of the group and the institutions of that group which serve to maintain its unity, like the family, legal, political and economic institutions and, most important for our purposes, education.

This is a very broad definition: the question really is how useful is it? Does it add anything of value to, say, the definition of an 'ethnic' group? Certainly, as in the discussion of subcultures (see Chapters 4 and 7), it can be a useful tool for analysis. In addition the very broad and all-encompassing nature of the definition links in with the earlier discussions of diversity, helping to demonstrate that the educational problems raised in urban schools by that diversity are not very readily solved. So, in a roundabout manner, because of its lack of specificity the term is helpful, in that terms like 'cultural diversity' and 'multi-cultural' enable us to make the analysis more complex rather than oversimplified. Having said that, it is important to reiterate the view put forward earlier: that the cultural diversity in urban schools is an issue because of the power relationships between the various groups concerned.

The *dominant* view of 'British' culture would be along the following lines:

Language:	English (+ Welsh in Wales)
Religion:	Christian (Judaic tradition acknowledged)
Gender relations:	Women's place is in the home
National history:	Anglocentric (i.e. English rather than British)
Family history:	Nuclear family (husband, wife, in that order, plus two children)
Skin colour:	White
Diet:	'Western European'
Main cultural tradition:	'High' culture (Shakespeare, Mozart, Rembrandt)
Personal interaction:	Respect for one's 'betters'
Preferred spatial location:	Rural/ex-urban

The list could go on. What is clear, however, is that what is being described as 'British' culture is in fact the culture of only a small section of the population, albeit the dominant one — in broad terms, the white upper middle class. What is also clear is that this list embodies much of what dominates the curriculum in the urban school system where many children do not speak English as their first language, are not Christians, are female, have histories that relate Britain to many other parts of the world, come from extended or single-parent families (seen by many, incorrectly, as 'abnormal'), are black, have different dietary habits, who prefer to spend an evening at White Hart Lane rather than at Covent Garden, believe in co-operation, that respect has to be earned and that living in the countryside is either boring or something that their parents escaped from. Paul Harrison's account of life in the inner city (1983) reveals most sharply how alien this dominant perception of British culture really is to many urban people.

The education system's response to diversity

In the nineteenth-century urban school, the key issues relating to diversity were those relating to class and religious difference. Chapter 1 has outlined some of the debate about these two areas within urban schooling systems. Language issues were there, notably with regard to Welsh, but that was and is mainly an issue for non-urban areas. The provision of equal opportunities for girls in education was an issue but a comparatively minor one when compared with the more famous successful struggle for women's franchise rights.

However, the emphasis in this chapter is more directed to those minority ethnic groups whom the education service began to see as a 'problem' in the period since about 1950. They shared the same forms of inadequate and inappropriate educational provision as working-class children and most girls; in addition, those minority groups who were perceived as being physically different, i.e. black, suffered from a further level of discrimination, namely racism, in the wider society as well as in the schools that they attended.

There are at least two levels to this racism as it was, and still is, manifested in schools. The first is the way in which the traditional urban curriculum looked at the outside world, the second the way the schools responded to a black pupil presence. The two levels interrelate and mutually reinforce one another, but it is useful at this point to look at each one individually to help clarify the issues involved.

First the curriculum; the decline of the British Empire was a remarkably fast event. Edwardian schoolchildren were reassured by their teachers that whatever their status in British society and whatever their living conditions in the sprawling urban conurbations, they were still members of a nation that led the greatest Empire ever seen. The large maps of the world that adorned their classrooms cast a rosy glow through the urban gloom. The following extract from a children's poem by Thomas Stevens published in 1902 gives something of the flavour of the views being espoused:

> B is a baby once known as a Boer,
> He was troublesome then, but all troubles are o'er:
> Now his trekking and wrecking and fighting are done.
> Britain welcomes in peace her recalcitrant son! . . .

D is a Dervish from sunny Soudan;
He dances no more his eccentric can-can,
But, trained to our manners, is eagerly fain,
When Britain once calls him to dance in her train.

E is an English babe, ready to take,
The yoke of the world, for humanity's sake,
So that every one knows, be it dreary or bright,
When it's England that leads him, the road must be right.

F's a Fijian, her hair like a mop;
Let others spin yarns, *she* can spin like a top!
Now she's winning her way to a place in our nation
By skipping from frenzy to civilisation.

G is a Gurkha — a big little man —
With a lion-heart under his covering of tan.
He's fond of his kukri, his gun, and his rice,
If the Empire requires him, it needn't call twice . . .

I is an Irish babe — sweet little Pat —
With shillelagh and shamrock to stick in his hat.
He has fought in his time; now no truer friend's seen;
We can wear our own colours while he wears the green.

J is a Jew with a ringleted head,
Who's up and about while the rest are in bed.
He's first on the steamer to sell you his wares,
And he'll never be missed but at dinner and prayers! . . .

M's a Masai baby, fierce, dark and strong —
Who steals neighbours' cattle and thinks it no wrong!
That's in East Africa, where they appear
To have manners and customs quite different from here.

N's a New Zealander, — Maori child —
Who hides in the bush, which is lonely and wild.
His life's like a gipsy's; he lives upon snails!
But he danced like a Prince for the Princess of Wales!

O is an Orange River Colony coon,
Who dances and sings by the light of the moon.
She's a Kaffir by birth, but our language she knows,
And she always gets blacker the bigger she grows! . . .

Babes of the Empire, from A down to Z,
Peace be the law where your banner's unfurled!
Happy of heart and contented of head —
Babes of the Empire that governs the world!

Although the Empire was lost, the attitudes that it engendered have
been slower to die. Three examples help to illustrate this. First, the
myth that the British gave independence willingly to the former
constituent parts of the Empire: that is, just as the British acquired it
for high-minded reasons, so they relinquished it for equally unselfish
motives. How is the history of the so-called Indian 'mutiny' dealt with
in schools even today? Secondly, having lost political and, increasingly, economic domination over an Empire, the British still maintain a

belief in a moral ascendancy over the Commonwealth as it is now called, particularly the so-called 'new' Commonwealth (i.e. black) countries; what could be called the 'at least under us the trains ran on time' syndrome. Thirdly, and perhaps most important of all, the view, well expressed in the poem, that black people were childlike, ignorant and capable of only menial jobs, the 'Africa never invented the wheel' syndrome. (Neither did Britain if the question actually matters.) Thus, the curriculum of schools still is affected in subtle and crude ways by the heritage of Empire: great explorers, theories of underdevelopment, an anglocentric curriculum that sees all that is part of the good, the true and the beautiful as coming from Europe, particularly from Britain.

Black pupils when they arrived in their classrooms found themselves perceived through this particular set of spectacles, being examples of the benighted foreigners to whom 'we' had brought 'civilisation' in the form of slavery, monocrop agriculture, and general economic and personal exploitation. That their parents were often in badly paid menial jobs confirmed this opinion and helped to confirm the children's status. Many could not speak English, 'they have no language', or spoke a dialect of English which was considered a block to learning — 'dialectical interference'.

> When teachers talk about classroom disruption, they claim it's because of mental adjustments or cultural shocks or cultural deprivation; they don't realise that they're the ones who are causing it.
> (A West Indian school leaver, quoted in AFFOR, 1982)

Thus to the racism that was encountered in the wider society was added an education that by its ignorance and undervaluation of blacks as people was another manifestation of that broader racism. Much of it was, in the words of the Rampton Committee Report (DES, 1981), 'unintended racism', but that is of little comfort to its victim.

> Unless it's going to take hundreds of years I can't see how you're going to change teachers' opinions because teachers are part of England. They're a cross-section of English society and if you look at English society you've got those who are racist and show it. They make racist comments and deliberately don't teach certain things. You've got those who are racist and don't realise it. I think they're more dangerous.
> (A black teacher, quoted in AFFOR, 1982)

Secondly, the educational policy response: this was officially categorised as 'assimilation' in Circular 7/65 in the belief that a national system of education was not designed to maintain different cultures. Behind this partially defensible idea was a deeper and more racist justification, clearly revealed in the Edward Boyle statement but echoed in many official documents at the time, namely that if there were too many 'immigrants' in any one school there would be more or less adverse reactions from the white majority. Circular 7/65 was quite explicit in advocating not only assimilation but also dispersal, because it claimed that if more than a fifth of the pupil population was 'immigrant', that is, black, serious problems would arise. The nature of these problems was not spelt out; there was no real need to, or so it was thought. Incidentally, it is interesting that the circular quotes the figure of a fifth of the pupil population with such authority as the tip-over point. The only justification for this was 'experience'.

The black children were in some cases 'dispersed', that is, moved out of their own neighbourhoods in order to be educated. The curriculum they were offered was an attempt to turn them into fully functioning members of the previously discussed British culture, skin colour excepted. Their religion, if it was not Christian, was ignored or abused, their customs in many cases opposed. Townsend and Brittan's 1972 study gives many examples of what can at best be called extreme insensitivity. Moslem girls in one school, who for religious reasons could not change for PE, were treated in the following manner. In the headteacher's own words, 'dissenting children were allowed to watch and after a few lessons soon fell into line' (p. 63). In the mid-1980s there are still schools where a mainly Islamic pupil population recites the Christian Lord's Prayer every day in assembly. Now, however, the Islamic communities have the confidence to question the validity of these practices and are, in some cases, wanting to set up their own schools under the terms of the 1944 Act, so that their religion and customs may not be so crudely trampled on (see p. 102 for a further discussion of this subject).

The religious issue is one that has still to be resolved in a satisfactory manner. This is even more true of the question of languages. Assimilationist policies saw, correctly, that English was the national language and that all children should have access to it. However, access to the school curriculum was denied to those children who came into schools without this tool. Under assimilation, the mother tongue, if other than English, was an impediment to be removed as quickly as possible so that the child could slot in to their place in British society. Even worse, those children who came in with English, but in a dialect that was unfamiliar, like those children of West Indian origin, were also considered non-English speakers. Hazel Carby's analysis of these early attitudes (Carby, 1982) makes horrific reading. She quotes references to West Indian dialect as an 'inadequate language', its speakers having only a 'partial mastery of English' and this 'deficiency' being a 'major factor in this culturally induced backwardness' of Afro-Caribbean children (pp. 187–8).

Such attitudes were part of the educational common sense of the time (the 1960s and early 1970s) so it is not surprising that black children did not achieve well in schools. They were not expected to and had also, naturally enough, started to reject their schooling as being both second rate and insulting.

With foundations like these, and reactions, perhaps best summed up in Bernard Coard's famous polemical book *How the West Indian Child is Made Educationally Sub-Normal in the British School System* published in 1971, it is not surprising that educational policies based on assimilation were generally discredited by the early 1970s. (Coard's book is also important because he brought to public attention the fact that disproportionate numbers of children of West Indian origin were being placed in ESN schools. (For further details on this see Chapter 6.) Far from being assimilated many were being segregated off. This is a feature of the urban schooling system that still causes much concern and disquiet to the Afro-Caribbean community.) The black communities rejected assimilation and their children continued to fail in the system. Indeed many of them still do, perhaps because assimilationist views are still widespread within the teaching profession, albeit in more disguised forms. The educational performance of certain groups, notably Afro-Caribbean and Cypriot children, is still low and cannot be explained away simply in terms of family background or some sort of innate intellectual inferiority (Taylor, 1981). But the view that it is the group's fault rather than the schooling system's is still widely held.

The move in educational policy towards cultural pluralism began to take place during the 1970s. In the main, it was a response by groups of urban teachers and policy-makers to the rejection, by pupils and parents from black minority groups, of educational policies based on assimilation. Much of the practice that followed, such as a more thoughtful attitude towards linguistic and dialectical variation and a more open response to the overt and covert racism in schools and society, was and remains important. However, there are black voices that maintain that the racist oppression is merely being continued, albeit in a more refined and subtle way. As Chris Mullard (1983) puts it, 'there appears to be only a change in the content of what is taught and not in the context in which it is taught' (p. 154). This is an important distinction and will be looked at in more detail in the final section of this chapter.

Cultural pluralism in education is, however, a many-headed object. It is a good example of C.S. Lewis's verbicide, that is, where words are appropriated to express a value position rather than to describe something in a clear manner. In the attack on assimilationist policies, cultural pluralism stood for radical practice in education. It implied a careful look at language, at religious issues, at pedagogy, curriculum content and the relationship between school processes and the racist practices and institutions in the wider society. Schools as part of that system were not excluded. In the name of greater racial justice, radical urban teachers were encouraged by certain urban LEAs to find space within the schools where serious questions of social justice and the nature of power relations could be explored with children. But for the majority of children, little had really changed. Cultural pluralism as a label was attached to a variety of practices that could readily be identified as assimilationist in result if not in content. Inspectors and advisers were appointed to 'deal' with multi-ethnic or multicultural education. However, many found that they were being seen as having an interest only in educational 'problems' that affected black pupils and ensuring that ESL provision was more widespread and effective. Crucial aspects of the concept were, and are, seen as beyond their educational brief. Black children continued to do badly in schools, when compared with their peers, and particularly at the 16+ level.

Although it is inaccurate to see these changes in any strict chronological manner, it is likely that the 'events' in British cities in 1981 in places like Brixton and Toxteth marked a significant break with many policies of the preceding twenty or so years. The debate is more sharply focused than previously and there is a greater sense of public urgency (born, perhaps, more from fear of public order breakdown than concern over previous debates of inopportune and ineffective action). In addition, the voice of black protest, which has always been there, has forced itself into the public debate and can no longer be ignored. This is not to suggest that there has been a significant break, rather a change in emphasis which seems to offer a more optimistic view of changes in the urban school over the next decade in response to the issues involved. In the last section of this chapter, the implications of this will be briefly examined.

ANTI-RACIST TEACHING AND THE URBAN SCHOOL

Towards the end of the 1970s central government, concerned about the education of ethnic minorities, set up a formal committee of inquiry into the educational performance of minority groups under the chairpersonship of Anthony Rampton. It was given the almost impossible brief to submit a report on one specific community, the West Indian (sic), within an extremely short time-span: some eighteen months. Two views can be held as to why this group was especially selected. The charitable one is that it was the community about whose educational performance there was the most concern and worry. A more cynical view would qualify that concern and worry by saying that this particular group's dissatisfaction with education was most likely to lead to open conflict unless something was seen to be being done, and speedily. The city riots of 1981 show that if there was such a fear it had some justification.

When the report did come out (DES, 1981) it was not the powerful cogently argued document that many had hoped for. With the unfortunate sub-title of *West Indian Children in Our Schools*, the interim report still painted a bleak picture of children of West Indian origin in the British school system. Much was blamed on what the report, somewhat disingenuously, called 'unintentional racism'. In other words, the education service was racist but it did not mean to be. As an excuse it ranks alongside the 'I only meant to tap him with the iron bar' school of not-guilty pleas. The report did however make a great number of sensible suggestions as to how things might be improved, even if most of them were somewhat modest notions of reform. There were changes in the committee following the presentation of the interim report, and a new chairperson, Lord Swann, was appointed.

The irony of Lord Swann's report is that it has been in many ways overtaken by events before its publication. The ILEA had, in 1983, produced a series of documents (ILEA, 1983a) that put forward a much more radical line on the issue, arguing that for the inner-city schools under its control, a more definite anti-racist stance should be adopted. By this, the authority meant that children should be made aware of the nature of racism and the power relationships that underpinned it. The ILEA documents put forward strategies that are worthy of attention. Most notable of these are:

1. Each institution was to make an anti-racist policy statement.
2. Each institution was carefully to review its curriculum in the light of the statement.
3. Greater black representation at all levels of the authority was to be secured.
4. This work was to be done to a definite timetable and its effects carefully monitored.

Two points stand out in the documents, however, which make the achievement of such objectives somewhat problematic. The first is that the theoretical parts of the document are less rigorous than they might be. It is claimed, for example, that the terms multi-ethnic, multi-racial and multicultural are, to all intents and purposes, interchangeable. This is, as has been demonstrated earlier in this chapter, a too-simplified view. So the aim of producing an intellectual justification for the policy is not as strong as might have been hoped for. Secondly, the delivery of the initiative does not take fully into account the *de facto* autonomy of schools and teachers. A downward and imposed model of educational change usually stands little chance of success in the British context.

However, it has to be said that the documents and policies are the result of as wide-ranging a consultation process as has previously been seen. The views about the education of minorities are drawn from the expressed views of members of those groups — an unusual process in educational policy-making. More, it is an important demonstration of how seriously one urban education authority takes the issue of racism in society. (This initiative is described in more detail in Chapter 8.)

However, such a commitment needs to be carefully operationalised. The overall aims may be clear to a greater or lesser extent but what does this actually mean for practice within the urban school? Some aspects of the emerging good practice are described below in terms of issues that have previously been mentioned.

Aims

A commitment to an education that provides for the needs of *all* children is by nature anti-racist and positive towards the diversity present in the urban classroom. As such, education would need to tackle the key issue of inequality in society. What are the consequences of this for current primary aims of education in British society, namely social cohesion and individual opportunity? If major redistributions of power are envisaged how can this be achieved in a peaceful and democratic manner? The education system is only one structure through which a redistribution of power and wealth can be achieved. It certainly cannot be successful in isolation. However, if educational institutions were to work in this direction they would need to abandon the aim of equality of opportunity in favour of that of equality of outcome (see Chapter 6). The difficulty is that this would seem to be in conflict with deeply treasured values of individualism and competition. This is, of course, a concern not specific to this chapter but to the whole book.

Pedagogy

Much has been written about the changes in content that are required in the curriculum (Jones and Klein, 1980; Lynch, 1983) if it is to reflect accurately the real diversity of British society and to correct the Eurocentric distortions that have been accumulated over the years. As important is the pedagogy that is employed with this content, new or old, and the processes by which such pedagogy is negotiated between teachers and taught. A curriculum that aims to combat inequalities in society but that is unilaterally conceived and taught may well replace one form of domination by another. An anti-racist pedagogy would need to recognise the validity of the pupils' own experiences and use these for work, discussion and explanation. It will need to treat subjects that have previously been forbidden in classrooms: How do black children feel about racist graffiti? Why is it senseless as well as insulting to call Bengali pupils 'Pakis'? What advantages are there for white people in the elimination of racism? These questions will demand an openness and responsiveness of pedagogy at both the primary and secondary level.

Language

Many teachers still cling to outmoded views about the nature of English and the place and status of non-standard dialects in the classroom. To this is now added the further issue of bilingualism. As was indicated earlier, many schools still see bilingual children, particularly if their first language is not English, as being disadvantaged if not actually deficient. Teaching English as a second language is perhaps the easier issue although by no means satisfactorily resolved. For example, most urban school teachers have to come to terms with the fact that their classrooms will contain, for the foreseeable future, children whose proficiency in English is such as to hold them back if adjustments in curriculum and pedagogy are not made.

More difficult questions are raised by a consideration of the role of other languages in the curriculum, especially those that unlike French and German have had no traditional status. For example, in an area where Bengali is a major community language, should non-Bengali speakers have the option of learning Bengali rather than French? Would not Hindi, Bengali and Spanish, for example, be more useful languages, in international terms, to teach to 'A' level as well as more accurately reflecting the languages of British cities? More radical still, should speakers of languages other than English have the option of not merely being taught their mother tongue, as English speakers are 'taught' English, but of having part or all of their total education in their mother tongue? There is now an increasing literature on this and related topics (e.g. Edwards, 1983; Linguistic Minorities Project, 1983a, 1983b).

Religion

Controversy has surrounded attempts by minority religious groups to open state-funded schools for their co-religionists in many urban areas, e.g. Ealing, Bradford. The religious settlement contained in the 1944 Education Act was intended principally for the Christian sects and certain sections of the Jewish community. Now Hassidic Jews and Moslems, among others, are requesting that the same dispensation should apply to them. These attempts have been bitterly opposed by urban local education authorities such as Bradford. The argument is that the creation of such schools would be divisive. Proponents of this argument do not propose to abolish the separate Protestant, Catholic and Jewish schools that exist under the Act. The argument must then be seen as discriminatory and potentially racist. Blocked in their attempts to set up voluntary-aided schools, some Moslem parents in inner-city areas are beginning to found private schools. Although there is official opposition to the idea of such separate schools, on the grounds of supporting a cohesive national system, this openly avoids the present existence of publicly funded denominational schools, principally Anglican and Roman Catholic. This issue will not go away and the present system is likely to continue to be regarded as discriminatory by the religious groups concerned until a solution is reached.

Positive discrimination

Few terms in this area arouse such ire as this one. This use of words is unfortunate as the principle is not to give more to some groups at the expense of others, but to restore to them what current practices deny them. Thus black teachers, like female teachers, are disproportionately underrepresented in the top levels of teaching systems. Few argue that this is because of lack of ability or experience, but then few go on to say that there is probably something in the institutional arrangements that causes this, racism in the case of black teachers, sexism in the case of women teachers. In a similar way, the governing bodies and other administrative structures in urban schooling systems are predominantly white (and male). To remedy this state of affairs, positive discrimination is needed. However, it is likely to be opposed, along similar lines to the opposition aroused by the ILEA's attempts following their new anti-racist policies. For example, headteacher autonomy and 'freedom' may be used to legitimate racist and sexist practice.

Performance

Few issues raise as much heat as the discussion of the educational performance of black children. Certain groups of minority children consistently underperform in relation to their white peers on various standard measures of achievement, most notably in public examinations. The factors that underpin this disquietening state of affairs are hotly disputed. Some argue that it is the home background and lack of parental support that is the main cause, a deficit position which is contested by the groups themselves as well as many educational professionals. Others argue that teachers' stereotypical reactions to children may be an important factor. This whole area is one that requires substantial further research.

These few examples indicate first the complexity of the issues raised by diversity in the urban schooling system and secondly the bitterly contested nature of the debates involved. Teaching in Britain has traditionally been a conservative profession. The changes to meet the demands of a just culturally diverse schooling system put enormous strains on teachers and the schools within which they work. However, to continue to fail children in the manner done in the past is increasingly an untenable option in urban schools.

GUIDE TO FURTHER READING

The literature on this area is still somewhat sparse. For a general overview, the Open University course on *Ethnic Minorities and Community Relations* (E354) (1982) is a useful introduction, as is Block Five from the Urban Education course E351 entitled *Race, Children and Cities* by Rosalind Street-Porter (1977). A persuasive overview is that edited by John Tierney (1981), *Race, Migration and Schooling*. David Milner's *Children and Race: Ten Years On* (1983) is a comprehensive social psychological account. The Rampton Report,

West Indian Children in Our Schools (DES, 1981), and the final report of the Swann Committee are useful sources of data.

NOTES ON THE SCHOOLS LANGUAGE SURVEY FINDINGS
(Figure 5.1)

Basis of the SLS data collection

The data of this Schools Language Survey are based on pupils' self-report, mediated through teachers and inevitably collected in a range of differing classroom situations. Readers should bear in mind that:

1. The survey questions were designed to elicit reporting of even modest language skills and, therefore, make it impossible to comment on the level of language ability of the pupils, either in oral or in literacy skills.
2. The process of recording the data inevitably involved some element of interpretation by the teacher of what the pupil reported speaking, reading or writing.

Naming of languages

The level of detail in a pupil's answer or teacher's reporting of it may be affected by very local factors (even to the level of what other pupils in the class have said, or the kind of relationship between teacher and pupil). One tendency is for some teachers in classes where there is a large number of pupils of one language group to give detailed information about dialects and places of origin, while in classes with fewer pupils answering 'yes' to the first SLS question ('Do you yourself ever speak any language at home apart from English?'), or where there is a wide range of languages, little more than the language name is given.

The method by which pupils and teachers (neither of whom may have a detailed knowledge of the linguistic background) were asked to record answers to a single question meant that some answers referred to the local spoken dialect used at home, some to the regional standard spoken language and others to the language of community loyalty or even the language of literacy.

Thus, for example, a number of pupils with a Pakistani background may have reported speaking Urdu when in fact it is likely that their first spoken language is a regional variety of Panjabi, and that Urdu for them is a language of literacy which may also be a second spoken language. Other children of similar language background may have reported speaking Panjabi.

The term used to refer to a language or dialect also varied according to the pupil's or teacher's perception of the status of this language or dialect in the wider community, either in the country of origin (e.g. Urdu given for Panjabi), or in England (e.g. 'Pakistan' given for Panjabi, 'Italian' for Sicilian, 'Indian' for Hindi, Panjabi or Gujerati).

'Creoles' refers to a large group of diverse languages which we divided into two main categories: 'French-based' and 'English-based and all other Creoles'.

'Chinese' is a group including all language labels referring to one of the regional Chinese languages (e.g. Cantonese, Hakka, and the general label 'Chinese').

In other categories simple language labels, and those that give more detailed geographical or dialect specifications, were all grouped together under the name of the national or regional official language (e.g. Kutchi is subsumed in the Gujerati group and Sicilian in the Italian group).

Literacy is to be interpreted in the broadest sense, that is, 'Pupils have reported that they can read and/or write one or more of the spoken languages given, or have reported one or more separate languages of literacy'.

6

The debate about 'special needs' in urban schools

THE ISSUE AND ITS SCOPE

Urban education as a field of study has tended to include those educational problems most highly visible in urban areas and actual and proposed policy solutions. It is therefore perhaps surprising that the theory and practice of special education has not previously been seen to be a vital element of urban education. Certainly the large-scale surveys would seem to show a formidable concentration of children with *special needs* (to adopt the most recently fashionable euphemism) in inner-city areas.

Table 6.1 *Children with 'special needs' in England and Wales*

Category	Number
Blind	1 221
Partially sighted	2 456
Deaf	4 267
Partially hearing	6 006
Physically handicapped	16 138
Delicate	6 272
Maladjusted	20 995
Educationally subnormal (moderate) (ESN(M))	81 011
Educationally subnormal (severe) (ESN(S))	34 137
Epileptic	1 332
Speech defect	2 308
Autistic	974
Total	177 117

Source: Adapted from statistics in Booth, 1982.

Note: The terms mild learning difficulty (MLD) and severe learning difficulty (SLD) are now replacing ESN(M) and ESN(S) respectively.

The recent government inquiry in the area (the Warnock Report) adopted the formula of *children with special needs*, which includes not only those children receiving formal special education but also those in remedial and disruptive classes, thereby covering about 20 per the school population (Warnock *et al.*, 1978). What then is the extent of current institutional intervention?

In 1977, according to the DES, there were 177 117 'pupils ascertained as handicapped and attending special schools or classes or awaiting placement' in England and Wales. (All statistics in this paragraph are from Booth, 1982.) Table 6.1 gives details of the categories of the children in special education according to the DES statistics. However, Booth indicates that other DES sources make clear that this is very far from the whole story:

> Any estimate of the extent of the need for special education has also to take into account the children who spend at least part of their time in special classes set up on the initiative of individual schools. In 1976 classes of this kind were attached to 10,845 maintained schools in England and Wales — nearly 40 per cent of all maintained primary, middle and secondary schools. They made provision for varying periods of time each week, for 494,248 pupils, of whom 458,087 (4.7 per cent of the school population) had difficulties in learning or problems of an emotional or behavioural nature, or both. The great majority (82 per cent of the 458,087) spent less than half, and only 12 per cent spent more, than three-quarters of their time in these special classes (Booth, 1982, p. 9).

The earlier figure of 177 117 represents almost 2 per cent of the total school population for 1977, which was 9 million. If this is added to the 4.7 per cent in other special provision, then the number involved represents 6.7 per cent of schoolchildren in England and Wales. Moreover, an appreciably larger number of children are likely to come into contact with this provision at some point in their school lives.

An important point to note about these statistics is that the majority of these children are being grouped in the categories of which the definitions are the least clinical and most susceptible to *social construction* and administrative convenience. That is, notions of good behaviour and even good performance tend to be based on the subjective (and differing) standards and tolerances of the people who establish the definitions. As Tomlinson has indicated, even categories such as 'partially hearing', which appear to be based on an objective criterion are constructed through a sequence of fluctuating criteria and subjective judgements (Tomlinson, 1982). But the socially constructed nature of handicap is most apparent with regard to so-called maladjusted and educationally subnormal (moderate) (ESN(M)) children, who represent more than half of those 'ascertained as handicapped'. Furthermore, those children who fall into the exceedingly loose category of having 'difficulties in learning, or problems of an emotional or be-havioural nature, or both' (see above) (what child has not experienced emotional problems and some difficulties in learning?) represent nearly all those in non-ascertained (i.e. non-special school) forms of special provision. Indeed, it is in this non-ascertained provision, with its vague definitions and criteria of assessment, that the greatest recent growth is taking place, particularly in the various euphemistically named disruptive units (HMI, 1978).

Given this state of affairs, it is necessary to make some distinctions not between *types* of children but between the various *categorisations* to which children are subject and the commensurate institutional interventions. Three levels of special need categorisation may be distinguished: first, there are those categories that rest on apparently sound clinical assessments. These are blind and partially sighted, deaf and partially hearing, physically handicapped, ESN(S) (severe — the new label is children with severe learning difficulties), epileptic, speech defect and the highly contentious group, autistic. Secondly, there are the vague categories covering the majority of children in special schools, namely ESN(M) and maladjusted. The third category covers all those 'remedial' and 'disruptive' children perceived to have special needs but not actually placed in a special school, the non-ascertained group.

These three levels may broadly be called clinically constructed formal special education categories, non-clinically constructed special education categories and non-formal special education categories. Although brevity insists that these be shortened in usage to clinical special education, non-clinical special education and non-formal special education, the full origination of the names of these groups of categories does not need to be borne in mind.

The majority of children are actually in the last group of categories and those who attend the associated forms of provision did not, until April 1983, have the rights to formal assessment (see below) which at least are guaranteed by the formal special education referral proce-dure. Rampton (DES 1981) saw this as cause for serious concern, particularly with regard to West Indian children. Indeed it is not impossible that this piecemeal, temporary and usually part-time provi-sion was often established precisely in order to circumvent the costly and time-consuming special education procedures which guarantee some minimum rights to children and parents. In addition, this form of provision avoids the necessity to pay special school allowances to teachers or to provide a preferential ratio of welfare assistance. It is the groups of children in the non-clinical and non-formal categories who are more likely to be concentrated in urban areas. These categories would be widened to include even more children, if the Warnock Committee recommendations were followed in full, simply on the basis of their perceived special needs. However, it is necessary to keep children in the clinical categories of handicap in mind, as the stigmatisation and segregation that they are subjected to may also point to the apparently arbitrary limitations of the mainstream school system and to the wider function of the notion of mental and physical handicap in society.

One final tentative point may be made on the differences between the children placed in each of these three groups of categories and this concerns social class. Andrew Sutton (1981) reports research which shows the number of voluntary organisations for the visually impaired, hearing impaired, deaf-blind and ESN(M) both at the national level and specifically in Birmingham. For the visually impaired there are six in Birmingham and seven nationally, for the hearing impaired there are four in Birmingham and three nationally, for the deaf-blind there are two in Birmingham and none nationally, and for the ESN(M) there are none in Birmingham and one nationally. Given, then, that there are vastly more children categorised as ESN(M) than as any other category, the disproportionately small number of voluntary organisations catering for their interests and those of their parents might seem to be surprising. If, however, one assumes that middle-class parents are much more likely to create and participate in such organisations, then one may further suggest that the category of ESN(M) draws overwhelmingly from the less economically and socially privileged classes. This argument does demand rather large assumptions, but in the absence of other data, it does at least put some flesh on the bones of Tomlinson's assertion that children classified as ESN(M) and maladjusted are drawn almost exclusively from the least-privileged sections of society, namely, the urban working class (Tomlinson, 1981; 1982).

THE LEGITIMATION OF SEGREGATION

At this point we need to examine some everyday concepts that make it easy for people to think of handicapped children as radically different and needing to be separated from ordinary children, that is, the *legitimation of segregation*. Special education has traditionally been perceived to be a matter of benevolently providing the best special provision for children who are in some way handicapped. The dramatic expansion in special education that has occurred in the cities of England and Wales since the 1944 Education Act has been almost ubiquitously regarded as a solid improvement in the conditions of the least fortunate in our society. Special schools have preferential pupil/teacher ratios, they have specialised equipment and ancillary help, specifically trained staff and access to the professional experts who are qualified to help such children. The picture is of a smiling 8-year-old Down's Syndrome child in a bright, well-equipped classroom with a competent-looking young teacher adjusting some piece of technological apparatus in the background. The emphasis is on help, and studies of special education have likewise tended to focus on the most efficient methods of helping those unfortunates with special needs; they have appropriately emerged from the disciplines of psychology or even medicine. These traditional perceptions of special education doubtless give one version of the social realities. It is a perception based on the acceptance of dominant ideologies of intelligence, behaviour, normality and individualism. It is from within these four interlocking concepts that practitioners and theorists derive legitimations for the practice of special education if such were ever seen to be necessary.

However, at the outset one might ask whether these professionals do not have a vested interest in the institutions and practices that they are justifying and often seeking to expand. As Patricia Potts (1982) states:

> So, more professionals are recruited for the increasing numbers of children they have identified as having special needs, as if the failure to do their job in terms of problem-solving justifies the proliferation. It sounds like policing. But it also shows that, while the professionals in special education have considerable power to influence the lives of their clients, the options over which they have control are not, perhaps, those which would make a fundamental difference to disadvantaged children. And if professionals were in a position to improve the disabling social, economic or personal lot of their present clients, what implications would this have for their own continuing careers? (p. 6).

This is not to say that professionals knowingly and ruthlessly devise theories and practices to exploit children in order to advance their careers and the extent and status of their groups. Rather the legitimations used in this area are seen to be not only true but self-evident: they are perceived as linking together in a coherent way and are rarely questioned. Furthermore, they are inseparably linked to those ideas that are part of the accepted ideology of the dominant social and economic groups, institutions and practices. Thus, the legitimations of special education are linked with the wider ideologies of individualism, intelligence, behaviour and normality that underlie much educational practice in England and Wales. Each of these four connected ideologies that are used to legitimate special educational provision needs to be examined in more detail.

Individualism

The idea of individual differences is deeply embedded in contemporary Western thought. Children and adults are seen as having different intelligence, abilities, interests, skills, strengths and weaknesses. With regard to education this stress on difference is enshrined in the 1944 Education Act. At the top end of these various ladders of differences are those people who exhibit an apparent excellence in a specific field: successful sports people, musicians, actors and actresses, artists and writers are subjected to a high degree of social approval and adulation. The stress on excellence is also a stress on the competition through which excellence is seen to be proved. Thus, alongside large-scale jamborees of competitiveness such as the World Cup, there are also contests to find the Brain of Britain or the *Woman's Own* supermum, or the best businessman (sic) of the year. At the bottom end of these ladders are those physically less able to compete and those who fail in the various contests of excellence. Of course there are still sports and even Olympics for the disabled so that they are not deprived of the competitive ethos, but such competitiveness is not regarded as legitimate for the low-status mentally handicapped. Individual difference, then, as a legitimation of special education is linked to a high regard for what is considered to be excellence and to a stress on many forms of competition.

This competitiveness need not be seen as inherent in the human character: it is, or, to be more specific, its European manifestations are, a major feature of much of Western society. Groups as different as Sioux Indians and Japanese schoolchildren tend to find such overt and all-embracing forms of educational competition rather disgusting (Erikson, 1965). But this stress on individualism pervades the whole education system of England and Wales. It is one of the main rhetorics of teachers even when they have little awareness of the actual differences among their children. Children are constantly assessed on ability and performance; their work and behaviour is endlessly marked, graded, judged and commented on. Children are placed in rank in their class, streamed according to ability, setted according to attitude and in some cases segregated into special education where that is seen to be appropriate to their individual needs. Whatever else may appear on the formal curriculum of urban schools, competitiveness is compulsory at most stages and it is one of the lessons best learned by pupils.

The hidden curriculum of competition and individualism in schools serves to ensure that the legitimacy of this type of activity and its rhetoric is socially reproduced, that is, that it is passed on to succeeding generations.

This stress on competition and individualism is not unconnected to the organisation of industry and commerce. Competition in a 'free' market was seen to be the driving force of capitalism by Adam Smith, whose theories have recently been revived by both economists and politicians. According to this view, the most efficient business produces the cheapest, highest-quality product and service, thereby providing the public with the best facility. Such theories may well be subtle and illuminating, but the realities of educational life for many children in urban schools can be seen as a cruel parody of them. For example, and this point is developed further in Chapter 7, in the labour market, people with different skills obtain different jobs and different rewards. Competition for the best jobs is fierce and, it could be argued, those people in the most powerful and best regarded positions are the ones best equipped to fill them. It is in schools that the individual differences relevant to such a competition are discovered, either encouraged or remedied, and ultimately quantified and *commodified* (made into saleable packages) through the process of certification. Actual questions of differential access to educational and professional opportunities according to gender, race or class may therefore be ignored as the clever children, and those who work hard, do well at school and thereby prove themselves to be suitable for subsequent powerful and well-remunerated positions in the labour market.

Perhaps few people in education continue to work in such crude terms, but the motivation of examination success and resultant career prospects are still held out to secondary pupils in inner-city schools even at a time of high unemployment. The children perceived to have special needs are the ones who will be least successful in these life competitions: they will have least access either to job satisfaction or to the affluent consumer lifestyle so valued in our society. If this failure is due to their individual differences then it could be claimed that it is clearly not due to any marked unfairness in the educational or economic systems.

Intelligence

Intelligence is such an important aspect of the rhetoric of individual differences that it is difficult to realise that it is a concept of comparatively recent origin. The theory of intelligence may be seen to involve five linked and highly questionable conceptions:

1. that intelligence is a common factor that explains a person's performance over a wide range of mental activities;
2. that this factor may be measured by intelligence tests and presented as a numerical IQ (intelligence quotient);
3. that this intelligence is subject to relatively little change throughout a person's development;
4. that this intelligence is largely a product of a person's genetic endowment rather than of environment;
5. that some racial groups have on average a higher intelligence than some others.

The first of these statements, that concerning the existence of a general intelligence, is perhaps the least contentious. Yet Evans and Waites (1981) in a review of the literature suggest that there is little evidence to support this notion either from researchers working on the functions of the human brain or from psychological investigations other than those concerned with the validation of IQ tests, which might well be taken to be tautological (i.e. true by definition). The argument that a 'g' factor is indicated by the fact that there is a high degree of internal validity between the various sub-test scores of IQ tests and the overall scores is purely tautological as the tests have been designed, developed and refined specifically and expressly to exhibit this validity. Intelligence tests, then, claim to measure a factor the existence of which still remains to be proved.

Statistical objections to IQ tests concern also the spread of scores. To claim that these tests spread children and adults according to a normal distribution curve which therefore relates intelligence firmly to various physiological human attributes is to ignore the fact that again they have been adjusted and refined precisely so that scores should fall on this curve. Furthermore, Galton's most basic numerical assumption — that the normal curve of frequency applies to psychological variables — has never been adequately shown to be true. Without this assumption ordered scales could not be converted to equal intervals, not mental tests scaled in terms of standard deviations or some fraction thereof, nor intelligence be conceived of as a quantity to be measured against a norm (Evans and Waites, 1981, p. 43).

The notion that intelligence is fixed and not subject to human development is one that has very pessimistic implications for teachers, as it implies that education can do little more than encourage already existing abilities. That case studies have shown remarkable improvements in IQ as a result of specially designed interventions may indicate

that this aspect of intelligence theory is as fallacious as those mentioned above, or it may merely reflect persistent inaccuracies in the
tests.

The genetic aspect of the theory of intelligence and the attempt to
link this to notions about racial differences have been brought back
into recent controversy by people such as Jensen, Herrnstein and
Eysenck. Their theories have been much contested by writers like
Chomsky and Labov. A worrying aspect of the debate is that the data
derived from Burt, on which so much of the theory of intelligence
rests, have been shown repeatedly to be culturally biased. The history
of IQ testing perhaps entered its terminal phase with Judge Peckham's
ruling of October 1979 against the Californian education authorities:

> defendants have utilised standardised intelligence tests that are racially
> and culturally biased, have a discriminatory impact against black children,
> and have not been validated for the purpose of essentially permanent
> placements of black children into educationally dead-end, isolated and
> stigmatising classes for the so-called educable mentally retarded (Evans
> and Waites, 1981, p. 10).

The judge further said that 'the experts have, from the beginning, been
willing to tolerate or even encourage tests that portray minorities,
especially blacks, as intellectually inferior' (p. 11). He places the IQ
testing movement within its historical and social context:

> We must recognise from the outset that the history of IQ tests and of
> special education classes built on IQ tests, and of special education classes
> built on IQ testing is not the history of neutral scientific discoveries
> translated into educational reform. It is, at least in the early years, a
> history of social prejudice, of Social Darwinism, and of the use of scientific
> 'mystique' to legitimate such prejudices (p. 10).

However, since these tests are still a crucial aspect of special education
assessment in the UK as well as being part of its legitimating ideology,
the contrast with prevalent opinion in the USA is informative.

The theory of intelligence, like the notion of individualism, may be
seen to be part of the overarching ideologies of Western society. Evans
and Waites cite these extraordinary examples of questions from the
comprehension sub-tests of Stanford–Binet and WISC, 'Why is it good
to put money in the bank? Why is it generally better to give money to
an organised charity than to a street beggar?' (pp. 130–81). The
intelligence that the tests purport to measure is socially and culturally
biased, being defined in terms of the knowledge of the dominant
economic group in that society. These instruments and the theory from
which they derive have been, however, widely used to determine
general educational policy, to make decisions concerning groups of

children, and even to institute eugenics legislation (Kamin, 1974). Moreover, educational measures of the concept of intelligence have not been confined to the placing of children in ESN(M) schools. Simon has criticised the 11+ selection examination as the apotheosis of IQ testing, whereby the entire secondary system was stratified for decades (Simon, 1971). This is a good example of where policy for children with special needs can be seen as an extension of more general educational policy. It may be that it is not the needs of children that are met by special schooling but the needs of schools and teachers who are becoming increasingly unwilling or unable to cope with anything but a narrow range of individual difference. If the same legitimations are being used to justify mainstream practice as to excuse separation and segregation, then it may well be that to insist that these processes should be reduced to an absolute minimum could benefit the education not simply of children perceived to have special needs but indeed of all those in urban primary and secondary schools.

Behaviour

The theories of deviance and labelling derived from Goffman have been adopted to show their educational implications by Hargreaves, Cicourel and Kitsuse (Hargreaves *et al.*, 1975). An act thus only becomes deviant when a second party perceives it to be such. It is not the person who commits the act who creates the deviance but the second person who labels it. Different schools have different standards of behaviour and even within the same school the line between the acceptable and the deviant will vary from teacher to teacher; indeed, the same teacher may have different criteria on different days, at different times of the day or with different classes. Furthermore, the way in which a teacher implements standards of behaviour may differ between children; Cicourel and Kitsuse have shown that teachers are much more likely to be tolerant of white middle-class children than they are of black and/or working-class pupils. One teacher's disruption can be another teacher's creative lesson. It is against this that one must see the growth in England and Wales over the last ten years of what can only be called a new type of child, the disruptive child. Children, like teachers of course, vary in their behaviour; very few are disruptive in all lessons, at all times and in all parts of the school; even fewer are similarly difficult at home or the youth centre. It is therefore inaccurate to talk about disruptive children as a hard and fast category.

In fact, the phenomenon of difficult behaviour in class is not a recent development. Bowman has convincingly shown how since the 1944

Education Act the mushrooming of maladjusted schools has provided a safety valve for the placement of children who, although their behaviour differs markedly from those traditionally understood (i.e. within a Freudian or psychodynamic framework) to be maladjusted, do present apparently unacceptable problems of disruption to mainsteam schools (Bowman, in Swann, 1981). The placement of large numbers of so-called conduct-disordered children is one of the main grievances of teachers in such schools. Nevertheless, places were still not sufficient enough or easily enough available, and so the new on- and off-site units came into existence. The units have distinct advantages over maladjusted schools, as far as primary and secondary schools are concerned, in that children can be placed in them without the embarrassing and delaying safeguards of special-education procedures and with only minimal consultation with parents. They have become an outstanding example of segregation legitimated on the basis of behaviour. If a teacher or a head (and the use, for instance, of the language of human bodily functions in front of the headteacher is probably more likely to lead to referral to such a unit than the same piece of trenchant advice offered to the French assistant) decides that a child's behaviour is disruptive, without even the need to set down specific criteria, then simply at that teacher's behest the child may be removed from all or part of his or her curriculum and indeed from mainstream education altogether.

> If you were walking along the corridor and you heard a bell you were supposed to go down on your knees. One day, I was reading a book in the corridor when I heard a bell. The priest came walking up and he said, 'Kneel'. I said, 'What?' He said, 'Kneel!' I said, 'Who do you think you are? King Arthur?' I was suspended for that.
> (Stephen Rice, aged 16. Elswick, Newcastle upon Tyne, quoted in White and Brockington, 1983)

This is not to say that this legitimation has reference only to disruptive units. As Tomlinson (1981) has shown, it is a major rationale for referral and placement in the formal special education categories of ESN(M) and maladjusted. The extreme of this continuum are those children in CHEs (community homes with education) who are removed from the mainstream curriculum because of behaviour that probably did not even occur in school. Here the definitions of behaviour are more openly defined, being enshrined in legislation, but the criteria by which the police apply this legislation in deciding whether or not to press for prosecution is less objective and favours children from middle-class backgrounds. These children tend to be overlooked in discussions of educational stigmatisation: indeed they were not included in the data at the beginning of this chapter. Yet Swann states:

> The numbers of children involved are not insignificant: in 1976 there were 6784 children in CHEs. As a comparison in the same year 3585 children were ascertained as blind or partially sighted, yet these children received far more attention and educational resources (Swann, 1982, p. 11).

The legitimation of the importance of behaviour is less directly linked to those of individualism and intelligence. It does, however, link with the requirements of industry and commerce for an obedient and non-disruptive labour force. This is demonstrated by the fact that the behaviours valued in school are those of punctuality, politeness to authority figures, neatness, the withstanding of boring routines with a minimum of complaint, and being a good loser and a magnanimous winner. The behaviours disapproved of are those that break the rules, such as violence, noisiness or movement, those that question or abuse authority, and those that fail to conform to work requirements. There is thus a strong relation between the acceptable/unacceptable behaviours of school and those of the workplace, and the inculcation of the appropriate behaviours is an important function of schools.

Normality

The theories and practices of special education often reproduce and legitimate further those ideologies on which they themselves are predicated. An example of this is the notion of normality and abnormality or health and sickness. The concept of health itself has been criticised as an attempt to make absolute what can only be relative. It is not possible to speak of anyone as being completely healthy. We are all sick in some degree. The importance placed on this sickness is a matter of individual anxiety and social pressure. The idea of mental health and illness is even more open to question. There is a tendency to describe as mental illness behaviour patterns that are the result of unhappiness, tiredness or a commitment to different standards. This tendency has taken on a political aspect when people who think differently from those in power have been described as mad and even incarcerated as a result of this description.

There is a continuing tendency to turn physical fitness and firm-mindedness into fetishes. On the other hand, the continual growth of the medical profession has led to a morbid concern with health and to the increasing medicalisation of a whole range of social problems. People who are handicapped or different may well be seen as being 'odd', people to stay away from. In this kind of social climate, people shudder at the sight of thalidomide victims, prefer not to live near 'mental' hospitals and are unwilling for their children to be educated alongside the partially sighted. It is these attitudes towards the handicapped that we refer to as *stigmatisation*. The separate education of children with special needs and the various other forms of institutional segregation and stigmatisation serves to legitimate in turn, for both the hale and the halting, the inferiority of the latter. Both actual separation and the idea of radical difference are reproduced with resultant limited morbid preoccupations on all sides. Thus the separation of the handicapped and the non-handicapped serves only to perpetuate mutual ignorance and prejudice.

THE PROCEDURE OF INSTITUTIONALISED STIGMATISATION

Rather than examining a range of illustrative examples of the practice of special education, it may be possible to understand it through a general analysis of the processes that highlight some of their significant functions. The model used is simply an adaptation of the medical model: referral, assessment, formulation, intervention and evaluation. The stages are by no means clear-cut: in practice they tend to overlap both chronologically and theoretically. For example, an intervention designed to help a child overcome specific reading difficulties may involve a great deal of reassessment at various stages of the process which helps to generate more accurate and up-to-date formulations and thereby modify the programme. At the outset it is as well to emphasise that although these procedural stages may have the clinical clarity of routine, in fact they are social procedures specifically modified by the participants in each individual case and context.

Referral

There are several crucial questions concerning the procedures of referral: these questions are political as well as technical. Who has the power to refer whom to where/whom? What is the technical and political derivation of this power? The most frequent course is for a teacher to notice difficulties with a pupil in terms of behaviour or learning progress. The teacher might then perhaps mention these difficulties to a headteacher or someone with a relevant specific responsibility. If the actual aim of the teacher is the removal of the child from some or all lessons, either in the interests of the child, the teacher or the rest of the class (these are often rationalised as being identical), then this involves a further referral outside the school. Alternatively, it may more simply involve discussion of a possible placement within the school's own facilities such as remedial, opportunity or disruptive classes or units which may be on- or off-site. However, at this stage there is the possibility for disagreement and differences between those with control of resources and the person making the referral. For example, the teacher and the head might both wish to place a child in the remedial class but the remedial specialist may object, without necessarily assessing the child, on the basis that the class is temporarily full: this in turn may be part of a bid to obtain greater staffing and/or resources. Quite often referrals are made by teachers in pressurised urban classrooms who would like to be relieved of a particularly difficult child. Pressure of this sort from teachers is likely to be opposed by specialists in the school and by those in authority if they either oppose the practice of removing children from class or if they doubt the impartial wisdom of particular teachers or their neutrality with regard to a specific child.

Parents may also refer children, and this is more likely to happen within the clinically formal group of categories. In these cases the referral in the first instance is likely to be to the family's general practitioner. However, children with partial hearing loss or with a speech defect are often not actually referred until they come into contact with the screening process which many urban authorities have instituted at reception level. In these cases, if the doctor accepts the referral then it is more likely that formal special-education procedures will be instituted. Some forms of non-clinical, non-formal special provision accept referrals from the children themselves: thus truancy centres in some urban areas (e.g. Tower Hamlets in ILEA) may locate some of their client children simply as the ones who walk in off the street and ask to attend simply because they 'can't stand school'. Finally, referral to special education may come indirectly from the police, the juvenile courts or social services.

When a child is referred to a specific person this is usually for the purpose of assessment. If the projected placement is within school this may be a specialist teacher or counsellor. If the projected placement involves formal special education, then referral is likely to be to an educational psychologist or, much more rarely, to a physician. In this way the decisions concerning referral can very largely determine the outcomes of the assessment process, irrespective of the ascribed needs of the child. The decision whether or not to make a referral, and if so to whom, is one usually taken by those with technical knowledge and/or political authority within schools. Their decisions are likely to be influenced as much by political as by technical considerations: for instance, are parents likely to co-operate with special-education referral, to ignore it, or to oppose it vocally? Are teachers likely to organise collective complaints if a certain child whose behaviour is considered grossly inappropriate is not removed?

Where a referral is made by a court or indeed by a specially convened case conference, there may be competitions of interest between various institutions represented (social services, mainstream education, special education, health service, psychological service, juvenile bureau), each either attempting to take control of the child's case or to pass it on to someone else. A child's future educational career, and hence subsequent life opportunities, may depend on the decisions concerning who refers him/her to whom or where. In most cases this is further complicated and made more arbitrary by the pattern of special-education facilities available within an area of the city or within the local education authority as a whole. Both Swann and Woolfe (cited in Swann, 1982, p. 71) have shown how the pattern of provision restricts and dictates the types of referral that are possible within a specific area. In other ways too, a child's educational career may be determined by fortuitous events: for instance a child manifesting behaviour that those in authority take to be confrontational may find him/her treated as delinquent if this is first manifested to the police, as 'hyperactive' or 'conduct disordered' or even 'pre-psychotic' if it is first brought to the attention of the medical profession, or in need of special education if a child's counsellor, teacher or educational psychologist first takes notice. Similarly, a child who cannot hear very well in one school, or even classroom, may be asked to sit nearer the front: in another, a referral may be made that will eventually lead him/her to spend two-thirds of his/her school career in a specialist unit 20 miles away from home.

Assessment

Assessment then may take place after the important decisions have already been made or when they have been severely restricted. Seminal questions concern who has the right to consent or dissent. For instance, only educational psychologists are allowed to administer IQ tests and this has become the basis both for their academic training, now usually certificated at Master's degree level, and for the powerful and well-paid professional position they have developed in local educational authorities over the last fifty years. Both the academic legitimations and the high pay and status are connected with the socially pivotal procedures they administer and their function as social gatekeepers:

> For if the human wreckage produced by the way society is organised can be discreetly removed, processed and returned in reusable form by these social garbage workers, then not only will the service avoid producing disruption itself: it will prevent the disturbance which might result if the evidence of the political system's failure to meet human needs were left in our midst (Ingleby, 1976, p. 155).

Exclusive use of IQ tests has become more entrenched as medical practitioners are dissuaded from and become more reluctant to use them. It provides the educational psychologists with an overlap between technical and political authority which has been reinforced by the 1981 Education Act. Where an authority has no adviser and the summary and recommendation part of the new procedure is left to educational psychologists, their power has become formidable indeed.

The methodologies and instruments of assessment may be discussed in five main groups: clinical procedures, consultations, observation, questionnaires and tests. Medical methods of assessment would include hearing and vision tests as well as those more specifically clinical, such as electroencephalograms (EEGs). Consultations simply denote conversation that the assessor might well have with heads, teachers, parents or children to elicit descriptions of behaviour, learning problems or histories. The case studies in Booth and Statham (1982) illustrate the relatively greater weight given by assessors in favour of professional opinion as against the accounts of parents.

A more impartial technique and one increasingly used in many cities is classroom observation procedure. Here the assessor — often an educational psychologist — attempts to observe the referred child in interaction with the teacher and other children in the classroom. Attempting not to draw attention to him/herself the assessor may use various observational schedules and various criteria (for example time spent on- or off-task, time spent out of seat, etc.) in observing a class over a length of time — which may be as little as one hour or more than a week. The resulting data may have some claim to objectivity and measurability (it may therefore be replicated at a later stage to ascertain any change in behaviour or performance) but of course the presence of the observer in the classroom could have an interfering effect on the child or the group. For this reason a more sophisticated version of this assessment technique consists in instructing the class teacher(s) in the methods of classroom observation. Some specific and timed observation then becomes part of their teaching repertoire. Here assessment has some overlap with intervention as, in the process of observation, the teacher's perception of the classroom situation may alter and this may lead either to the conclusion that the child is less of a problem than was originally thought or that there are a range of tactics that could be adopted in the course of lessons which would help improve the behaviour or performance.

IQ tests have already been mentioned, but there is also a wide variety of tests, questionnaires, grids and scales which may also be used in the assessment process. Achievement tests may be used to compare a child's performance in specific subjects with national norms, thus clarifying a teacher's impression of a child's academic progress. Reading tests in particular are used to show how a child's performance compares with that of others and this is usually expressed as a reading age. Some non-verbal tests, such as Raven's Matrices or Goodenough, purport to give a guide to the child's general ability. Other questionnaires, such as the Bristol Social Adjustment Guide or the Rutter B Scale, may be used to try to give some measure to the child's classroom behaviour. Such instruments are usually completed by the teacher(s) and hence they give not a measure of the child's behaviour but rather a measure of a specific teacher's perception of this behaviour within the selective context in which it has been encountered and observed. There are also tests and questionnaires, such as the Rorschach, the Junior Eysenck Personality Questionnaire and the Children's Apperception Test, which actually aspire to give some indication of a child's personality. The categories of these particular instruments tend to be loose and subjective, either leaving much to the interpretation of the assessor or being largely derived from the interpretation of the person who invented the questions. Although the use of personality tests is in practice largely confined to educational and clinical psychologists, and in some cases doctors, all the tests mentioned above are freely available for use by teachers. Indeed a knowledge and experience of such instruments may well be a large part of the professional expertise of a remedial specialist or schools counsellor. This expertise may well be founded on a rather unquestioning acceptance of their virtue, validity and impartiality: it may well also lead to a confusion between completing instruments and measuring children.

> I was labelled dyslexic right from the start and they tried tae put me in a mentally handicapped school. It was only because my Mum and Dad fought for me (saying there was nothing *that* wrong with me) that they allowed me intae a 'normal' school; but even there they split me off and made me go intae a reading unit. Right until secondary school I was always something special in the class because I'd be taken out for an hour every day.
> (Maureen McLaughlin, Edinburgh, quoted in White and Brockington, 1983)

Formulation

The process of formulation is perhaps equivalent to diagnosis in medical practice. It implies that after assessment has taken place there is a period of reflection and possibly discussion in which assessment findings are correlated and possible intervention and placement strategies are considered in the light of how they match the specific individual needs of the child in question. That this process does not take place with any reliable regularity is indicative of the amount of faith that those responsible for decisions with regard to special education place in their assessment techniques and instruments. If a non-English-speaking 11-year-old scores 69 on the full scale of the WISC then some consideration and discussion is necessary before blithely assuming that his/her educational interests would best be served by placement in an ESN(M) school. Yet this has happened. The procedures recommended by the 1981 Act, and in particular the drawing up of the summary and recommendations, would seem to provide ample opportunity for formulation. However, the consultations necessitated by a multi-disciplinary ascertainment may unfortunately often prove to be a dispute between the professionals of different orientation rather than the formulation of a negotiated consensus. In such disputes the decision will ultimately rest not with the person who has the most detailed knowledge of the child under consideration or the one who has the most detailed perception of his/her special needs, but will rest with the professional group with the greatest political authority. Educational psychologists have gradually been assuming this power in the urban education authorities of England and Wales, and they have been confirmed in it by the 1981 Education Act.

In the USA, by contrast, no individual professional group has this power and more importantly the parents must be consulted at the stage of formulation. Indeed, under recent US legislation (Public Law 94–142) it seems to be the parents who are the ultimate decision-making authority. This contrasts strongly with England and Wales, where parents can still be made to send their children to a special school against their will. However, the regulations for the implementation of the 1981 Act (Circular 1/83) do make it clear that parents must be consulted and involved in the formulation process. Furthermore, parents are to be given access to the professional records on which decisions may be based. This might emphasise to professionals that they should collaborate with parents rather than attempting to manipulate them.

Intervention

Within the medical model the stage of intervention may be known as treatment, or even, to Hellenise, therapy. The orientation of a response to educational special needs may be social work, medical, psychiatric, psychological or psychodynamic as well as specifically centred in the classroom. A full discussion here of intervention is inappropriate because it might draw the central focus away from the crucial issues of segregation and stigmatisation. (The Guide to Further Reading at the end of the chapter should be referred to if more information is needed.) Recent literature has shown an encouraging trend away from benevolent paternalism and a psychological microview towards a more sociological and comparative approach: however, here it may be sufficient to mention some issues more germane to the subject of urban education, namely placement and behaviour modification.

Special-education placement may be categorised according to four criteria (see Figure 6.1): residential/non-residential; full-time/part-time; temporary (i.e. with a date of return to mainstream agreed in advance) or permanent; within the building and institutional framework or outside it. A concern for the educational placement effects of categorisation might point for instance to the custodial sentences for young offenders to CHEs. Many such institutions now consider themselves to be therapeutic, and education is seen as an important aspect of the 'treatment' they offer. Such community homes provide education on-site for the incarcerated children and adolescents who therefore do not attend the local schools. The curriculum in such institutions is usually not comparable to that of the mainstream, due to limitations of resources and staff skills. The children spend their school hours with the same judicially deemed deviant peer group with whom they are living. Since many CHEs are situated in remote rural areas, the urban children, deprived of contact via the local schools, often meet very few people and acquire little familiarity with the local environment. Their therapeutic curriculum of rearing goats, clay modelling and growing vegetables may be of dubious relevance to them when they are eventually returned to the city. The purpose of magistrates and social workers deciding to send children to such institutions is presumably not punitive (leaving aside the 'short, sharp shock' model of detention centres). Children are sent to CHEs for periods of up to several years at a time to 'help' them to become people who do not break the law. The point is that when children are sent to this highly expensive provision they are also being sentenced to an

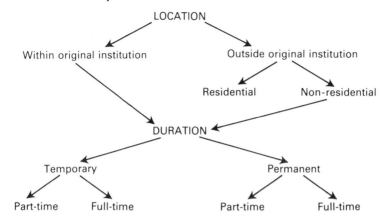

Figure 6.1 *Special education placements.*

inferior education, a deficient curriculum and a consequent restriction of their life chances. Few children leave CHEs with examination results satisfactory enough to enable them to continue their education. Perhaps few such children would have succeeded in mainstream schools: but their opportunities would not have been so arbitrarily restricted by a court of law acting in conjunction with therapeutic educators. In considering the high rates of recidivism it might not be inappropriate to recall that these children have been deprived of even the chance of educational and commensurate success through the normal processes. Placement in a CHE may be seen, therefore, as a sentence to an inferior education.

> There was a special class in the school and they tried quite hard to help me, but I think I needed someone to push me more than they were prepared to. Maybe they thought if they pushed me too hard I would leave or go off. It wasn't so much the school that was a washout. Maybe *I* was a washout. Maybe the school wasn't at fault. Perhaps it was *me*.
> (Gordon MacMillan, aged 23, Baptist Mills, Bristol, quoted in White and Brockington, 1983)

If CHE placement represents the negative aspect of segregated educational provision, behaviour modification might offer some of the techniques necessary to enable children with special needs to succeed in mainstream schools. Behaviour modification has, however, become a contentious issue. It is claimed that it is successful in helping to resolve or at least ameliorate a wide range of learning and behaviour difficulties. However, if its success is as clear as its adherents claim, if it is more than another fashionable whimsy like child analysis, then it represents teachers and educationists with a dilemma that is social or even ethical rather than technical. Is it acceptable to alter children's behaviour in a way contrary to their apparent wishes? Does this not interfere with cherished freedoms of the individual? But if a child's choices are going to lead to a maladjusted school, a psychiatric hospital unit or a junior Borstal, does it not seem to be justifiable to usurp the child's freedom of choice at one stage so that he or she may have a substantially increased repertoire of choice at a later stage? If a behaviour modification schedule or a programmed learning scheme with contingent positive reinforcement can help to keep a child in touch with his/her peers and with the mainstream curriculum, then in the long run it actually gives him/her a freedom of choice over a range of options that he or she would not otherwise have had. This is made even clearer by the fact that many behaviour modification programmes used in schools, particularly with adolescents, are actually agreed upon with the child, the programme designer and another party such as a headteacher or parent or guardian. Of course it is still possible to say that the child was coerced into this choice, but since the success of such programmes usually depends on the motivation of the child, such coercion would actually be counter-productive.

This subject is important for two reasons: first because the libertarian position with its antagonism to behaviourism and behaviour modification may be serving to restrict the range of options and interventions available to children with special needs; secondly, these types of interventions are quite possible in mainstream schools. Although purists such as Berger might have difficulty in acknowledging such reinforcement strategies and behaviour programmes even as part of a scientifically oriented behaviour modification (Berger, 1979), such interventions nevertheless represent a series of positive strategies which are readily available to class and subject teachers in mainstream schools to help children with special needs. One could even go further and suggest that many of the so-called techniques of behaviour modification in the classroom actually represent little more than good pedagogical practice which has always stressed a positive attitude, rewards, structured progress and careful ongoing assessment. Indeed they closely resemble the practices of those inner London schools that Rutter *et al.* (1979) found to be the most successful. Indeed, perhaps if these skills were more prevalent among teachers in mainstream schools, not as an emergency kit for dealing with designated problems but as part of their everyday teaching repertoire, then more children would be likely to have greater success both in their academic and social development. Such skills ironically would possibly obviate some of the need for more formal behaviour programmes on the Berger model and for the more segregated forms of intervention for children with special needs.

Evaluation

Evaluation may be applied both to the case of the individual child and to the effectiveness of various types of provision. In the USA, Public Law 94–142 insisted on a regular review of each case. There are no such safeguards in England and Wales except where they have been insisted on by individual LEAs, headteachers or other responsible persons. In order for a child to return to mainstream school in England and Wales it is often necessary for the whole special-education referral process to be repeated in reverse. When a mainstream school is attempting to have a child removed, there is some pressure on this process that normally allows it to retain its momentum. Whether there is usually such forceful pressure to return a child to mainstream school is doubtful. Furthermore, parents and children are not always aware of the possibility of reversing the process, and the professionals concerned may have no interest in initiating it. Heads of special schools are unlikely to see their schools as a restricting environment that is influencing a child adversely so they will rarely initiate the process. The educational psychologists for their part are likely to lose all contact with a child once placement has been achieved: indeed this may be perceived to be the successful end of intervention and involvement. (Although there is likely to be contact between special schools and educational psychologists, this may well involve a different person or even area.) Once more, the crucial issues are to do with power as well as techniques. By what level of success against what criterion may a child be referred from special to mainstream school? Are these criteria known to the child and parents or guardian? Are they indeed known by the head, teachers or educational psychologists?

Whereas at referral the loose procedures of remedial and special classes and off-site units were seen to be likely to place a child at a disadvantage, at the stage of evaluation and reintegration this very laxity may prove an advantage. Where no formal procedures are necessary and there are closer contacts with the teachers in the mainstream (as there are for a remedial department, say, as against an ESN(M) school), it is often possible to experiment and to adapt methods of reintegration. A child may join his peers for some subjects initially; this may then be increased to more time and the speed of reintegration slowed or hastened according to the relative success. Any sort of part-time, local provision is going to have advantages in this respect over full-time and/or distant interventions.

But evaluation should be applied not merely to the children but to the various types of special education. Do special schools actually work? Of course it is almost impossible to agree the criteria by which this question could be answered. But it is surely reasonable to ask whether the benefits that a child received from a special school are greater than those that could accrue from individual assistance in the mainstream. Against this it would be necessary to assess whether the social restrictions placed on a child by attending a special school, unit or class are more tolerable than the risks of the child being seen to be different in the mainstream. Here some criteria may be agreed, such as progress in reading age scores, improvement of teacher ratings on behaviour scales and, not least, the opinion of the child and parents or guardians. Many of the questions below are based on an attempt at such an evaluation (Coulby, 1981). Given the quality of educational research, the lack of data on these evaluative issues is perhaps surprising. If a child of 11 has a reading age of 7, is his/her reading likely to improve most in the next two years by leaving him/her in his/her normal class without special help? By providing some help in specific lessons? By withdrawing him/her part-time to a remedial class? By full-time placement in a remedial class? By attendance at an ESN(M) school? By social work with his/her family? By involving the parents in a reading and listening scheme? By psychotherapy? In the case of such intervention how long would progress be maintained after its cessation?

Even if we knew the answers to these questions — and to be fair we are not entirely in the dark — there would certainly be many other factors to take into account before making a decision on the future of the child, but more evaluative data on which to make a prediction would be helpful. Of course, if such information did exist this is not to say that decision-makers would always be aware of it or take notice of it. It is many years since Tizard's evaluation showed the ineffectiveness of child guidance clinics in helping children (Tizard, 1973), yet this in no way inhibited their continuance and even growth. Professional interests and the legitimation of dominant groups through the medicalisation of such problems, often associated with urban poverty and oppression, may prove to be more important in determining the existence of a provision than whether or not it is actually successful in helping those to whom it is ostensibly addressed.

THE EFFECTS AND FUNCTIONS OF SPECIAL EDUCATION

As has been emphasised in this chapter, one of the main effects of special education on the children who are involved in it is to attach a stigma to them. This stigma may concern the high degree of concentration paid to a physical difference — 'spastic' is a word of abuse in many mainstream schools — or the attachment of an apparently hard and fast psychological or medical label to a difference in behaviour or learning progress. These latter labels are quickly translated back into the more common parlance of nutty, stupid, etc. Human differences will always exist: it is the social process of labelling, institutionalisation and segregation that transforms difference into stigma. Whatever progress special schools may make with pupils in academic and social terms, against this must be set the underlying bitterness that the stigmatisation of placement must only serve to generate and reinforce. Hargreaves has shown the effect on children of finally accepting the label that educational institutions have attempted to place on them (Hargreaves *et al.*, 1975). Apart from the personal resentment, there is also the likelihood that performance will be diminished and that predictions about handicapped — or delinquent — careers will become self-fulfilling. The segregation instituted by placement in a residential maladjusted school or a distant school for the blind may become ossified in adult life into the incarceration of prison or the long-term hospital ward. It is important to remember that these life-careers often had their inception in well-intended decisions and placements made by teachers and psychologists in educational institutions.

However, in general, the functions of special education are closely connected with the reproduction of the system of stratification of society in accordance with the division of labour appropriate to capitalist economic requirements. It does this by the reproduction of the ideologies of individualism, intelligence, behaviour and normality. At the bottom of the competitive education system of England and Wales, especially in inner-city areas, are those who fail dramatically at school work, those whose behaviour or appearance offends the values of teachers and headteachers, and those physically unable to compete successfully in the great race of free-market competitive individualism. These children not only fail to achieve certification; they often acquire the stigmatising labels that they are themselves socialised into accepting. Instead of being given access by education to the institutions that lead to wealth and power, they endure an inferior curriculum in the presence of their deemed deviant peers. Their place in the labour market will be at the very bottom — unskilled, low-paid jobs with little security and untouchable status; in times of recession they will provide the labour reserve army of the unemployed. Tomlinson points out that the eventual employment of those with special needs has always been a predominant concern for those interested in their welfare, lest they be unemployable and thus constitute a drain on the resources of the state and/or dominant group (Tomlinson, 1981, p. 28).

Given the complication of the class structure by the pattern of divisions of race, it is not surprising that those people pulled into the urban economy during the period of rapid growth should find their children grotesquely overrepresented in special schools, classes and units. Black children are prepared by the ascertainment and separation processes of special education for their role at the bottom of the hierarchy of the labour force. Life in the ghetto and the ghetto job are prepared for in the ghetto school. Placement of some children in special education might serve to encourage the others. If children see their peers whose progress or behaviour has been repeatedly criticised by teachers in the mainstream removed summarily to a special class, school or unit, then this is likely both to give them the impression that the teachers' comments are based on justifiable criteria that can be reified in institutional placement and also to motivate them to do their best to conform to accepted educational standards of progress and behaviour. Special education thus functions as a major force of social control not only for the children who have contact with it, but for all the children in the educational system. Deviance and difference in mainstream schools is minimised by the removal of whole sections of children and by the tacit threat of removal hanging over the others.

Consequently, a final effect of the existence of special provision is the avoidance of change in mainstream schools. If so-called different and difficult children are expeditiously removed, then schools do not need to evolve the curricula and pedagogy which would, with appropriate administrative and architectural (such as lifts and ramps) change, have allowed these children to remain with their peers. That some radical, innovatory and caring teachers also end up working in special schools and units also removes a pressure on urban schools to adapt. Ironically, such adaptations would be likely to benefit all children in terms of a more relevant and stimulating curriculum and a more caring and flexible administration and teaching style. Both handicapped and non-handicapped urban pupils then serve to gain by the reduction of such stigmatising processes and institutions.

GUIDE TO FURTHER READING

Anyone interested in finding out more about special education can do no better than consult the excellent Open University material for the course on Special Needs in Education (E241). One of the readers for the course, Swann (ed.) (1981), *The Practice of Special Education*, presents a wide range of perspectives on current policy. Insight into school practice in integrating children with special needs can be gained from Hegarty *et al.* (1981), *Educating Pupils With Special Needs in the Ordinary School.* For the wider implications of segregation and the distorted nature of the growth of comprehensive schooling, see Hargreaves (1982), *The Challenge for the Comprehensive School.*

For a vigorous critique of the concept of IQ, see Evans and Waites (1981), *IQ and Mental Testing.* It is worth looking also at the elegant paradigm argument in this field by Kamin (1974), *The Science and Politics of IQ.* With regard to the nature of ESN(M) education in Birmingham, Tomlinson (1981), *Educational Subnormality*, examines in detail the racist and anti-working-class nature of special-school provision. This analysis is carried further in Tomlinson (1982), *A Sociology of Special Education.* As a further outline of how to integrate children from the perspective of a class teacher, see Leach and Raybould (1979), *Learning and Behaviour Difficulties in School.*

7
School and work

INTRODUCTION

By way of introduction we would like to quote the following comment from a young person on a Youth Training Scheme course:

> In my opinion the new Youth Training Scheme is exactly the same as the old Youth Opportunities Programme. I think it is just a way of keeping down the unemployment figures. Maybe if the Government spent less money on nuclear weapons and stopped losing money because of the EEC, then more jobs could be created in areas of high unemployment.
>
> Of what I have experienced so far on the YTS, it is just like being back at school in the first year. We are starting off again with the basics instead of being taught more advanced adult work. As for the point of work experience, well maybe it is useful but what if you haven't got a job at the end of it? That year on the YTS could have been spent trying to find a more permanent job.
>
> By the end of the first year of the YTS there will be thousands of youths like myself applying for one job, all with the same qualifications and certificates, which will not be of any use because everyone will be equally skilled.
>
> If you do get a work experience job then you will be lucky if you last much longer than your year on the scheme, because in my view most employers just take you on because: (a) they don't have to pay you; and (b) after the first year another YTS student can fill your place.
>
> If anyone reading this wonders why I am on a training scheme it is because the money is better than Social Security and it is slightly less boring (*Times Educational Supplement*, 11 November 1983, p. 16).

The changing pattern of employment

The employment pattern of British cities has changed dramatically over the last decade. Unemployment in many large cities such as Glasgow and Liverpool has been a permanent feature for a number of decades. Figure 7.1 indicates the change in the job pattern for the GLC (Greater London Council). It is typical of what has happened in other

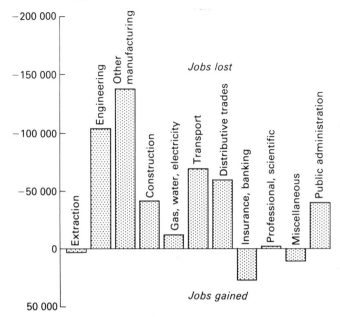

Figure 7.1 *Job losses in London 1975–83. From the GLC Economic Policy Group, 1983. Reproduced with permission.*

large cities. A quarter of a million jobs have been lost in manufacturing and engineering alone. Where London is perhaps not typical is in the increase in jobs in commerce and banking. The lost jobs are largely in those sectors of the economy that previously employed large numbers of working-class men. Between 1978 and 1982 one in six jobs were lost in the manufacturing industries in London (GLC Economic Policy Group, 1983, p. 1). The reasons for the changes are not our concern here but they include the world recession, government policy (encouraging the growth of new towns and development areas, 'the cuts'), the decline of heavy industry under competition from abroad and the introduction of microprocessing. The full effects of these are yet to be revealed but Figure 7.2 indicates, in the case of London, that the traditional image of the manufacturing city must be revised. Some 40 per cent of London's jobs are in the public administration, professional, scientific, commercial and banking sectors. Again, while London's role as capital city and banking centre may make it atypical, the likelihood is that these employment areas have cushioned the city against the worst effects of the increase in unemployment. Other cities may have experienced the decline in manufacturing and traditional industries (such as steel in Sheffield, shipbuilding in Newcastle upon Tyne) without the benefit of these other job sectors. Moreover, it

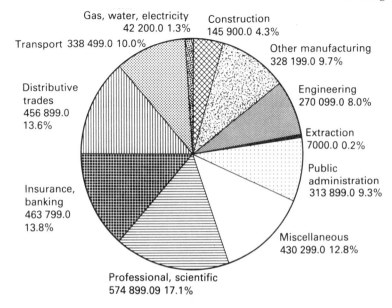

Figure 7.2 *Where Londoners work. (Note: Miscellaneous services includes sport, leisure and tourism; extraction includes mining, quarrying and agriculture.) From the GLC Economic Policy Group, 1983. Reproduced with permission.*

ought to be noted that many traditional manufacturing sectors (for example textiles in Leeds and Manchester) have been in decline for a much greater length of time than just the last decade.

The gender division of labour

Work in cities is not only divided according to the rewards and status of the various jobs. It is important to see work as still largely divided according to gender. Men seek work in manufacturing, heavy industry, vehicle driving, management and the professions. Women are employed as cleaners, secretaries, typists and shop assistants. The pattern is still for men 'bosses' to have women secretaries. This *gender division of labour* is something that schools and colleges help to perpetuate. It is necessary to be aware of it at the outset as job aspirations and relevant education and training may be very different for boys and girls in education systems where this division of labour is reproduced. If this pattern were to be broken down changes would need to take place not only in schools but in the organisation of the workplace itself.

The youth labour market

For young people in cities there have been two recent changes that have entirely altered the relations between school and work: these are the rapid growth in youth unemployment and the almost total decline of apprenticeship schemes (Youth Task Group, 2 February 1982). (Though, of course, we should remember that it was almost exclusively young men who obtained places on apprenticeship schemes in the past.) In response to these changes various government schemes have been introduced to provide young people with training and to prevent them going straight from school to the dole queue. These schemes have now been consolidated in the Youth Training Scheme (YTS) which aims 'to provide all young people participating in the scheme with a better start in working and adult life through an integrated programme of training, education and work experience' (Youth Task Group, 4 March 1982). Later in this chapter we will describe and analyse the YTS scheme in some detail and see how it exemplifies (or not) various theories about education and work. However, first we wish to examine some commonsense notions about school and work.

Equality of opportunity?

One of the main ideals behind education in the UK may be seen as equality of opportunity. Given equal opportunities children may compete fairly for the glittering prizes of education which are usually seen as GCE passes and university degrees. To suggest that equality of opportunity does not lead to equality of attainment may sound self-evident to British ears. The point, after all, is to have a race in which children start from the same spot: they can hardly all be expected to finish at the same time (or finish at all). Yet, as long ago as the mid-1960s Coleman, working in the USA, had suggested that equality of opportunity should be redefined as equality of attainment. After a large-scale study of black and white groups in schools in the USA, he concluded that:

> *The difference in achievement* at grade 12 [school leaving age in the USA] between the average negro and the average white *is, in effect, the degree of inequality of opportunity*, and the reduction of that inequality is the responsibility of the school. This shift in responsibility follows logically from the change in the concept of equality of educational opportunity from school resource inputs to effects of schooling (Coleman, in Raggatt and Evans, 1977, p. 64, our emphasis).

Coleman is suggesting that the race is rigged or, more seriously, that a race is the wrong metaphor for schooling systems. Children with different backgrounds and interests, some with various forms of handicap, should not be seen as competing in a race, no matter how fair. Schooling should concentrate on diminishing the variations in the level of attainment with which children leave school. To concentrate instead on the rules of the race must tend to emphasise competition and continue a system within which many children are judged to be losers.

Coleman's concept of the equality of attainment or equality of outcome has not replaced equality of opportunity as an aim of education in either the USA or the UK. It has, however, been espoused, albeit in part and tacitly, by those educators who have worked towards such progressive reforms as comprehensivisation, mixed-ability teaching, equal curricular experiences for boys and girls, common leaving certificates at 16, open access to higher education and recognition on the part of schools of the importance of the language, customs and culture of pupils and their families. The crucial point, however, has reference to the subject of school and work: even equality of attainment could never lead to equality of jobs. Even if a utopian school system were to turn out children who were all achieving equally, they would then be placed in a job market where gross inequalities of rewards, conditions and status persisted. (It is, of course, possible to make a further leap of the utopian imagination and conceptualise a society in which such inequalities did not persist. Such musings are, however, rather remote from the subject of school and work in the UK.) The *stratification of the labour market* is such that public and private employers actually require young people with different skills at different levels. Industry, commerce, the professions and service facilities need some young people with a high level of specific specialised skill. They also need people with low-level skills or virtually no skills at all. If schools do not produce unskilled and unqualified young people, then they will fail to meet one of the demands of the labour market.

In taking this argument towards the edges of absurdity we are assuming one important proposition: that the labour market determines the pattern of education and not vice versa. If schools were to produce children who attain equally at, let us say, 16, this would not, of itself, produce a utopian, egalitarian society. People at the workplace would need to generate tests and training to differentiate and stratify the equally-achieving school leavers. That schools themselves produce a highly stratified output of school leavers may be seen as a response to the needs of the *mode of production* (that is, the way that industry, commerce and public facilities are organised) for a differentiated and stratified workforce. In considering school and work, then, we may expect the needs of the labour market to determine patterns of education rather than the ideals of educationists to influence the pattern of the labour market.

Urban unemployment

As the number of unemployed people has increased over the past decade the number of young people out of work has grown even more sharply. These figures were provided by the MSC in 1982:

> Unemployment overall quadrupled between 1975 and 1982. Despite the intervention of large-scale special employment measures — notably the Youth Opportunities Programme — unemployment amongst under 18s multiplied five times over the same period. And the prospects are even worse: without policy interventions we estimate that 57 per cent of 16 year olds and 48 per cent of 17 year olds in the labour market will be unemployed by 1984. In 1983/84 of just over 500,000 16 year olds leaving full time education, only just over 200,000 are likely to find jobs (Youth Task Group, 2 February 1982).

This unemployment was distributed unevenly between groups and areas across the country. Certain cities — Belfast, Liverpool, Newcastle upon Tyne — had especially high levels of youth unemployment. Inner-city areas in particular had high concentrations of out-of-work young people. Hackney in inner London provides a vivid example:

> In April 1981 when the average rate for Hackney males was 18.3 per cent, it was 29.2 per cent for sixteen-to-nineteen year olds, the highest rate in Greater London. . . . Among females the overall rates were lower but the effect of youth even more disproportionate: 24 per cent of sixteen-to-nineteen year olds were out of work, almost exactly double the female average (Harrison, 1983, pp. 125–6).

Between a quarter and a third of young people in inner-city areas, then, are unable to find work. If we consider black groups separately from white, then the figure is even more disturbingly high. *The Times Educational Supplement* reported that:

> Youth unemployment in 1981 was no worse among Asians than whites, but markedly worse among West Indians — 28 per cent of men were registered as out of work (compared wth 11 per cent of whites). The proportion of Asian women aged between 16 to 24 who were in jobs or looking for work was lowest of all the groups (*Times Educational Supplement*, 4 November 1983, p. 1).

The figure for 'West Indians' (many of whom were probably born in Britain) does not take account of the different age groups of unemployed people. Black young people living in inner-city areas are likely then to be subject to dramatically high levels of unemployment.

Simultaneous with the world recession and Britain's relative economic decline has been the steady decrease in employment opportunities
in the inner cities. Traditional small-scale manufacturing in East
London for instance has been declining, partly under pressure from
planning legislation. Metal-bashing industries in Birmingham, Coventry and Wolverhampton have been among the worst casualties in the
recession and of competition from cheaper imported goods. New
manufacturing industries, including those involving the much-invoked
'high technology', are frequently set up on green-field sites, in the new
towns, in development areas or in the new city of Milton Keynes. The
computer industries, for instance, tend to be located in the pale British
equivalent of silicon valley in the upper Thames area. The high rates of
inner-city areas, restrictive planning legislation, high levels of trade-
union activity and difficulty of road transport access have all tended to
make these areas unattractive to industry. Up until the mid-1970s
there were actually advertising campaigns in London to encourage
industrial and commercial employers to move out of the city. Ex-urban
development areas offer tax and rate concessions, good motorway
links, a largely non-unionised workforce, attractive locations and
often relatively cheap housing for pioneering executives. Industry and
jobs have left the inner cities, leaving areas like Attercliffe in Sheffield
or Wapping in East London as deserted industrial museums, dark
monuments to a vanished prosperity. It is interesting to see the way in
which this decline is described by the MSC: 'local communities are in
decline because they lack the skills required to attract inward investment or enable new local enterprises to flourish' (NTI, 1981, p. 10).
We will return later to the fallacies of explanations that try to equate
shortage of jobs with shortage of skills.

The competition from cheap imported goods from the Third World
is connected with both unemployment and low wages. In an attempt to
match Third World prices, many small enterprises appear to be
attempting to compete with them by paying low wages rather than
shifting to a more advanced technology. This process is vividly described by Harrison:

> This is creeping underdevelopment, in which parts of the country regress
> towards an economy of coolie labour, the creation of a Third World
> country in our midst, in the inner cities and the peripheral regions like
> most developing countries, Britain is becoming a dual economy, with a
> backward sector of low-paid, labour-intensive industry and a vast reserve
> army of unemployed, and a more modern, well-paid, capital-and-
> knowledge-intensive sector. That division reflects and deepens social and
> geographical inequalities between inner city and suburbs or new towns
> (Harrison, 1983, p. 70).

In addition, the increasing preponderance of transnational corporations has meant that manufacturing plants can be closed down at will and production shifted to low-wage countries. The result can be an intensification of unemployment in the metropolitan countries and pressure upon workers in countries like Britain to accept lower wages or else face the threat of company closure. It is in this changed and still rapidly changing market for manpower that we have described that urban school leavers find themselves looking for jobs.

EDUCATION, TRAINING AND (UN)EMPLOYMENT

The lack of skills argument

As urban unemployment grew during the 1970s criticism began to be expressed from several quarters about the quality of secondary education. The cry from employers, epitomised by Weinstock's notorious 'I blame the teachers' article in the *Times Educational Supplement* (Weinstock, 1976), was that young people left school ill-equipped for the world of work. They did not even have basic literacy and numeracy skills; they were badly disciplined and unable to fit into the demands of the workplace; they did not value the important contribution of business and commerce to our national wealth, indeed to our whole civilisation; instead of practical, technical or scientific studies they preferred to waste their time on subjects like English or, worse still, their teachers led them towards dangerously left-wing attitudes via such subjects as sociology. At the same time young people and their parents also expressed concern that schooling was becoming irrelevant to their needs, that it was not going to 'get us a job'. These complaints came not only from employers and their right-wing political supporters. At a conference sponsored by among others the Child Poverty Action Group on Education and the Urban Crisis, John Bazalgette noted in a comment echoed by many other contributors:

> One of the greatest weaknesses at the present moment is the detachment of teachers and educators from the changes in economic and technological structures. . . . Employers and managers are desperately worried about the effects of this upon young workers. They certainly do not come and talk to teachers because of the entrenched hostility between the educational system and the employment system. The only people who are tackling that hostility are the children, as they leave one group for another (Field, 1977, p. 107).

James Callaghan, when Prime Minister, orchestrated such comments in his famous Ruskin speech which initiated the so-called great debate on education. These comments and the subsequent debate took place as statistics were emerging that seemed to show that the educational service at all levels was failing since youth unemployment, especially in the inner cities, was steadily rising.

These arguments were based on some largely unexamined assumptions which on inspection may be seen to be fallacious. Stage one of the argument is that youth unemployment is caused by lack of necessary skills (the quotation from the MSC above provides an illustration of this). Stage two of the argument is that it is the fundamental duty of schools to provide young people with these skills. Taken together, the argument then states that young people cannot get jobs because they are not properly qualified, because they do not have the skills relevant to the new technological needs of industry. In contradiction to stage one we would assert that young people cannot get jobs because there are no jobs. If industry required special skills it would rapidly establish apprenticeship schemes so that young people could acquire them. But, as we have seen, apprenticeship schemes have been cut. To place responsibility for youth unemployment on the young unemployed is a classic case of blaming the victim. Capitalist industry and commerce is employing a smaller workforce; this is due to influences such as world recession, lack of investment and the increasing use of microprocessor technologies, not to the failure of young people to acquire relevant skills or of educational institutions to provide them. Stage two of the argument implies that young school leavers are the ones who take on highly skilled jobs. This is rarely the case. Skilled and professional work are usually taken by people who have studied for 'A' levels or for degrees. It may be that at this level there is not a sufficient emphasis on science and technology but this is largely a separate argument from that concerning the pre- and post-16 education of young people who leave school at the earliest possible date. Nevertheless, the education service has been used as an available scapegoat for unemployment.

The MSC and YTS

Perhaps, as a consequence of this, schemes that set out to ameliorate youth unemployment and to give young people a 'better' training have emanated not from the Department of Education and Science or the local education authorities but from the Department of Employment. The agency responsible for these developments has been the quasi-autonomous non-governmental organisation (Quango) known as the

Manpower Services Commission (MSC). Acronyms abound in this area and we must introduce at least two more: the first important scheme established by the MSC for young people was the Youth Opportunities Programme (YOP) in 1978; this was replaced in 1983 by the extensive and apparently permanent Youth Training Scheme (YTS). Much of the rest of this chapter will be concerned with an examination of the role of the MSC in the education and training of young people, and particularly with the YTS. However, it is important to stress that the discussion of school and work is not limited in its relevance to those involved in further education or even those in secondary schools. The relationship between school and work begins in the infant school. Processes of, for instance, social control and the gender division of labour are important from the very earliest years of schooling. Discussions and theories relating to education and work, then, are of utmost relevance to all teachers involved in urban education.

YOP was a programme to provide school leavers with a work-experience placement, without any guarantee of a job at the end of it. 'Jobs not Yops' became a common piece of graffiti on the walls of inner cities during the 1980s. Its successor, YTS, was established very rapidly to provide not only work experience, but high-quality on-the-job training and supervision plus thirteen weeks of education. The scheme is voluntary but open to all school leavers, both those who find a job and those who remain unemployed. In addition, some people over the age of 17 who have no work and have not been on the scheme are also eligible. The scheme aims 'to provide positive opportunities for disadvantaged groups' (Youth Task Group, 3 December 1982) and so it was further thought desirable that '18 year olds with special needs (e.g. disabled young people) should be covered' (Youth Task Group, 4 April 1982). This age limit for those with special needs was raised to 21 in 1983. In the first year of the YTS 460 000 places were to be made available to young people at a cost of over £1 billion. In the event the take-up rate was, from the outset, considerably lower than expected. However, the scheme is a major and long-lasting contribution to the education and training of young people in the cities of the UK.

The Technical and Vocational Education Initiative reflected the wish of the MSC to see its 'vocationalist' philosophy, as enshrined in YTS, permeate the secondary school curriculum. As a pilot scheme in a number of LEAs, TVEI envisaged an enhanced vocational, technical and practical education for the 14–18 age group. Where the initiative was piloted, MSC funds were channelled to schools for additional staff and equipment. Funds from the MSC have made generous provision in, for instance, Bradford secondary schools and allowed the development of several significant curricular innovations.

The MSC is not itself in the main responsible for delivering the training provision. YTS programmes are delivered by two distinct methods. In the first (Mode A) the employer is responsible for (say) 200 trainees, and arranges on its own premises 'a complete programme of education, training and work experience' or 'a local education authority assumes responsibility for (say) 500 trainees. It provides them with education and training and arranges for them to be placed, within the authority or with other employers, for periods of work experience' (Youth Training Group, 1982, Diagram 1). Smaller employers may group together in a local Chamber of Commerce scheme or become managing agents themselves using further education provision to supply the education component. In the second scheme (Mode B), the MSC is itself the managing agent but it still largely relies on other institutions to deliver the training service: 'MSC arranges with a voluntary organisation or a consortium to assume responsibility for (say) 50 trainees and provide education, training and work experience for them in a training workshop' (Youth Training Group, 1982, Diagram 1). This arrangement is perhaps most suitable for young people leaving special schools. Alternatively, 'M.S.C. arranges courses of F.E. or training with local contractors and also arranges linked work experience with employers' (Youth Training Group, 1982, Diagram 1). Each mode involves work experience, training and education. Mode A is most suitable to those young people actually in employment (by far the minority). It has in fact proved the most popular option with all young people. The shortage of applicants on Mode B schemes has presented difficulties for some institutions, particularly FE colleges, which had anticipated higher numbers. Trainees are paid £25.00 per week (1983) for the entire duration of their course. At the end of the course it is hoped that trainees will have acquired certain 'core skills':

> Through the medium of both planned practical experience and off-the-job training a scheme must provide for young people to make progress in five course areas: (a) number and application (b) communication (c) problem-solving (d) manual dexterity (e) introduction to computer literacy and information technology (YTS 1983, p. 4).

That 16-year-old school leavers are assumed to be lacking in these skills may be taken as implicit criticism of the education service.

There has been considerable condemnation of the YTS. Interestingly, however, the Labour Party has voted in favour of its continuation. Despite its critics, then, the scheme would seem to be here to stay. Our stance towards the scheme is largely critical but it is worth also making some positive comments. The YTS is bringing about 'a revolutionary change' (strong words, these, from David Young, the then Chairperson of the MSC) 'in the way we train our workforce in general and our young people in particular' (YTS, undated, p. 1). The change is actually neither as new nor as revolutionary as it has been portrayed. Horne has shown the similarity between the YOP and the YTS and the 'dole colleges' established to train and control young jobless people during the period of high unemployment before the Second World War (Horne, 1983). While it may not be quite so revolutionary, the YTS is giving or attempting to give a large part of the age group a meaningful preparation for working life. Learning from the bad reputation of YOP, the MSC has, in its publications and statements, constantly tried to emphasise the high standard of the training: 'the quality of training provided within the scheme and in individual establishments must be assured' (Youth Training Group, 1982, 3.15g). The commitment to thirteen weeks' education and particularly the repeated emphasis on computer literacy and information technology as compulsory glossy components forms part of this 'quality'. Likewise, the MSC emphasises that there should be genuine on-the-job training and has established a rudimentary supervisory provision to ensure that this takes place. It is likely that some of the schemes — say the Mode A schemes established by national organisations such as the National Westminster Bank or the Post Office — will offer young people a range of experiences and training that they could not hope to find at school or perhaps even at FE colleges. (The beneficiaries of such schemes may turn out to be those young people with jobs assured by such employers rather than those who face the dole after the completion of their YTS year.) There is a commendable emphasis on opportunities for girls in the MSC rhetoric and an insistence that young black people be given an equal chance. Indeed, the MSC may be ahead of employers, trade unions and schools in its insistence that 16-year-old young women leaving school have a role in the workplace that stretches beyond the typewriter or the tea-urn. It may be difficult to transform this commitment into practice, but present gender divisions in FE colleges have set a standard that it should not prove difficult to surpass. The skills and images of domesticity, caring and secretarial efficiency are transferred almost without question from the colleges to the workplace (Gibb, 1983; Blunden, 1983). The MSC has ensured that handicapped young people should be able to participate in the YTS. For many people this will postpone, if only temporarily, the point in their lives when there are few options left except Social Education Centres.

The ideology of vocationalism has become even further entrenched with the introduction of a plan for a new 17-plus national certificate known as the Certificate of Pre-Vocational Education (CPVE). With much haste in the spring of 1984, the Joint Board for Pre-vocational Education, a group of bodies concerned with further education, prepared a sixty-page consultative document sent out to every secondary school and FE college in England and Wales inviting comments on the CPVE proposals. The certificate was to be based upon both existing pre-vocational courses and new, board-designed or school/college-designed courses. According to the plan, CPVE programmes would have to include a balance of 'liberal' and 'vocational' studies, learning through practical experience, work experience, careers education, and student involvement in planning, organising and assessment of their learning.

Although aimed at a broader attainment range than YTS, CPVE none the less was not seen as a universal 17-plus certificate; the academic 'O' and 'A' level track is to remain as the major educational pathway for the select few. Indeed the then chairperson of the Joint Board was reported as saying that the CPVE has much in common with TVEI and YTS — as the 'vocationalist' family — in that they were all responses to unemployment (*Times Educational Supplement*, 11 May 1984).

The statisation of expenditure

Castells suggests that one of the most important ways in which capitalist businesses manage to maintain their profit levels in the urban context is by transferring large components of their essential expenditure on to the state (Castells, 1977; 1978; 1980). Roads, port facilities, research and development are all examples of provisions that are essential to the survival of capitalist businesses and industry. However, these are not paid for directly by capitalist organisations, but the expenditure, taken by the state, is shared among the population at large. Capitalist interests, then, only pay a small component of this charge. For Castells, the most important dimension of these state expenditures are those concerned with *the reproduction of labour power*. This means those facilities that allow a skilled, healthy, docile workforce to be perpetuated from one generation to another. Crucial institutions in the reproduction of labour power are those concerned with housing, education and health. That the workforce should be housed, healthy and trained is obviously necessary to the continuation of the capitalist mode of production. Yet, in these areas too, much of the cost of the provision has been shifted via the state on to the population at large. Castells calls this the *statisation* of expenditure. These two concepts are central to Castells's work. For him the process that structures urban space is the reproduction of labour power.

The statisation of provision is a process likely to lead to *urban conflict* (i.e. conflict not necessarily predicated on class opposition) because the state will be unable to pay for enough facilities to meet popular demand. In recession we have seen such conflicts over the closure of hospitals and educational cutbacks in cities in the UK. The YTS would seem to be a choice example of statisation in Castells's terms. The MSC's own documentation makes no attempt to conceal this when it states that employers 'have a very great deal to gain from a scheme which increases the number of trained young people but costs them no more than the present arrangements (and perhaps less)' (Youth Training Group, 1982, 2.6). Indeed, given the decline of apprenticeships where employers provided the training and paid the trainees, and the rise of YTS where the employers pay neither for the training nor the allowance of the trainees, it is certainly going to cost them a good deal less. The expense of industrial training had previously been transferred from indivdiual employers to Industrial Training Boards relating to specific industries. Now that most of these have been wound up, the responsibility for training has been shifted via the state quango of the MSC from the employers on to the public at large. Whether this statisation of provision will lead to urban conflict in Castells's sense remains to be seen. The state rather than employers is now, however, the target for whatever dissatisfaction is generated by the quantity or quality of youth training provision.

Correspondence theory

Bowles and Gintis claim that in 'capitalist America' there is a correspondence between the practices and ideologies of schooling and those of the workplace. This *correspondence theory* relates to some of the ideas mentioned in Chapter 4, such as those concerning the hidden curriculum and the notion of educational institutions as the ideological state apparatus. However, correspondence theory is particularly interesting in this context as its main emphasis is on the links between school and work:

The educational system helps integrate youth into the economic system, we believe, through a structural correspondence between its social relations and those of production. The structure of social relations in education not only inures the student to the discipline of the work place, but develops the types of personal demeanour, modes of self-presentation, self-image and social-class identifications which are the crucial ingredients of job adequacy. Specifically, the social relationships of education — the relationships between administrators and teachers, teachers and students, students and students, and students and their work — replicate the hierarchical division of labour. Hierarchical relations are reflected in the vertical authority lines from administrators to teachers to students. Alienated labour is reflected in the students' lack of control over his or her education, the alienation of the student from the curriculum content, and the motivation of school work through a system of grades and other external rewards rather than the students' integration with either the process (learning) or the outcome (knowledge) of the educational 'production process'. Fragmentation in work is reflected in the institutionalised and often destructive competition among students through continued and ostensibly meritocratic ranking and evaluation. By attuning young people to a set of social relationships similar to those of the work place, schooling attempts to gear the development of personal needs to its requirements (Bowles and Gintis, 1976, p. 131).

This long and dense quotation applies to practices that are in operation at all levels of schooling in UK cities as well as in 'capitalist America'.

At primary and secondary school, children learn to be punctual, they learn that tasks are split up into certain time periods, that work is different from play, that they must try to be neat and productive in their output. These are all skills that are directly necessary to the young adult's effective functioning at the workplace. Perhaps even more important they learn that some subjects (academic ones) are more important than others (practical ones). They learn that some children are more 'intelligent' than others and they become aware of their own position within this hierarchy and come gradually to accept it. They are thus prepared for work which is stratified in terms of its status and rewards and for accepting uncomplainingly their own position within that hierarchy. Finally, through examinations and certification, schools actually participate in determining each individual's position within the stratified labour force.

Some people don't like school, 'cos it's so rigid. You start at 9.00 a.m. and leave at 3.30 p.m. You have to do it every day from Monday to Friday. Your only days off are Saturday and Sunday. But it'll be exactly the same when they start work except that you get paid for going to work and you don't get paid for going to school.
(Tracy Atkinson, quoted in White and Brockington, 1983)

The education system provides an essential function for capitalist industry and commerce. It is a further step from this statement to the more rigorously Marxist position of Bowles and Gintis that the needs of the productive base accounts for the existence and nature of the educational superstructure. However, the formation of the YTS would seem to provide a good illustration of the application of correspondence theory. The orchestration of complaints about the lack of connection between schooling and work could be interpreted as evidence of capitalist dissatisfaction that the correspondence principle was not being successfully implemented. Since, in employers' terms, schools appeared to have lapsed from correspondence, a new system of mechanisms was introduced, via the MSC, to ensure that the needs of the workplace were more fully and adequately met. While the state appears to have made a provision, at some cost, to meet the needs of capitalist interests, we do not assume that all employers will necessarily be happy with the new scheme. YTS and the Technical and Vocational Education Initiative (TVEI), which provides money in certain selected areas for specific programmes of technical education in the fourth and fifth years of secondary school, would seem to be palpable evidence that the demands for vocationalism to be reintroduced into education appear to have been met in general terms. (By vocationalism, we mean the notion that training is more important than abstract education.) However, whether these schemes manage to meet the needs of specific employers will only be seen after they have been in operation for some years.

YTS – who participates?

By the autumn of 1984 the YTS scheme had become a major dimension of post-compulsory education, capable of catering for up to 400 000 young people each year. Much of the rest of this chapter therefore deals with this scheme in some detail.

As indicated above, educational institutions are important mechanisms for reproducing stratification in cities. In order to understand how this operates it is necessary to ask which children participate in YTS programmes. It could be argued that a course of training and work experience would be useful and genuinely educative for *all* children. Would not some workshop or technical experience widen the mind and increase the range of skills of the future lawyer, business consultant or research chemist? But the group of young people who are successful at school in conventional terms are unlikely ever to be involved with the YTS. It is those young people who did not accept or pursue conventional school values, who 'failed' their education, who will end up on YTS programmes. In British cities this means that the young people will be almost exclusively working class, both black and white. The YTS is one in a long sequence of educational and training schemes designed for other people's children.

Now that YTS is a permanent national provision it consolidates the tripartite system at 16-plus. 'O' levels and CSEs replace the 11-plus as the exams that determine into which strata of education and training a pupil should progress. Those with successful GCE and CSE examination results proceed to take 'A' levels, in the sixth form or at college, the first option being most likely. Those who only manage a few examination passes proceed to study for BTEC (business and technical education) awards either in the sixth form or at college, the latter being the most likely. Those with no examination passes or those with grades where success is equivalent to failure will, if they are lucky, find a job (which may well involve placement in the YTS in the first year of work) or otherwise gravitate towards a YTS course as unemployed trainees. For all these groups, but in a steeply increasing order of likelihood, there looms the probability of short- and long-term unemployment. Pupils from middle-class families are the ones most likely to stay on into the sixth form and go to university, those from working-class backgrounds are the ones likely to leave school at 16 with few or no meaningful qualifications (Halsey *et al.*, 1980).

> Working class people are directed towards the factories by schools and the middle class are directed towards university. Even at thirteen and fourteen you could tell which kids were earmarked for that, and we never ever mixed with them.
> (Tory Crimes, quoted in White and Brockington, 1983)

YTS and the nature of skills

The prediction of widespread unemployment for young people who have completed YTS programmes perhaps needs some elaboration. After all, the MSC have persistently argued that skills are transferable and that if young people learn one set of skills they will be able to utilise them in different contexts according to where opportunities arise in the workplace. This conception of transferable skills has been substantiated for the MSC by, among others, Tina Townsend's study of 1000 jobs in London (Hayes *et al.*, 1983). Her argument has been widely criticised:

> To give one of Townsend's examples, when students are taught that the 'skills' of massage work and dough kneading are identical, they are taught that performance is independent of any understanding of the whole process or end product and does not depend for its meaning on content or cultural connotations. Students consider this absurd. And rightly (SSEG, 1983, p. 16).

Skills that are considered transferable in this way are scarcely skills at all. Real skills of use in the workplace include at least two categories: wider educational skills such as numeracy or programme design; technical or craft skills such as those traditionally associated with skilled workers. The skills with which the YTS is concerned, far from guarding against unemployment by their transferability, are largely the skills of unskilled work.

> Two weeks after leaving school I was offered a job at Lipton's super-market. It was a six months scheme. They had me brushing the floor and washing the sinks — silly little things, so that you weren't learning anything.
>
> (Denise Hegyesi, quoted in White and Brockington, 1983)

In this context it is possible to see why the so-called social skills loom so large in YTS programmes. The social skills of deference, obedience and politeness to the employers may well be the most important as well as the most transferable skills of unskilled work. Of course, these are not the only contents of social skills courses. Many include useful elements such as how to complete a job application form, how to phone for an interview or how to claim unemployment benefit. But such courses are about getting and keeping jobs: they therefore must concentrate on how to please employers. Elements such as how to dress for an interview, how to speak to your employer, how not to make trouble at work can also be included. There would be nothing more sinister here than a fine and overt example of social control (see Chapter 4) and its relation to the workplace were it not for the political climate within which the YTS has come into being. Just as the first trainees were beginning their YTS programmes in the autumn of 1983, Mr Peter Morrison, Minister of State at the Department of Employment, issued a draft instruction to those institutions providing the thirteen weeks' off-the-job training. This instruction was to forbid them to include in their course matters relating to 'the organisation and functioning of society unless they are relevant to trainees' work experience' (*Times Educational Supplement*, 16 September 1983). After some embarrassment and dissent from the MSC this statement was subsequently withdrawn. However, the overt emphasis on training rather than political education remains. If the lecturers or teachers are not to discuss the organisation and functioning of society with young workers, may they not be seen as positively concealing from their students crucial ways of understanding their new role as work-people? In this context the social skills that they are encouraged to teach them may seem close to indoctrination.

It is from this perspective that we must examine David Young's claim that the YTS is generating 'a more versatile, well-motivated and productive workforce which will benefit the future economic well-being of the nation' (YTS, undated, p. 1). If more versatile means more easily pushed around, well-motivated means frightened of the poverty associated with unemployment and productive means worse paid, then the future economic well-being will clearly only benefit certain small sectors of the nation. Trainees may come to appreciate 'the importance of industry' but issues of industrial conflict and, presumably, trade-union traditions and philosophies, are under the threat of total censorship. This seems a little one-sided. We must stress that we are not against the teaching of social skills *per se*. Social skills teaching can be useful especially in contexts where students can negotiate which skills they themselves see as important and where the wider implications of learning and following socially accepted behaviour patterns can be brought up and discussed. Social skills training in a context of political censorship or one-sided ideological emphasis must be seen as an overt attempt to create a compliant, pacific, deferential workforce, happy to do the least regarded and least rewarded jobs in industry and commerce. (The issue here is similar to the contrast between valid socialisation and invalid social control discussed with regard to infant schools in Chapter 4.)

This discussion of the content of social skills training is perhaps just one aspect of the issue of the threat to a wider conception of education posed by a narrow, partisan vocationalism. The limited concept of training is seen as being useful to the individual in finding employment and useful to society in providing a relevantly skilled workforce to generate wealth for 'the nation'. By implication, a wider concept of education is seen as being effete and concerned with academic non-essentials. The language of popular journalism, working-class youth and industrial and commercial spokespersons would seem to be in accord. This rhetoric not only ignored conceptions of education of the whole person or education as individual fulfilment, it also overlooks those young people who will be able to consolidate their non-vocational academic skills into well-paid jobs via 'A' levels and university degrees. Employers who take on young people with these qualifications seem undeterred by the fact that they have little work experience, have not been taught social skills and might even never have been on a YTS programme. Finally, given that many young unemployed people will remain unemployed following their YTS year and that the future seems to hold a pattern of working life in which we will all enjoy or endure more 'leisure', then it may be that wide educational skills and interests would actually prove quite useful to those hard-headed working-class youths.

Health and safety

Having examined the way in which the YTS initiative provides an illuminating example for some urban educational theories we will go on to examine some of the further implications posed for both school and work by the introduction of this innovatory scheme. Before doing so, however, a tangential criticism of the YTS needs to be noted, that concerning health and safety. There is a risk when little supervision seems to be provided in the scheme for young people having their first contact with potentially dangerous work environments. With regard to the YOP it had been noted:

> In some cases the problem was demands for work in unsafe conditions. As a Parliamentary answer revealed, over a mere 12 month period (1980/81) there were 2,011 YOP trainees involved in accidents, including 5 deaths and 23 amputations — a totally unacceptable rate of injury (SSEG, 1983, p. 7).

A newspaper report from Scotland provides a frightening example:

> The horrific accident in which 16-year-old trainee Sean O'Brien was burned to death in an engineering firm while on a pilot scheme for YTS could have been avoided had he been properly supervised, a Scottish court ruled last month. After hearing how Sean received total burns when his paraffin drenched overalls were ignited by an industrial heater, Sheriff John Boyle fined Rosehall Engineering Ltd., of Coatbridge, £800 for breaches of safety law.

Sheriff Boyle criticised the lack of supervision:

> These two young men were placed in the company's care for work experience. They had none before. . . . Considering their youth and inexperience, mistakes, even a degree of irresponsibility were to be anticipated. That supervision was sadly lacking. . . . No particular course of action seems to have been given to the boys. No-one came to look at what they were doing (*Safety and Fire News*, October 1983).

The scheme whereby the MSC gives prime responsibility to its managing agents may lead to nobody being quite in charge of matters such as training quality and health and safety. Although apparently sophisticated and cost-effective, the principle of divided responsibility can lead to serious consequences.

YTS and (un)employment

Among the issues raised by the formation of the YTS is the accusation that its only real purpose is to massage the unemployment figures. The high level of youth unemployment, particularly in the inner cities, is both politically unpopular and potentially dangerous in that it may well be a major contribution to urban riots such as those in Brixton, Toxteth and Moss Side in the summer of 1981. By 1982 as many as '553,000 young people were on YOP schemes and therefore not registered as unemployed'. Predictions from the MSC indicated that 'without policy interventions we estimate that 57 per cent of the 16 year olds and 48 per cent of the 17 year olds in the labour market will be unemployed in September 1984' (SSEG, 1983, p. 7). Since it is unlikely that placement on YTS will lead many young people to obtain jobs that they would not otherwise have obtained anyway (that is, YTS is hardly likely of itself to generate many new long-term jobs), the attempt to disguise the full extent of unemployment may be seen as an acceptance of joblessness rather than an attempt to improve it. If the YTS offered young people a worthwhile programme of education, training and work experience, if, say, it formed part of a comprehesive 16 to 19 provision for all young people, then it could be seen as a valid method of simultaneously reducing youth unemployment figures. This, however, does not seem to be the case. A further insight into the workings of YTS may be revealed by observing the effects of the scheme on the youth employment market itself.

That reduction in the youth unemployment figure was a major motivation behind the creation of the YTS was first revealed in a confidential government document leaked to *Time Out* shortly before the General Election. According to this document, the YTS would have the further benefit of reducing the entire youth wage:

> In a paragraph headed 'It makes young people pay for their training', contained in a list of the scheme's advantages, the report says: 'Young people, . . . would receive a modest allowance well below the normal wage. It would be possible in time to prescribe a lower training wage for those being trained by their employer (including apprentices). This would be a means of achieving a particularly desirable objective — the lowering of the training wage which is unlikely to be achieved voluntarily (Rose, 1983, p. 6).

Traditionally, of course, apprenticeship has been accompanied by a low wage and, even in the past, by the system of payment by apprentices (or their parents) to master craftsmen for the privilege of training. Yet, with apprenticeship came the acquisition of real skills and a body of knowledge that guaranteed the trainee a future career in an established trade. Given, however, the virtual abolition of apprenticeship (and the future career prospects that went with it), the YTS allowance of £25 per week has had the effect of forcing down the wages of the last remaining apprentices. Thus: 'The Electrical Union recently agreed to a cut in the employers' apprenticeship rate from £41.64 to £27.88 per week' (Rose, 1983, p. 6). The wages of all young people, and indeed of older men and women too, are under threat from the low level of the YTS allowances. If employers can take on young trainees whom they do not have to pay at all then why should they employ older people on an even marginally reasonable wage? This leads to the further issue of *job substitution*.

> You've got to be careful that YOPs don't take jobs from other people. If they started cutting grass for the Council, for example, it would do all the people who cut grass out of a job.
> (Phil Bird, quoted in White and Brockington, 1983)

Job substitution is the practice whereby someone doing a job is sacked, or not replaced when they leave, in order to take on a YOP or YTS trainee. The MSC is alert to this risk and in an attempt to avert it established the '2:3 rule' for managing agents of YTS:

> For the Managing Agent's Fee and Block Grant to be paid, Managing Agents must agree to recruit trainees that [sic] are genuinely additional to the recruitment that would have taken place anyway. The ratio of normal recruitment to additional places has to be 2:3 in 1983/84 and provided this ratio is met or bettered the MSC will make the funds available for *all* the young people taken on. Normal recruitment will usually be based on the number of 16 year old school leavers recruited by the Managing Agents and/or his subcontractors in 1982 (YTS, 1983, p. 5).

For every *additional* three places the employer provides, s/he can be paid for two more young people who would normally have been taken on as trainees/apprentices. This seems to be a once and for all rule established in 1983 and once the ratio has been established there seems to be nothing to stop employers taking on a different group of government-paid trainees every year. David Young made clear the advantages of this arrangement to employers, writing in the journal *Director*: 'You now have the opportunity to take on young men and women, train them and let them work for you at our expense, and then decide whether or not to employ them' (quoted in Rose, 1983, p. 7). With this kind of encouragement it would not be surprising if the 2:3 rule were flouted and job substitution were to become the rule:

> The biggest abuse has been the use of trainee labour to replace real jobs. The MSC admits that without the unions' notification it is powerless to prevent this, and that at least 30 per cent of YOP schemes were 'job substitution' (meaning the true figure was far higher). In YTS this abuse continues, since the MSC continues to permit it (SSEG, 1983, p. 8).

Within this environment of job substitution, the lowering of wages and a general free-for-all for employers, it is not surprising that blatant examples of exploitation of young people are beginning to emerge in the trade-union journals. One example will suffice:

> One USDAW official told us of his fruitless attempt to act for trainees in a supermarket chain in the northeast, where employers had insisted the scheme include overtime and Saturday working (for trainees only and with no extra pay). The MSC turned its back and permitted such abuse to continue (SSEG, 1983, p. 8).

THE IMPLICATIONS FOR TEACHERS

This example of the YTS raises many practical implications for teachers in secondary schools and FE colleges. What advice should secondary teachers give their school leavers with regard to YTS? Should FE lecturers embrace YTS as the best, indeed the only, further education available to many young people, thereby abandoning any commitment they might have to a wider concept of education? Is it possible to ignore the YTS and to insist on offering a more liberal education to young people? Some lecturers and colleges may choose to recognise that YTS is now a permanent feature of training and attempt to manipulate and change it from within. It is difficult to see how this can be done given that the colleges have so little time and authority compared to the employers. However, examples of more positive practice are beginning to emerge. At one urban college the MSC refused to extend the thirteen-week education period to allow for recently arrived immigrants to have extra English language teaching. The local authority also refused to top up the MSC financing. The college set up a scheme whereby the young people could take a 21-hour course on English language for a term (without losing their social security entitlements), then proceed to the thirteen weeks component of their YTS programme. By the end of this period the young people's English was sufficiently competent to allow them to proceed with some success to the work experience and on-the-job training components of the YTS. Questions concerning school and work ultimately apply to teachers in all levels of educational institutions. Do we educate and train children for a capitalist industrial society or for a society that does not exist?

Before trying to wriggle out of this cleft stick let us examine the proposition (derived from Bowles and Gintis whose work was discussed and quoted earlier in the chapter) that our present schooling is designed to educate and train children for capitalism. In British cities it is possible to examine the mechanisms and ideologies whereby the stratification of labour in the capitalist workplace determines (or, more mildly, is reflected by) the pattern of stratification in educational institutions. The mechanisms of stratification include the existence of private and 'public' schools where middle-class parents can purchase privileged access to prestigious higher universities for their children. There is an illusion that UK cities have 'gone comprehensive' but many urban education authorities still have a selective system that retains grammar schools. The remaining schools may have been redesigned as comprehensive but the change here is little more than cosmetic. Some authorities, such as Calderdale, are having their attempts to establish comprehensive secondary schools repeatedly vetoed by the Secretary of State. The practice of rigid streaming can mean that children are stratified even within the common schools. This is not merely an issue for secondary schools, a surprising number of primary schools retain the apparently unjustified practice of streaming from an early age. Banding the curriculum, often at the end of third year in secondary schools, is frequently the mechanism whereby many pupils are made aware of their position within the stratified hierarchy of perceived ability, and this position is consolidated and refined. Special schools create an entirely separate and segregated stratum of children (as described in Chapter 6). Examinations and certification make children acknowledge, and ultimately accept, how their abilities are valued, and provide for employers and educational selectors a quantified label from which they can determine the appropriate level of entry into the workplace.

These mechanisms are legitimated by a series of taken-for-granted ideologies, many of which are analysed in other chapters. The nature of a fixed, measurable, inherited intelligence, which determines ability across a whole range of subjects, is examined in Chapter 6 where both its scientific fallacy and its political usefulness are exposed. The linked ideologies of individualism, competition and equality of opportunity have been mentioned in this chapter and are also discussed in Chapter 4. Another important source of ideology is the *essentialist* conception of knowledge. This refers to the belief that some skills and subjects are more worthwhile than others. English, science and maths, for instance, are seen as somehow better, more important, than woodwork, Bengali and sociology. It is seen to be a pre-eminent part of a school's task to retain 'standards' in these essential disciplines. Naturally the children who achieve well in the high-status subjects are perceived to be more intelligent than those who achieve in the low-status subjects and therefore they are selected for superior job prospects. Yet this ideology too appears to have little impartial basis (in this case in *epistemology*, the study of knowledge). Are the skills of literary criticism at a higher level than those of technical drawing? How could such a decision be made? What criteria would be involved? In many cases the status ascribed to a given subject may result more from its historical importance (the role of Latin in secondary schools, say) or from Eurocentricity (why is so much French taught in urban schools when large fractions of the population speak Bengali, Punjabi, Turkish, Urdu and Gujurati?) than from its epistemological worth. Yet from the primary school onwards some activities are regarded as being of academic worth and others are perceived to be peripheral ('they study Arabic in their Koranic classes on Saturday') or recreational ('stop playing with that Lego and get on with your work'). Just as the ideology of intelligence is the psychological legitimation of stratification, so the ideology of essentialist knowledge and standards are its epistemological legitimation. These beliefs help to support a stratified school system that serves to reproduce stratified urban labour power. These mechanisms and ideologies do not determine stratification in the workplace. They are rather the institutional and intellectual reflections of the need of capitalism for a trained and ideologised (that is, educated in essentialism and competitive individualism) workforce.

Such an analysis seems to leave little space for teachers to develop curricula and institutions that offer positive possibilities for young people in urban schools. One possibility seemed previously to be to concentrate on 'the successful pupil from a poor home'. By promoting such pupils and encouraging their education through to university it was hoped that the ideology of equality of opportunity could be seen to be working in practice. The residual working-class enthusiasm for grammar schools would seem to imply a belief — held despite the indications of more than a generation of experience — that the promotion of individual success would somehow help the whole group. Unfortunately, promoted working-class young people often attend universities in cities other than the ones in which they grew up and go on to professional work in yet other cities. They do not return to the inner cities of their childhood to attempt to ameliorate conditions, but rather use their education to escape from these conditions. Of course such professionals may then go to a different city or a different part of the same city to 'help' the working class or black people by becoming social workers, teachers or probation officers. In such cases they may well be unaware of their function of social control. The alternatives facing the urban teacher, then, would seem to be education for reproduction, education for escape, or education for utopia. While this sounds rather grim, it is possible for teachers to strike a balance between these elements that might provide some dimensions of a meaningful curriculum for many urban children. These possibilities are discussed in Chapter 8.

GUIDE TO FURTHER READING

On the relationship between education and work there are two key texts: Willis (1977), *Learning to Labour*, and Bowles and Gintis (1976), *Schooling in Capitalist America*.

Neither of these books is easy to read. A more accessible source and one that takes account of the growth of unemployment and MSC provision in the UK is Watts (1983), *Education, Unemployment and the Future of Work*. Gleeson, (ed.) (1983), *Youth Training and the Search for Work*, contains critical analyses of the emerging new pattern of further education. A further critique that embraces the whole state educational provision is contained in the course material to the Open University's course *Society, Education and the State* (E353), especially units two and four.

A more establishment perspective can be gained by studying the publications of the Manpower Services Commission, especially MSC (1981), *A New Training Initiative*, and the Further Education Curriculum Review and Development Unit. In the case of the latter, see FEU (1979), *A Basis for Choice*, and FEU (1980), *Developing Social and Life Skills*.

8
Initiatives and innovations

> To create urban schools which really teach students, which reflect the pluralism of the society, which serve the quest for social justice — this is a task which will take persistent imagination, wisdom and will.
>
> (Tyack, 1974)

INTRODUCTION

The previous chapters have been critical of many of the practices inside urban educational institutions and of the theories behind them. We would wish to resist giving the impression, however, that nothing can be done because of the wider structures of the capitalist state. These structures may constrain the ability of teachers and administrators to make positive innovations (ideologically based decisions of central government to cut back public spending are a case in point). Nevertheless, there are opportunities and possibilities for those working in urban schools to plan and implement initiatives that may help to brighten the basically gloomy picture painted in the preceding chapters. Indeed, with regard to some policy aspects in some urban areas these initiatives are already under way. However, the temptation to conclude on a note of bright cheerfulness needs to be resisted if the realities of urban schooling in Britain are not to be misrepresented. The thrust of the book has so far been to stress the importance of the social structure, and the changes in that structure, in relation to what goes on in urban schools. As we have seen, a depressing scenario has been presented in which urban teachers and pupils are caught up in a complex process of labelling, selection and social reproduction.

The point, however, is to suggest a positive basis for teacher action. Notwithstanding the structural constraints upon urban education, teachers, both collectively and individually, have a responsibility to reflect on their actions and attempt to initiate change. It is possible to cite what we consider to be good practice at the LEA institutional and classroom levels. What we are not suggesting is that good practice can come about without confronting bad practice — but that is easier said than done. Teachers in urban schools, it could have been claimed, have a difficult enough time as it is without making a further rod for their own backs by challenging such features as institutional racism, the social control basis of education, and the socially reproductive nature of the curriculum. It often seems enough for urban teachers to get through the teaching day with physical and mental health still intact.

However, until fundamental social changes are accomplished generations of working-class and black children will be confined to the scrap-heap of a society dominated by a bankrupt ideology and an unjust set of social and economic relations. It is the moral and social responsibility of all those who wish to see progressive change in urban education to involve themselves on a day-to-day basis in action that will contribute to such change. Such action can range from the development of more liberating forms of social relations in the classroom through to greater co-operation with other teachers by which an increasing awareness of their structural location can come about. This latter aspect might involve not only the development of an alternative set of norms within the school to those that dominate the education system as a whole (and have become conventional wisdom in individual schools) but also the revitalisation of teachers' unions and so to the recognition of the political character of pedagogy.

> A lot of teachers believe that everything they tell us is gospel, but we had a good English teacher who'd listen to us. We'd go miles off the subject but we'd listen to his points, and we'd usually come to some sort of compromise. It wasn't just somebody standing at the front saying, 'I'm right — you listen'.
>
> (Wanda Raven, quoted in White and Brockington, 1983)

Progressive action on the part of urban teachers may demand a fundamental rejection of the many questions posed by recent governments, by the Manpower Services Commission, and by 'spokespersons' of industry. But rejection must be accompanied by an alternative set of questions which together redefine the agenda: how do we reject authoritarian social control as a legitimate function of urban schools? How can we treat pupils in urban schools as individuals who have had a wealth of experience rather than as predefined categories? How can teachers become more aware of educational racist practices and attempt to counteract them?

These sorts of questions should not necessarily be seen as aimed at teachers as isolated individuals who are to undergo a kind of personality change. We ought, perhaps, to be somewhat critical of this kind of psychologistic approach; no amount of attitude change is going to alter a situation where underlying institutionalised practices are paramount. The social existence of teachers, like everyone else, helps determine their consciousness. However, schools can and do provide opportunities for discussion among teachers, pupils and, sometimes, parents. Issues are raised; frequently, connections are made with the 'outside world'; occasionally, routine practices are changed. It is, after all, possible for teachers as well as pupils to resist, for they too feel the sharp constraints of educational institutions.

With regard to possible initiatives in the UK, these may be made by an individual teacher or department, by a whole school or by a local education authority. Initiatives at any level may spread either by influencing other participants at the same level or those at other levels. An anti-racist policy developed by one department may, eventually, spread to influence a whole school. One school's attempt to integrate children with special needs may provide a successful example that leads to a change of policy right across a local education authority. These are examples of policy being changed from the bottom up, as it were. Attempts to change policy from the top downwards are unlikely to be successful unless they succeed in winning the collaboration and enthusiasm of those participants at other levels. Thus local education authority or national policy changes must win the support of teachers and heads before successful implementation can commence. It is worth considering that 'bottom-upwards' influence can be an important element in changes at local and national level. The recommendations of the Plowden Report, for instance, which were subsequently highly influential, were apparently based on what the committee members perceived to be good practice in a number of schools.

This chapter will first examine the extent to which schools and teachers have the autonomy to make initiatives in urban areas, and the relationship between this autonomy and the wider structures of the state and the economy. It will then go on to examine some of the initiatives that have recently been made in urban educational institutions with regard to the issues addressed in the four previous chapters.

RELATIVE AUTONOMY AND URBAN EDUCATIONAL INSTITUTIONS

It is possible to make a (somewhat simplistic) distinction within social science theories between those that are deterministic and those that are voluntaristic. Marxist theories in particular have often been criticised for their determinism. Marx, it is alleged, saw history as an inevitable movement in the direction of capitalism which would then

equally ineluctably lead to revolution and the establishment of socialism. Furthermore, the base-superstructural theory (outlined in Chapter 2) seems to indicate that all social processes and institutions are
determined by the nature of the organisation, ownership and control
of the means of production. Marx's theories then may be seen as
historically and economically deterministic. This criticism applies less
comfortably to many of the subsequent writers in the Marxist tradition
such as Gramsci who argued that human actors played their part in the
continuation or overthrow of capitalism. It has been suggested that the
mode of production was the outcome of struggle between groups and
that the results of this struggle were not historically determined in
advance by theory or dogma. The dangers inherent in this 'vulgar'
determinism — that human beings are seen as passive pawns in the
movement of historical forces and that therefore individuals and
groups need not struggle to improve their conditions, these anyway
being predicated in the mode of production and impervious to any kind
of change which does not take place on this site — have then, to a large
extent, been acknowledged and overcome by many Marxist writers.
Voluntaristic human action is now an accepted principle within much
Marxist theory. History is seen as the result of conflict and struggle: the
future cannot be prophesied but will depend on the results of a struggle
which is in progress now.

The economic base is still seen as being the predominant influence
on forms of social organisation, but it is not the only influence (as
Engels, Marx's collaborator, pointed out). Cultural and political
processes and institutions are also accepted to be of major importance.
Within these aspects of the social structure individuals and groups have
autonomy to improve or worsen their conditions. Indeed, struggles
and changes in these areas may have some influence on the economic
base itself. Change of this sort, however, is still regarded as unlikely,
and Marxists still look to the organisation of the means of production
as the predominant element in understanding a given form of social
organisation.

One of the formulations of non-deterministic Marxist social science
has been the elaboration of the concept of *relative autonomy*. It has
been suggested that the state in particular has a certain degree of
autonomy relative to the mode of production (Poulantzas, 1978;
Castells, 1976a). Although there is seen to be an important relation
between the economy of a nation-state and its political institutions and
processes, it is accepted that these are a separate area of conflict and
not directly tied to the base. Thus apparently similar modes of
production can exist alongside widely differing political systems, not
only between nation-states but also within them following electoral or

revolutionary change. The relative autonomy of the state makes it a crucial site for struggle given its control over the military and police institutions and given that its high-spending potential makes it an important participant as investor and/or consumer in the mode of production itself. Individuals and groups who are in conflict at the site of the means of production may then shift their stuggles backwards and forwards into the political domain. To those familiar with politics in the UK this phenomenon is highly visible: of the two major parties one is financed and largely controlled by the collective organisations of labour, and the other is (appreciably more generously) financed and largely controlled by capitalist enterprises. When a party takes control one of its main tasks is to try to intervene to the benefit of its supporters in struggles located in the workplace. The history of trade-union legislation over the last decade provides an obvious but not isolated example.

Before making the relevance of this to urban educational institutions clear, a further step in the argument needs to be taken. It may be suggested that just as the state has some autonomy relative to the economic base, so some state institutions have a limited degree of autonomy relative to those forces that control the state itself. Particularly in large institutions, those that are not rigorously centralised, and those with high levels of staffing and expenditure, there is sufficient autonomy for individuals and institutions to initiate and implement policies that might be tangential or even contrary to those of the state itself. Educational institutions in the cities of the UK may be seen as fitting into this category. We may see these institutions then as having a double level of relative autonomy: first, they have some autonomy relative to the state that ultimately controls them; secondly, this state itself has some autonomy relative to the economic organisation upon which it is ultimately based. Far from being condemned to a determined position of reproducing the workforce for capital in terms of skills, ideology and stratification, those who work in such institutions have some degree of space in which to initiate their own policies. The boundaries of this space will be tested and reached from time to time: local educational authorities may intervene to restrict school initiatives (William Tynsdale, Risinghill, Madeley Court); central government spokespersons may oppose more widespread initiatives (peace studies); capitalist organisations may reassert their influence over the state and its educational institutionalism (the post-Ruskin new vocationalism and the rise of the MSC discussed in Chapter 7). Nevertheless, within this constrained and contested space, urban schools and teachers can make and are making important developments to correct some of the injustices that have been highlighted in the four preceding chapters.

Before going on to discuss a few examples of these developments it is important to stress that they are limited and are relative to local and national state control which is itself ultimately predicated on the capitalist mode of production. Bowles and Gintis (1976), in their final chapter, in bright optimism talk about the need for a 'long march through the institutions'. This is perhaps to be unduly hopeful. We have already mentioned instances where the relative nature of the autonomy of educational institutions has been forcefully reasserted. If teachers and schools all over the cities of the UK were to make radical innovatory policies would not this lead to similar intervention? It might, but on the other hand if the conflicts over education become more ideologically and geographically widespread surely they would lead to even greater space being gained for innovation. The sad truth of course is that it is highly unlikely for such a movement to become widespread. Teachers and educational institutions are more frequently highly resistant to change and innovation. Indeed it is in the nature of the institutions (dominance of examination boards at secondary level or hierarchical organisation of the teaching force itself, for example) and in the ideologies and attitudes of urban teachers (their inherently pro-*status quo* nature so well revealed in Grace, 1978), that the limits of the autonomy are most clearly seen. A long march through the institutions may not be structurally impossible but it becomes exceedingly unlikely when both the institutions and the marchers are seen as highly resistant to change. The socialisation of teachers and the way in which they are hierarchically organised in schools render them unlikely candidates for Althusserian heroism, so that the innovations and developments to which we point are far from widespread. This is not the same, of course, as saying that they could not be radical even if they wished, and that their radicalism would either fizzle out or be crushed by state interference.

Rather, our perspective emphasises educational institutions as sites of conflict. Conflict and resistance have already been discussed in Chapter 4. However, it is not only between pupils and teachers or the school that conflicts arise. There may be significant conflicts between groups of teachers and between teachers and those in authority. The issues over which conflicts arise may well overlap with those that lead to pupil resistance. Thus teachers may find themselves faced with pupil apathy or disaffection when attempting to teach a curriculum over which they are themselves in conflict with colleagues or headteachers or examination boards. Of course pupil resistance can always be appealed to as a legitimation by conflicting teachers without them necessarily endeavouring to locate its precise causes. The curriculum, the patterns of social control, the nature of contact with parents and the community, procedures for evaluation and assessment are all matters about which teachers differ. They will be negotiated and agreed through staff discussions and compromise with more or less influence from the headteacher according to his/her authoritarianism and the relative trenchancy of the teachers concerned. Many of the disagreements will be so trivial as to provide only a small spark in the school day. Nevertheless, it is important to remember that differences exist even on small issues and that the accepted 'reality' of schools is one that has emerged as a result of social processes at the micro level.

Over some issues, differences may resemble more a conflagration than a spark. Groups of teachers may be in bitter opposition one with another; senior staff may side with one group or attempt to arbitrate; sometimes local authority inspectors, officers or politicians may be involved; occasionally parents and children may be drawn into the conflict and give support to one or more groups. We are not only alluding here to those *causes célèbre* which occasionally feature in the national press and in the rhetorical extravagances of Westminster politicians, for these form only a small part of educational conflicts. Urban schools in particular are sites of struggle and many long- and short-term conflicts arise in them which never even percolate into the local press. These conflicts are the processes by which the autonomous space for teachers to make radical innovations are normally negotiated.

We are not then talking about external reified structures in education and society which prevent any autonomy of action on the part of individuals or groups. Rather, we are asserting that these very structures (school knowledge and ideology, certification and stratification, notions of intelligence, essentialism and hierarchy, racist tests, procedures, curricula and teacher attitudes) are the product of conflict within various sites. There are many such sites, economic, political, religious or domestic. For women attempting to assert the right to have a responsible job and to share household chores a major site of conflict may be the family. But educational sites are of similar importance for they are another major institution in the reproduction of labour power (see Chapter 2). To assert that the structures of society and education are the product of conflict is to reveal them as vulnerable to change and revision. By contesting the structures at the points where they seem to be inhibitingly oppressive and by following through this contest into conflict, teachers can reveal the nature of the societal structure for themselves, their colleagues and their pupils. They can also change them. Educational structures have been changed in the past and can be changed in the future, but not without contest and conflict over the important issues. This argument may, of course, be generalised to the wider structures of the economy and society. Here too conflict may lead to space won for innovation and to a reduction of the oppressive structural processes. Castells points to the importance of conflict in urban areas and the way in which this has sometimes gained important benefits, liberties and operational space for oppressed groups.

This section is being argued with some degree of generality and there is a risk of ignoring how these conflicts feel to teachers in urban schools. Often those responsible for trying to implement policy innovations in urban education institutions — be they teachers, heads, inspectors or politicians — may feel that they are banging their heads against various brick walls. It is easier to write about conflict than to engage in it. Many young teachers often experience the personalities and the structures of their first schools as far too powerful and rigid for them to change. Urban schools are a familiar graveyard for the idealisms accumulated at college and university. The modification of idealism through contact with the everyday world of school may, however, not lead to its demise but rather lead into its transformation into something more vigorous and adaptive. It is these modified idealisms on the part of young teachers that will provide an important drive towards change in urban schools. It is the force of the ideals that will provide them with strength for the conflicts when often it may seem that all they are achieving is sore heads. As well as disillusionment, young (and even old!) teachers have managed to achieve many innovations in the policies of urban schools which have lifted some of the oppressive weight of the structures from themselves and their pupils.

INITIATIVES IN URBAN EDUCATION

> The contradictory ideologies of individualism and cooperativeness that are naturally generated out of the crowded conditions of many classrooms also provide countervailing possibilities . . . just as blue- and white-collar workers have constantly found ways to retain their humanity and continually struggle to integrate conception and execution in their work (if only to relieve boredom) so too will teachers and students find ways, in the cracks so to speak, to do the same things.
>
> (Apple, 1982)

Ideology

In examining some initiatives that affect the issues discussed in Chapter 4 we will look at four main overlapping areas, curriculum, pedagogy, assessment and the hidden curriculum. It needs to be emphasised at the outset that the issues here are central to the function of schooling and initiatives may therefore be seen as harder to implement and less likely to have successful results than may be the case with regard to, say, race or special education.

The curriculum in the UK may be characterised as *essentialist*: that is, it is based upon the belief that certain forms of knowledge are intrinsically more worthwhile than others and that pupils, particularly those perceived as 'able', should be given access to the higher forms of knowledge. Physics is seen as being more worthwhile than craft, design and technology, biology than horticulture, Latin and French than Bengali and Turkish. In many ways curriculum initiatives may be seen as attacks on this essentialist conception. Primary schools in British cities have, over the last thirty years, moved more towards a *pragmatic* curriculum: that is, one based on identifying problems and attempting to solve them, the subject of the problem being of secondary importance to the generation of skills in hypothesising and testing solutions. Within this progressive primary curriculum, still much influenced by the writings and work of Dewey, subjects are treated in an integrated way and children are encouraged to develop and follow their own interests provided these lead them to encounter problems in a creative manner. This is still far from the curriculum norm in British urban classrooms (Bennett, 1976) but it remains a celebrated model that is being developed and to which primary teachers may turn for the legitimation of innovatory practices. In most schools in the UK — indeed in an increasing number, given the decline of middle schools — this integrated approach, where the children are taught largely as one group by one teacher or team of teachers in one room or suite of rooms, is sacrificed at secondary transfer. At the age of 11 pupils are perceived to benefit more from the essentialist curriculum expertise of teachers in the secondary school than from this integrated approach. Many primary teachers would suggest that this is debatable. At primary level particularly, but not exclusively, innovations have suggested alternatives to essentialism that are either less elitist or more integrated.

A clear example of this is to increase the range of foreign languages taught in urban schools. Urban areas in the UK now contain a vast variety of languages spoken in the home. The last language census in the ILEA indicated that the children in the Authority's schools spoke 147 languages between them. Other cities such as Birmingham and Bradford have a similarly (though not so extensively) polyglot population. The principal languages spoken by the children and families include Bengali, Punjabi, Urdu, Hindi, Gujerati, Arabic, Swahili,

Turkish, Greek and Spanish. Yet the foreign language taught in urban secondary schools is predominantly French with perhaps the possibility of some German or Spanish. Not only are children not given access by urban schools to skills of literacy in their own language, but one of their strengths remains unconfirmed by the education system so that they cannot gain qualifications in their own language/s, and the implication is given to all children and their parents that the languages spoken by, say, people from the Indian subcontinent are intrinsically less valuable, less educational, than those spoken by Europeans. This situation is being remedied very slowly, partly under the influences of the EEC directive which insists that children should be able to learn their mother tongues in schools.

In primary schools initiatives have been made, often with the help of EEC funding, to teach children literacy skills in their own mother tongue in school time rather than through supplementary schooling (discussed below):

> Between 1960 and 1980, Bradford was also the site for the . . . EEC Mother Tongue Pilot Project which was one facet of the Community's general preoccupation with the right of migrant workers' children to receive instruction in their own language and culture. In the final year of operation, 107 lower and middle school children had daily lessons in Italian, or Punjabi (Jeffcoate and Mayor, 1982, p. 28).

Similar schemes have since been initiated by the EEC to teach, for instance, Bengali as a mother tongue in the East End of London and Turkish in Haringey (Commission of the European Communities, 1984). In other primary schools, developments in this direction are now occurring. At secondary level too, it is now becoming possible for children to study their own mother tongues and to be examined at CSE and GCE. Of course it is not easy for the schools to implement this, particularly where, as in some schools in Brent, Hounslow and the ILEA, they may have forty or more languages spoken in one school. A further difficulty is that the schools have employed French teachers and this is the discipline still encouraged in universities and colleges. Many teachers are addressing this issue seriously and some urban education authorities have now accepted that general policy initiatives (showing political commitment at a level less remote than the EEC) are essential. However, the time still seems far off when secondary schoolchildren in Birmingham will be taught Bengali rather than French at secondary level. Yet Bengali is, in international terms, a more significant language than French and there are certainly more Bengali than French speakers in Birmingham. If all children were to learn, say, Bengali instead of French (in areas of different language concentration it may be Punjabi or Turkish, etc.) then communication between different language groups in urban areas would certainly be encouraged and pupils would not need to go on a weekend trip to Calais to practise their French.

The growth of social education and active tutorial work in some urban secondary schools may be seen as another potentially innovative development. However, it is not the curriculum change *per se* that is important here since social education can be taught along the lines of the social-skills lessons criticised with regard to YTS in Chapter 7. Where social education is a curriculum offering for those considered less able to follow the more 'academic' subjects, then the pupils are likely to learn more about the organisation of society from the way in which they were selected for the classes than they are from the content of the lessons. But when social education is part of a compulsory core curriculum for all pupils and where it can help pupils understand their place in society, where it can address issues such as youth employment or the division of labour in society, then it will share with a few other curriculum developments, such as some peace-studies courses, the possibility of reversing the process of ideologisation that takes place in urban schools. Indeed, discussions of the nature of ideology may themselves be an important component in such a curriculum. These developments are not necessarily confined to one department: English and media teachers may help pupils look critically at TV programmes and texts such as newspapers and magazines; science teachers may see the social responsibility of science as an important component of their lessons; home economics teachers may discuss the nature of domestic work and how it is shared out among a family or group of people living together.

This leads to another hopeful innovation which may be called the breakdown of the sexist curriculum. One aspect of the essentialist curriculum was that it was taken for granted that certain subjects were appropriate for certain pupils. This division was nowhere more apparent than with regard to gender: boys would appropriately study maths, physics, chemistry, woodwork, metalwork, football, cricket and rugby; girls would be more likely to study foreign languages, biology, home economics, hockey and netball. These divisions are gradually being broken down in some urban schools. It is now commoner for all children to study, say, home economics, craft, design and technology, and then to choose between them as options in the fourth year. This, of course, still leads to gender division though at least with a wider distribution of skills and knowledge.

Even such small innovations are less common with regard to sport, although in 'coeducational secondary schools there is a growth in the teaching of mixed groups' (Baylis, 1984, p. 18). Gender divisions are perhaps enforced most strongly in PE and sport although, as a recent ILEA report found, there is very little physiological reason for this:

> Linear regression of world best performances in running, cycling and swimming, indicate that women will 'catch' men in 50 years. Already teenage girls are swimming faster than Mark Spitz swam only a decade ago (Baylis, 1984, p. 18).

The gender division of labour is one of the most pervasive ideologies to which schools subject children. If this process is to be in any way reversed then the ideology itself needs to be addressed directly in a whole range of subjects. Further, the curriculum will need to change so that the gender division of labour is not replicated and reproduced in schools. This surely will mean radical changes in the way in which options are organised as well as a fundamental rethinking and reorganising of the role of sport and physical education in schools.

The discussion of mother-tongue teaching above could as appropriately have come under the heading on education for a multicultural society later in this chapter. Similarly, anti-racist teaching, which will be discussed there, is an issue that also influences the ideologies that are operant in schools and that they pass on to their pupils. As mentioned in Chapter 4, ideology not only penetrates what is taught in schools but also the way in which it is taught and assessed and that whole range of educational practices that we may loosely call the hidden curriculum. We go on at this stage to discuss developments in these areas.

Again developments are more readily identifiable at primary-school level. In urban areas, notably in Haringey but increasingly elsewhere, there has been a recent trend towards encouraging children to read at home and even in benefiting from the assistance of parents in teaching children to read (Tarrent, 1982). This has proved to be remarkably effective as far as teaching and encouraging pupils to read is concerned. It has also had the spin-off effects of encouraging and developing reading activities in the family generally and in strengthening links between parents and teachers. This is a significant innovation for schools in urban areas but it also points to a shift that has ideological implications. The question is whether schools are merely co-opting parents, guardians and older siblings to assist them in an educational task that only the head and teachers have defined, or whether there is a more substantial collaboration with parents over what is taught and how. Some primary schools also encourage parents into school either into a specially set-up parents room, or indeed into actual lessons and classrooms to assist with lesson preparation and teaching. At present the teaching task is largely defined by the school but the possibility for more radical innovations, with parents joining pupils and teachers in elaborating what should be taught and how this could best be managed, is, in such schools, obviously present.

In secondary schools such initiatives, along with just about anything else radical or innovatory, tends to be called community education. The term community when applied to schooling (as to health, social work or even policing) tends to attempt to evoke a favourable response without prompting questions about the social organisation of a given locality. Whatever rural villages may be, most urban areas are not communities: they are localities of sharp division, competition and conflict (see Chapter 2). To attempt in a well-meaning way to imply that there is actually a unity of interests among groups and that 'community' co-operation is the aim or the norm is to conceal from both the professionals and their clients one of the most important elements of urban life. This is not to suggest that we disapprove of many of the innovations carried out under the community education umbrella; on the contrary, but we are cautious about the attempt to define, co-opt and invade the 'community'.

Within the community-education movement in UK cities there have been many developments that have not been of this nature. The Abraham Moss Centre has long been celebrated for its open reception of local people and for their important place not only within the school building but also in planning the curriculum and the wider activities of school. Likewise, Sydney Stringer in Coventry has tried to involve parents and representatives of local groups at the very highest level of decision-making in the school (Fletcher and Thompson, 1980). In the ILEA, the 'Hargreaves Report' has advocated much closer links between parents and schools (Hargreaves *et al.*, 1984). For our concerns, what is important about such developments is that they attempt to break down the rigid boundaries between the teachers and the taught and that they open up the definition of school knowledge and school activity to discussion by a much wider group of participants. In this way they may influence two major aspects of ideology and social control within urban schools. First, they may undermine the notions of authority and hierarchy that schools presently inculcate so successfully by helping to make it clear that a wide range of people may participate in the definition and transmission of school knowledge, that teacher authority is not infallible, and that there are other ways of organising educational and social activities than one person giving the instructions and others following them. Secondly, it is possible that if this process were to be carried through it would alter the type of knowledge transmitted in schools away from traditional essentialism. It is not certain, of course, that teachers or heads would be enthusiastic about all the curricular suggestions that may be made by parents or representatives of local groups. How, for instance, would one respond to demands for racist ideas to be taught, or indeed for the traditional curriculum to be reinforced? There are no easy answers to these difficulties but it is possible that a new form of relationship between schools and the inhabitants of the localities they serve may lead to educational benefits beyond the initial breaking down of barriers.

That not all groups in urban areas are entirely satisfied with their schools is evidenced by the growth of another initiative, which was alluded to above, and which is variously called supplementary or Saturday school. These may broadly be seen as having two different sets of objectives. First, they have been established to teach children the language, culture and often religion of their families. Greek language supplementary schools for instance may have the teaching of Greek Orthodox religious beliefs as part of the curriculum. Koranic schools may be attended by Islamic children almost every night after school and here they can learn Arabic in addition to religious beliefs and practices. Secondly, supplementary schools have been founded to teach the same subjects that are offered in local schools. This type of schooling is particularly popular with children from Afro-Caribbean families. They attend the schools in order to be helped with homework or indeed given additional teaching and material on subjects they are covering in schools. These supplementary schools are often staffed by black teachers as well as by other helpers.

The two types of supplementary schools may each indicate a distinct criticism of local education authority schools: first, in that they do not offer the language and religious teaching appropriate to the needs of the children and the requests of the parents; secondly, in that the schools are so unsuccessful in transmitting their own curriculum that the children require additional help in order to understand it. The first of these criticisms may not be as forceful as the second as some groups may prefer children to learn their language and religion in supplementary schools precisely so that they can participate with all the other children in the full curriculum of mainstream schools. Some urban education authorities, such as the ILEA, have started to provide funding for a range of supplementary schools. Likewise, teachers from particular racial, linguistic or religious groups may teach in supplementary school as well as working in local authority schools. Nevertheless, this innovation in urban education has not developed within mainstream schools; rather, it is an attempt to compensate for their shortcomings.

As indicated in Chapters 4 and 7, the assessment procedures of exams and certification serve both to instill the ideologies of intelligence and competitive individualism and to facilitate control through the imposition of externally (and apparently arbitrarily) defined criteria of success. Innovations in this area have been few since the introduction of the CSE exam and the gradual abolition of the 11-plus. This is also the most difficult area for individual teachers or schools to challenge since they, like the pupils, are presented with an external reified set of conditions that they can neither control nor (except in rare cases) alter. Indeed, many discussions about the secondary curriculum seem to falter at the point at which teachers assert that there is little that they can do to change things because they have to conform to the exam system. This is not entirely the case since the range of different boards and the flexibility of CSE Mode 3 may mean that by shopping around or by persistently maintaining a point with the CSE board, it is possible to find certification procedures that are not too great a travesty of the curriculum that best suits the pupils' expressed needs and interests. It seems, however, that this is an area of innovation that requires a central initiative.

Although there have been protracted delays (to say the least) preceding the development of the common exam at 16-plus, there have recently been two other central initiatives which may well improve assessment procedures in urban secondary schools. First, the idea of drawing up pupil profiles for all school leavers which contain a positive record of all the skills, interests and achievements they have developed at school is being given positive backing by the DES. Such profiles are, of course, likely to be more relevant to pupils who leave school with four CSEs than to those who gain four 'A' levels. The main issue of gross inequalities of achievement is not softened. Indeed such profiles may be interpreted as another encroachment of employer-led vocationalism into the education of 14- to 16-year-olds, though this is perhaps to overlook the stress the proposals place on positive recording of achievement rather than negative cataloguing of failure and misdemeanours. The second initiative may well address the issue of inequalities of achievement that is central to urban secondary schooling. At a speech (appropriately enough) in Sheffield, the Secretary of State indicated that the DES was to initiate a shift from norm-referencing to criteria-referencing in the formal exam system. This means that instead of the examination system passing only a specific percentage of candidates who reach a certain, almost arbitrary level, all those candidates who exhibit a given range of knowledge and skills (which is of course specified, though not necessarily discussed, in advance) will pass. This may mean that a much larger number of pupils will in the future gain reputable certification at the end of their secondary schooling — such, indeed, is the Secretary of State's hope. The impact of such a change is likely to be even more favourable in schools in urban areas where underachievement has long been identified as a difficulty. Since this is a top-downwards initiative it will need to gain the co-operation of teachers: this would be more likely to be forthcoming if they (not to mention the pupils, parents and local spokespeople) had more say than at present in precisely what skills and knowledge are to be assessed.

Innovations in the curriculum have sought to make the social-control function of urban schooling less constraining or perhaps less visible. The rise of pastoral care and the parallel, and not unrelated, rise of disruptive units (discussed in Chapter 6) probably fall into the category of disguising social control. Discipline structure in schools now follows the rhetoric of answering the child's 'individual needs'. Within the framework of pastoral care, non-conformity in schools usually implies deviance on the part of the pupil and potentially on the part of his/her family. A rather invasive social work pattern can then be adopted by teachers. The result of such a model is likely to intimidate parents and children even further from urban schools. It is surely incommensurate with the 'community' approach to the curriculum mentioned above. Where social workers or educational welfare offices are based in schools, as in many urban authorities, and where they perceive their role as working with families rather than as, for instance, bullying non-attenders back to school, there is a possibility that a positive relationship with parents may be retained. This is not however a substitute for the close positive working relations over education (that is as opposed to distant, negative relations over behaviour) that many urban primary schools have developed with parents by involving them in their child's education and indeed in the workings of the school.

Real innovations in social control have come with the relaxation of unnecessary rules and discipline rather than with the psychologisation of their enforcement. The self-styled community-school movement has again been responsible for innovations in this area. Abandoning unnecessary and difficult to defend rules concerning costume and demeanour has led to more relaxed attitudes between staff and pupils in some urban schools. This is of course helped by closer involvement of pupils and their parents in the work of the school. Relaxation of school rules in institutions that seek to retain authoritarian structures of personal relations and curriculum can, of course, lead to the kind of urban classroom situation with which the national press seem to be exclusively familiar. Significant change in this area is an essential prerequisite if urban schools are to be more than institutions for the propagation of ideology and social control. It is an issue that is firmly within the responsibility and capability of schools and teachers.

Education for a multicultural society

> We are dealing with the fact of racism: for most of us this is not something of our making. Yet we are all touched by it. We must confront all the possibilities and manifestations of racism, in ourselves, in our actions and in our institutions.
>
> (ILEA, 1983a)

In the preceding section we mentioned several institutions, particularly mother-tongue language teaching and supplementary schools, which form important components in education for a multicultural society. In this section we will look at curriculum developments in multicultural education and then at initiatives made not by schools and teachers but by local education authorities. In particular we will concentrate on one urban authority — the ILEA — which in 1983 launched a major initiative on equality in schooling and in particular on anti-racist teaching. While we are cautious of our London-centrism and are certainly aware of developments taking place elsewhere on this subject, there is perhaps no need to be apologetic in this instance. The ILEA's claim to be a pioneering and progressive education authority is often misplaced: its policies on major issues such as special education often seem to be stubbornly unenlightened. However, the initiative on inequality has become perhaps the authority's main item of policy, it has been seriously researched and thought through and it is being pressed upon schools with an almost unprecedented determination. It seems then to be reasonable to pay it due attention. In examining this policy of the ILEA, or indeed that of many of the other urban authorities that have developed planning on this subject, it would be a mistake to see it entirely as an instance of top-downward innovation. The curriculum developments that we go on to discuss largely preceded local-authority planning, so that it was innovation and in some cases pressure from teachers and schools that led to the wider policy developments in urban education systems.

International and multicultural studies have been developed in both primary and secondary schools. They can form a guiding principle for the design of curricula in almost any subject or group of integrated subjects. More commonly, a 'multicultural' principle informs the teaching of social studies, history, geography, English, religious education and modern languages. The idea of multicultural studies as a separate subject on the timetable risks placing it in a ghetto of isolation. It is better seen as a principle that can inform all teaching and curriculum planning. Characteristically, in a primary school, children may study the movements of people, money and commodities that made up the slave trade. They may see how this influenced capital accumulation and industrialisation in the UK. They may compare these historical phenomena with the present economic life of the Caribbean area and with more recent demographic movement. The music and writings of people in West Africa, the Caribbean and the cities of the UK would provide a source of stimulation and information. In a secondary school pupils might study the history, economics and culture of India from the Mogul invasion to the present day. The religions of the subcontinent could be given a positive treatment and linked to economic patterns, class and caste systems, the legacy of colonialism and present-day political conflicts. Again demographic movement and imperialism would be important aspects. A wealth of cultural material from Mogul miniatures to *The Chess Players*, from the Taj Mahal to *Midnight's Children*, would provide valuable resources. At this level pupils might be expected to begin to grasp some of the patterns and determinants of the international division of labour itself.

During the 1970s such curricula were developed by teachers and schools in urban areas. These developments were, in the main, encouraged and consolidated by local authorities. However, they became subject to criticism from at least three different angles. First, there were those who thought that schools should concentrate exclusively on British history, society and culture. This assimilationist position, now discredited, was discussed in Chapter 6. Secondly, there were those who thought that multicultural education provided an inferior curriculum of curries and steel bands for the black children while the white ones were encouraged to succeed in the traditional subjects which actually led to academic and professional success (Stone, 1981). While this argument highlights the rather naïve quality of some early work in multicultural education, it only remains valid where the curriculum is divided on (presumably covert) racial lines. Since the proponents of multicultural education would see it as an essential aspect of the education of all children — indeed, as we have repeatedly stressed, actually as necessary in rural areas as in cities — the criticism is somewhat tangential. Thirdly, there are those who suggested that multicultural education did not address the issues directly enough (Mullard, 1980). The issues, from this perspective, are neocolonialism in the Third World, racism in the cities of the UK and international patterns of domination and exploitation.

This argument is behind the current shift in emphasis from multicultural education to anti-racist teaching. The shift is evident in the ILEA policy initiative which we discuss below. There are however two difficulties with this argument. First, it risks throwing out the baby with the bath water: perhaps multicultural education has not gone far enough, but it has certainly gone a long way and it would be a pity to lose that progress. Secondly, the argument criticises the innovatory work of many teachers in urban schools without acknowledging the progress that they made; it therefore risks alienating and confusing all except those who are nimble-footed enough to shift from one band wagon to another.

The ILEA policy is contained in five documents (ILEA, 1983a, 1983b, 1983c, 1983d, 1983e) which are broadly titled *Race, Sex and Class* but which are pre-eminently concerned with what they call multi-ethnic education and anti-racist teaching. At the centre of the policy is an insistence on overt statements of disapproval of racism in educational institutions themselves:

> There will be:
> 1. A clear, unambiguous statement of opposition to any form of racist behaviour. . . .
> 2. A clear indication of what is not acceptable and the procedures, including sanctions, to deal with any transgressions (ILEA 1983d, p. 5).

Schools have interpreted this to mean racist abuse by pupils, parents or staff, the wearing of racist insignia, writing of graffiti, or distribution of racist literature or attempting to recruit people to racist organisations. The ILEA policy, however, makes it clear that attention is not only to be directed towards these offensive manifestations of racist behaviour. Rather, this is a necessary foundation for a form of education that recognises that racism can be structural as well as behavioural. The policy therefore addresses itself directly to countering those structural elements in schools that may operate in a racist way. Within the opposition to racism quoted above is a declaration of a positive policy which represents a commitment to all children in inner-London schools:

> There will be:
> 2. A firm expression of all pupils' or students' rights to the best possible education. . . .
> 4. An explanation of the way in which the school or college intends to develop practices which both tackle racism and create educational opportunities which make for a coherent society and a local school or college community in which diversity can flourish.
> 5. An outline of the measures by which development will be monitored and evaluated (ILEA, 1983d, p. 5).

The policy then is directed not only to eliminate overt racism in schools but to try to reverse those educational processes that operate in a racist way — that is, to the disadvantage of minority groups. How does this affect the nature of school knowledge to which those concerned with multicultural education had paid so much attention?

One element of this is mother-tongue teaching and here the ILEA policy is firm and courageous, especially in view of the fact that 147 languages are spoken in the authority's schools:

> (i) It is the right of all bilingual children to know their own mother tongue skills are recognised and valued in schools.
> (ii) It is educationally desirable that bilingual children in primary schools should be given the chance to learn to read and write their mother tongues and to extend their oral skills in these languages.
> (iii) It is educationally desirable that bilingual children in secondary schools should be given the chance to study the language of their home as a subject of the school curriculum and to gain appropriate examination qualifications (ILEA, 1983b, p. 17).

Indeed, the new initiative goes potentially much further than this in accepting, in principle, the right of children to be taught in their 'own language'. The idea seems to be that children should receive all their schooling in the language of their home. The practical difficulties put this well beyond the bounds of possibility and firmly in the realm of 'principle'.

At the wider level of the curriculum, the ILEA's policy does not seem to aspire to go any further than multicultural education. Indeed, it restates that curriculum in disappointingly general terms:

> (a) Very young children need both an affirmation of the value of people of all colours and cultures and to be helped towards avoidance of stereotypes and misrepresentations which form at a very early age.
> (b) A wide range of content is important but it is essential that pupils develop analytical skills and can engage in an understanding of cross cultural perspectives and values.
> (c) Pupils and students must have opportunities to gain an historical perspective that is free from ethnocentric biases (ILEA, 1983d, p. 7).

Why only history? Surely it is possible to have ethnocentric perspectives on maths, science and literature too. The policy here seems to be actually abandoning ground won by the multicultural innovations — see, for instance, the stimulating inclusion of Maya number systems in ILEA's own SMILE maths scheme. One might have expected the policy to suggest that the curriculum addressed racism directly, say, by studying prejudices in UK cities or by looking at the forces that lead Anatolian peoples to go and live and work in the Federal Republic of Germany and Switzerland and how they are treated there. The final curriculum suggestion in the policy is patently absurd. In view of the ILEA's entrenched policy of segregating children into special schools and units on the basis of their perceived intelligence and behaviour (as discussed in Chapter 6), one can only read with irony that 'The whole curriculum must be open to all so that no sort of restricted access is given to some pupils because of stereotyped views of ability' (ILEA, 1983d, p. 7).

One aspect of ILEA's policy that indicated a radically innovatory nature is the insistence that in drawing up anti-racist statements, discussions should involve *all* members of staff. 'This programme will need to involve each member of the teaching and non-teaching staff and will need to see the allocation of specific roles and tasks to individuals or groups' (ILEA, 1983c, p. 3). Ancillary workers, cooks, lunchtime supervisors, caretaking staff all come into contact with children. It is essential that they are included in formulating anti-racist policy so that they can collaborate in its implementation. Furthermore, many of these workers may themselves be black; they may indeed be the only black workers in the school. This would mean that they will probably have more tangible experience of racism to bring to the discussions than the teachers themselves. If racist abuse and the use of carelessly racist language is to be prevented in the corridors, playgrounds and dining rooms as well as in the classroom, the close involvement of all workers in the school is essential. All this is clear and practical enough — the radical nature of the proposal is the idea that non-teaching staff might actually have anything valuable to say about education. Yet, if the kind of involvement of adults in the policy and work of schools (discussed above) is to be anything more than a cosmetic appeal to 'community', surely non-teaching staff are among the first groups who could validly join in such collaboration. Who knows, one day such a revolutionary approach might end up with all the workers in a school using the same staff room.

One of the most controversial aspects of the new ILEA policy is the firmness with which schools are being instructed to carry it out. Dates have been set by which governors and staff must prepare policy documents and anti-racist statements, review existing arrangements and curriculum policies, produce a timetable for change and make progress reports. These hurdles are not merely being monitored by the governors but by the Authority's officers. To this extent the policy is fiercely top-downwards. In many ways this makes it exceptional in educational policy in the UK. Such policy, whether at national or local level, is usually *enabling* — that is, it allows authorities, schools or teachers to make initiatives if they so wish, rather than *enforcing*, that is, insisting that specific policies be implemented in a particular way by a set date. The unusually enforcing nature of the ILEA policy has led to some resistance among teachers and heads. Of course a lot of this resistance comes from those who might not feel too enthusiastic about anti-racist education anyway, from those who resist any initiative because it might involve stressful change and work and from those who complacently assume that their existing arrangements cannot be improved on. The autonomy of headteachers to miseducate children in spite of directives from the elected representatives hardly seems a flag to which many will flock. However, there is perhaps some danger in rigidly specific directives: our own enthusiasms for the insistence that the Authority has shown that its policy be implemented might be considerably muted, for instance, if it were a pro-racist policy.

The education of children perceived to have special needs

> . . . we have made very clear our determined opposition to the notion of treating handicapped and non-handicapped children as forming two distinctive groups, for whom separate educational provision has to be made. It follows that we wholeheartedly support the principle of the development of common provision for all children.
>
> (Warnock, *et al.*, 1978)

Innovations concerning the education of children perceived to have special needs mainly concern ways of educating them alongside their peers in mainstream schools without segregation or stigmatisation. Teachers, schools and local authorities were developing ways of integrating handicapped children and of furthering contacts between mainstream and special schools before the 1981 Act and they continue to do so. Manchester has increased its support services; Sheffield has transferred some of its special-school teachers to a peripatetic role in mainstream schools; in Calderdale and the East End of London attempts have been made to use support teams working in ordinary schools — primary and secondary — to help prevent classroom disruption as an alternative to sin bins; Derbyshire integrates even severely handicapped pupils into its comprehensive system. Developments include the provision of resource centres, peripatetic teachers, special departments for the physically handicapped or hearing impaired, and close links between special schools and mainstream schools. However, these innovations remain sporadic and piecemeal. Indeed some authorities now have more children in special schools they they did before the 1981 Act. In ILEA, against a national average of 1.8 per cent of pupils in special schools, there has been a rise from 2.8 per cent in 1980 to 2.9 per cent in 1983. This rise is partly the result, however, of the increase in provision of special units attached to ordinary schools.

The effect of the 1981 Act and its implementation in 1983, then, does not seem to have been as definite an impetus in the direction of integration as many people had hoped. This is perhaps because, following the distinction made in the preceding section, it is enabling legislation rather than enforcing legislation; thus, authorities that already have investment in terms of plant, personnel and prestige in segregated provision are free to retain this using the get-out clauses of the Act. (These say that integration need not be implemented if it would either cost too much, not be to the benefit of the individual child, or interfere with the education of children in mainstream classrooms. Thus they are fairly wide categories of exclusion.) Initiatives tend to depend on individual schools, teachers or advisers having some commitment to integration and using the Act as a legitimation.

In some respects the 1981 Act seems almost to have made things worse. The Act does make explicit (enforcing) demands for paperwork in terms of written statements for children currently receiving special education and those being assessed. The Act:

> has a voracious appetite for paper in all forms. It takes a long time to goad into action and it needs far too many educational psychologists, teachers and administrators and other staff to keep it up to scratch (Peter, 1984, p. 35).

The extra staff being employed by local authorities often consist of educational psychologists, advisers and administrative staff: these may well function to preserve segregation rather than to erode it. The urban authorities mentioned above as having made significant innovations, had concentrated on employing teachers, either in mainstream schools or in peripatetic teams. It may be that one of the effects of the Act will be to have more educational psychologists filling in more forms about more pupils rather than to break down segregated provision. If anything, this is likely to perpetuate the ideologies discussed in Chapter 6 rather than to undermine them. Thus some commentators have concluded that the Act is distinctly unhelpful:

> The majority of LEAs who have no clear policy on integration or wish to avoid the issue altogether will be under no pressure from the Act to do otherwise. A recent survey of LEAs shows that the majority do not envisage any changes in their existing segregationist policies but that implementation of the Act is being confined to questions of assessment and the role of professionals (Bookbinder, 1984, p. 9).

Despite the imaginative innovations mentioned above, then:

too few LEAs show signs of long-term, systematic and wide scale planning
to accommodate more pupils in the mainstream (especially the disruptive
ones) (Peter, 1984, p. 25).

Perhaps it is a question here of whether we perceive the bottle to be
half full or half empty. The pessimist might dismiss the 1981 Act as a
failure because it was not sufficiently enforcing with regard to integration and because it is highly unlikely that there will be another
opportunity for legislation on special education within this century.
The optimist might say that given the relative autonomy of schools
from the state, enabling legislation was precisely what was required.
Within this framework schools and teachers will be free to experiment
with a range of different forms of integration, developing whatever is
best suited to the needs of their area and its patterns of mainstream
provision. It is then a matter of persuading local authorities, heads and
teachers of the benefits of integration: they will then gradually develop
that innovatory provision that will be all the more 'long-term, systematic and wide ranging' for having been locally generated and not
centrally enforced.

While perhaps tending more towards the pessimistic side of this
argument, we would stress that it is precisely within the area of
persuasion that innovations have been the most widespread. What the
Warnock Report and the 1981 Act have done is to put special education
on the agenda for most teachers. There is now much more discussion of
these issues at local level; special education has more prominence in
the initial training of teachers; it is much more likely to be included in
in-service courses. A notable example is the Open University's course
on *Special Needs in Education* (E241). This course is passionately
integrationist and it makes its arguments from a wealth of positions —
psychological, sociological, comparative, historical and medical. It is
written with the depth and clarity characteristic of the Open University's work on education. Given that it is a deservedly popular course, it
may well play its part along with other courses and discussion in the job
of persuasion — which is apparently necessary if the 1981 Act is to be
implemented in a meaningful way. The opportunity for teacher innovation in urban schools can most readily be taken on this issue.

School and work

The major top-downward initiatives of the MSC with regard to school
and work have been discussed in detail in Chapter 7. In many ways
these could be seen as an example of the point at which the relative

autonomy of teachers, schools and local education authorities is called to account. The influence of the economic base over the political superstructure can be shown in the formation of a new state agency to serve more effectively those needs for a narrowly skilled and disciplined workforce that were not being met by schools. The state in turn emphasised the limits of the relative autonomy of educational institutions and professionals by creating a new agency, replacing some of their main functions, to implement the policy of narrow vocationalism. The limits to the relative autonomy of schools have been made clear in this important area.

This is not to say that there is any inherent opposition between the aims of schools and those of the MSC. Where the MSC has been able to offer schools extra money to implement its policies, as in the case of TVEI (Technical and Vocational Education Initiative), they have flocked to take it. (This scheme offers selected local education authorities additional funding to set up technical curricula for the 14 to 16 age range. The money is often spent on expensive equipment. Some of these courses have provided interesting innovations, but a main difficulty seems to be that they tend to reinforce rather than undermine gender stereotyping.) The aims of the MSC, then, are probably not in conflict with the function of schools in urban areas — to reproduce a skilled, ideologised and stratified workforce — they are simply stated more overtly and clearly.

However, other initiatives are taking place in urban schools apart from those under the aegis of MSC. The gradual evolution of the new sixth form is an important example. Many schools and colleges have developed a flexibility in their curriculum options for post-compulsory pupils which allows for technical and vocational courses to be studied alongside the more traditional academic ones. Thus in many urban schools pupils studying for City and Guilds or BTEC qualifications are working alongside those taking 'A' levels. This allows for some flexibility in terms of subject options in that additional CSEs or 'O' levels, for example, may be taken at the same time as a vocational course. It also has the advantage of retaining a broad social mix at the upper end of schooling which previously has been dominated by the needs of those young people destined for college or university. The development of this comprehensive sixth form, which could clearly be located in a college of further education or a sixth-form college as easily as in a school, has been hampered by the Secretary of State's partiality for 'schools of proven worth'. When urban education authorities are reorganising they have often, as in the case of Manchester, attempted to set up a comprehensive 16 to 19 provision. However, this has frequently come into conflict with traditional, often grammar or ex-grammar, schools which have flourishing sixth forms of the pre-university model. These schools are frequently popular with middle-class parents who have therefore opposed the reorganisation proposals. In such cases the Secretary of State has insisted that schools with traditional sixth forms be preserved. This has resulted in some creaming off of pupils from the otherwise comprehensive provision. As mentioned in Chapter 7, a tripartite system now exists at 16-plus and is likely to be further reinforced by the development of 'a new 17-plus national certificate based on a year of "vocational exploration" and broad general education' (*Times Educational Supplement*, 11 May 1984) — the Certificate of Pre-Vocational Education (CPVE). Despite the suggestion that this new course would be aimed at a wider range of sixth formers, it is unlikely that it would be taken up by traditional 'A' level students.

Again it is in the area of curriculum that most autonomy is open to urban schools and teachers. Possibilities in this area have already been mentioned. The important innovations seem to be coming from those schools that are putting unemployment firmly on the curriculum (Watts, 1983). Where children are taught about national and international patterns of unemployment, what policies can be adopted to increase unemployment or to diminish it, there is less likelihood of them placing the blame on themselves rather than on economic structures.

It is perhaps to the distinction between what we call *vocationalist* (i.e. reproductive of the stratified workforce) and truly *vocational* education that attention should be drawn. The term vocational has become debased over the years so that it now has the sole connotation of manual work. Vocational education (or training) is for the masses — even when there are few 'vocations' that can actually be followed in practice. The term today has little relevance for the classical vocations: the church, the law, medicine, and so on. Yet a truly vocational education would be one that was applicable to all young people. The ideological divide between education and training would disappear as the vocational dimension gained greater importance in relation to the curriculum. In this respect we need to look beyond the taken-for-granted assumptions relating to the highly stratified occupational structure of capitalist society.

Consequently, we should begin to consider radical initiatives in this area that seek to break down the barriers between schooling and work. The present system merely perpetuates the quest for qualifications — whether in the form of the standard GCE/CSE certificates or in the form of YTS 'profile' certificates. These qualifications are themselves ranked into a stratified order, where some gain entry to jobs while

others simply remain as unsold, unmarketable goods. Such credentialism can neither create employment nor lead to any kind of understanding as to why unemployment exists and continues to grow. More
positively, a curriculum that incorporates a fundamental examination
of work in relation to both individuals and society would offer an
alternative basis for urban schooling. In this way, we might be able to
move away from the alienating and class-divided examination system
as it now exists, and away from statised management of unemployment
which masquerades as vocational training. In short, YTS, TVEI and
CPVE on the one hand and credentialism on the other would give way
to what some educationists would see as a *polytechnical* curriculum — a
curriculum that involved all young people in a school–work relationship.

At the same time, there would be a need to break down the elitist
conception of post-16 secondary education. The comprehensive sixth
form that has already been mentioned, in which there is a broad
mainstream education based upon the development of critical awareness, can in principle provide a buttress against the reproduction of the
social division of labour. It none the less demands not merely the
re-establishment of progressive traditions that prevailed during the
1960s, against the current reactionary trends of academic elitism for
the few and statised vocationalism for the masses, but much more, a
significant move towards a radically reconstructed urban education
system. Such a system must incorporate new institutional practices
anticipating a society in which political power and material resources
might undergo a fundamental redistribution.

GUIDE TO FURTHER READING

A helpful account of developments in community education is that
edited by Fletcher and Thompson (1980), *Issues in Community Education*. Hargreaves *et al.* (1984), *Improving Secondary Schools*, had
considerable implications for secondary school curricula and organisation. The ILEA policy documents (1983a, 1983b, 1983c, 1983d, 1983e)
provide guidelines for anti-racist teaching. Recent developments in
integrating children perceived to have special needs are described in
Booth and Potts (eds) (1983), *Integrating Special Education*. Watts
(1983), *Education, Unemployment and the Future of Work*, includes
fascinating details of how some schools are facing up to the issue of
youth unemployment.

Bibliography

AFFOR (1982) *Talking Chalk: Black Pupils, Parents and Teachers Speak About It*. Birminham: AFFOR.

Althusser, L. (1971) Ideology and ideological state apparatuses, in Cosin (ed.) (1972).

Apple, M.W. (1979) *Ideology and Curriculum*. London: Routledge and Kegan Paul.

Apple, M.W. (1982) *Education and Power*. London: Routledge and Kegan Paul.

Barton, L. *et al.* (eds) (1980) *Schooling, Ideology and the Curriculum*. Lewes: Falmer Press.

Barton, L. and Tomlinson, S. (eds) (1981) *Special Education: Policy, Practices and Social Issues*. London: Harper & Row.

Barton, L. and Walker, S. (eds) (1983) *Race, Class and Education*. London: Croom Helm.

Baylis, T. (1984) Jumping the sex hurdles, *Times Educational Supplement*, **3534**, 23 March 1984, p. 18.

Beck, J. *et al.* (eds) (1976) *Worlds Apart*. London: Collier Macmillan.

Bennett, N. (1976) *Teaching Styles and Pupil Progress*. London: Open Books.

Berger, M. (1979) Behaviour models in education and professional practice: the dangers of mindless technology, *Bulletin British Psychological Society*, **32**, November 1979, pp. 418–19.

Blowers, A. *et al.* (eds) (1982) *Urban Change and Conflict: An Interdisciplinary Reader*. London: Harper & Row.

Blunden, G. (1983) Typing in the tech: domesticity, ideology and women's place in further education, in Gleeson (ed.) (1983).

Bookbinder, G. (1984) Ambiguities and contradictions in the 1981 Education Act (England and Wales), in Swann, W. *et al.*, *The New Laws on Special Education*. Milton Keynes: Open University Press.

Booth, C. (1896) *Life and Labour of the People in London*. London: Macmillan.

Booth, T. (1982) *Special Biographies*. Milton Keynes: Open University.

Booth, T. and Potts, P. (eds) (1983) *Integrating Special Education*. Oxford: Basil Blackwell.

Booth, T. and Statham, J. (eds) (1982) *The Nature of Special Education: People, Places and Change*. London: Croom Helm.

Bowles, S. and Gintis, H. (1976) *Schooling in Capitalist America*. London: Routledge & Kegan Paul.

Bowman, I. (1982) Maladjustment: a history of the category, in Swann (ed.) (1982).

Braham, P. (1977) Immigrants and inequality, in Block II *Inequality in the City*, Course E361, Education in the Urban Environment. Milton Keynes: Open University.

Braverman, H. (1974) *Labour and Monopoly Capital*. New York: Monthly Review Press.

Burgess, E.W. (1925) The growth of the city, in Raynor and Harris (eds) (1977a).

Central Advisory Council (CACE) (1967) *Children and Their Primary Schools* (The Plowden Report). London: HMSO.

Carby, H. (1982) Schooling in Babylon, in CCCS (1982).

Carter, H. (1981) *The Study of Urban Geography*. London: Edward Arnold.

Castells, M. (1976a) Theoretical propositions for an experimental study of urban social movements, in Pickvance (ed.) (1976).

Castells, M. (1976b) Is there an urban sociology? in Pickvance (ed.) (1976).

Castells, M. (1976c) Theory and ideology in urban sociology, in Pickvance (ed.) (1976).

Castells, M. (1977) *The Urban Question: A Marxist Approach*. London: Edward Arnold.

Castells, M. (1978) *City, Class and Power*. London: Macmillan.

Castells, M. (1980) *The Economic Crisis and American Society*. Oxford: Basil Blackwell.

Castells, M. (1983) *The City and the Grassroots*. London: Edward Arnold.

CCCS (Centre for Contemporary Cultural Studies) (1982) *The Empire Strikes Back*. London: Hutchinson.

Central Advisory Council for Education (CACE) (1963) *Half our Future* (The Newsom Report). London: HMSO.

Coard, B. (1971) *How the West Indian Child is Made Educationally Sub-Normal in the British School System*. London: New Beacon Books.

Coates, K. and Silburn, R. (1970) *Poverty: The Forgotten Englishmen*. Harmondsworth: Penguin.

Commission of the European Communities (1984) *Report from the Commission to the Council on the Implementation of Directive 77/486/EEC on the Education of the Children of Migrant Workers*. Brussels: CEC.

Cosin, B.R. *et al.* (eds) (1971) *School and Society*. Milton Keynes: Open University.

Cosin, B.R. (ed.) (1972) *Education, Structure and Society*. Harmondsworth: Penguin.

Coulby, D. (1981) Disruption in the urban classroom: a model and a long-term evaluation of an innovatory response, MA thesis, University of London.

Dale, R. *et al.* (eds) (1981a) *Schooling and the National Interest*. Lewes: Falmer Press.

Dale, R. *et al.* (eds) (1981b) *Politics, Patriarchy and Practice*. Lewes: Falmer Press.

Dale, R. (1982) Education and the capitalist state: contributions and contradictions, in Apple (ed.) (1982).

Daniels, W. (1968) *Racial Discrimination in England*. Harmondsworth: Penguin.

Davies, B. (1976) *Social Control and Education*. London: Methuen.

DES (Department of Education and Science) (1981) *West Indian Children in Our Schools. Interim Report of the Committee of Enquiry into the Education of Children from Ethnic Minority Groups* (The Rampton Report). Cmnd. 8273. London: HMSO.

DoE (Department of the Environment) (1977) *Inner Area Studies: Liverpool, Birmingham and Lambeth: Summaries of Consultants Final Reports*. London: HMSO.

Dumont, R.V. and Wax, M.L. (1971) Cherokee School Society and the intercultural classroom, in Cosin *et al.* (eds) (1971).

Durkheim, E. (1956) *Education and Sociology*. New York: Free Press.

Edwards, V. (1983) *Language in Multicultural Classrooms*. London: Batsford.

Engels, F. (1969) *The Condition of the Working Class in England*. London: Granada (first published in English 1892).

Erikson, E.H. (1965) *Childhood and Society*. Harmondsworth: Penguin.

Evans, B. and Waites, B. (1981) *IQ and Mental Testing*. London: Macmillan.

FEU (1979) *A Basis for Choice*. London: FEU.

FEU (1980) *Developing Social and Life Skills*. London: FEU.

Field, F. (ed.) (1977) *Education and the Urban Crisis*. London: Routledge & Kegan Paul.

Fishman, W. (1979; 4th impression 1983) *The Streets of East London*. London: Duckworth.

Fletcher, C. and Thompson, N. (eds) (1980) *Issues in Community Education*. Lewes: Falmer Press.

Foot, P. (1965) *Immigration and Race in British Politics*. Harmondsworth: Penguin.

Friend, A. and Metcalf, A. (1981) *Slump City*. London: Pluto Press.

Fuller, M. (1983) Qualified criticism, critical qualifications, in Barton and Walker (ed.) (1983).

Gans, H.J. (1977) Urbanism and suburbanism as a way of life, in Raynor and Harris (ed.) (1977a).

Gibb, V. (1983) The re-creation and perpetuation of the secretarial myth, in Gleeson (ed.) (1983).

Giddens, A. (1981) *A Contemporary Critique of Historical Materialism*. London: Macmillan.

GLC Economic Policy Group (1983) *Jobs for a Change*. London: GLC.

Gleeson, D. (ed.) (1983) *Youth Training and the Search for Work*. London: Routledge & Kegan Paul.

Gordon, P. and Lawton, D. (1978) *Curriculum Change in the Nineteenth and Twentieth Centuries*. London: Hodder & Stoughton.

Grace, G. (1978) *Teachers, Ideology and Control: A Study in Urban Education*. London: Routledge & Kegan Paul.

Grace, G. (ed.) (1984) *Education and the City: Theory, History and Contemporary Practice*. London: Routledge & Kegan Paul.

Greenlee, S. (1975) *Ammunition*. London: Bogle-L'Ouverture Publications.

Hall, A.J. (1983) Cultural diversity and the urban Catholic primary school, MA dissertation. London Institute of Education.

Hall, P. *et al.* (1973) *The Containment of Urban England*. London: George Allen & Unwin.

Hall, S. (1977) Education and the crisis of the urban school, in Raynor and Harris (ed.) (1977a).

Hall, S. and Jefferson, T. (eds) (1976) *Resistance Through Rituals*. London: Hutchinson.

Halsey, A.H. (1972) *Educational Priority, Vol. 1. EPA Problems and Policies*. London: HMSO.

Halsey, A.H. *et al.* (1980) *Origins and Destinations*. Oxford: OUP.

Hargreaves, D.H. *et al.* (1975) *Deviance in Classrooms*. London: Routledge & Kegan Paul

Hargreaves, D.H. (1982) *The Challenge for the Comprehensive School: Culture, Curriculum and Community*. London: Routledge & Kegan Paul.

Hargreaves, D.H. *et al.* (1984) *Improving Secondary Schools*. London: ILEA.

Harrison, P. (1983) *Inside the Inner City: Life Under the Cutting Edge*. Harmondsworth: Penguin.

Harvey, D. (1973) *Social Justice and the City*. London: Edward Arnold.

Hayes, C. *et al.* (1983) YTS and training for skill ownership, *Employment Gazette*, August 1983, pp. 344–8.

Hegarty, S. *et al.* (1981) *Educating Pupils with Special Needs in the Ordinary School*. Windsor: NFER Nelson.

HMI (1978) *Behavioural Units: A Survey of Special Units for Pupils with Behavioural Problems*. London: DES.

Home Affairs Committee (1981) *Report from the Home Affairs Committee, Session 1980–1*. London: HMSO.

Home Office (1981) *The Brixton Disorders* (The Scarman Report). London: HMSO.

Horne, J. (1983) Dole schools, *New Society*, 1 September 1983, pp. 319–20.

ILEA (1977) *The Development and Future of the Authority*. London: ILEA.

ILEA (1983a) *Race, Sex and Class: 1. Achievement in Schools*. London: ILEA.

ILEA (1983b) *Race, Sex and Class: 2. Multi-Ethnic Education in Schools*. London: ILEA.

ILEA (1983c) *Race, Sex and Class: 3. A Policy for Equality: Race*. London: ILEA.

ILEA (1983d) *Race, Sex and Class: 4. Anti-Racist Statement and Guidelines*. London: ILEA.

ILEA (1983e) *Race, Sex and Class: 5. Multi-Ethnic Education in Further, Higher and Community Education*. London: ILEA.

ILEA (1983f) *Delivery of the Authority's Initiative on Multi-Ethnic Education in Schools*. London: ILEA.

Ingleby, D. (1976) The psychology of child psychology, in Dale *et al.* (eds) (1981b).

Jeffcoate, R. and Mayor, B. (1982) *Bedford: Portrait of a Multi-Ethnic Town*. Milton Keynes: Open University.

Jensen, A.R. (1969) How much can we boost I.Q. and scholastic achievement? *Harvard Educational Review*, **39**.

Jones, C. and Kimberley, K. (1982) Educational responses to racism, in Tierney (ed.) (1982).

Jones, C. and Klein, G. (1980) *Assessing Children's Books in a Multi-Ethnic Society*. London: ILEA.

Kamin, L.J. (1974) *The Science and Politics of I.Q.* New York: John Wiley.

Karabel, J. and Halsey, A.H. (eds) (1977) *Power and Ideology in Education*. New York: OUP.

Knox, P. (1982) *Urban Social Geography: An Introduction*. London: Longman.

Kramer, S. (1953) *History Begins at Sumer*. London: Thames & Hudson.

Labov, W. (1969) The logic of non-standard English, *Georgetown Monographs on Language and Linguistics*, **22**, pp. 1–31.

Lawson, J. and Silver, H. (1973) *A Social History of Education in England*. London: Methuen.

Leach, D.J. and Raybould, E.C. (1979) *Learning and Behaviour Difficulties in Schools*. London: Open Books.

Lees, L.H. (1979) *Exiles of Erin*. Manchester: Manchester University Press.

Linguistic Minorities Project (1983a) *Short Report of the Linguistic Minorities Project*. London: London Institute of Education.

Linguistic Minorities Project (1983b) *Linguistic Minorities in Britain*. London: London Institute of Education.

Lynch, J. (1983) *The Multicultural Curriculum*. London: Batsford.

Maclure, J.S. (1965) *Educational Documents England and Wales 1816–1963*. London: Methuen.

Mayhew, H. (1861) *London Labour and the London Poor*. London.

Miller, H.L. (1978) *Social Foundations of Education*. New York: Holt, Rinehart and Winston.

Miller, H.L. and Woock, R. (1970) *Social Foundations of Education*. Hirsdale: Dryden Press.

Milner, D. (1975) *Children and Race*. Harmondsworth: Penguin.

Milner, D. (1983) *Children and Race: Ten Years On*. London: Heinemann.

Manpower Services Commission (MSC) (1981) *A New Training Initiative*. London: MSC.

Mullard, C. (1980) *Racism in Society and Schools: History, Policy and Practice*. London: University of London Institute of Education.

Mullard, C. (1983) The racial code: its features, rules and change, in Barton and Walker (eds) (1983).

Navitt, M. (1979) *Unregistered Unemployment*. London: Youthaid.

New Training Initiative (NTI) (1981) *A Consultative Document*. London: MSC.

Newsom Report (1963) See Central Advisory Council for Education (1963).

Open University (1973) *Urban Education*, Course E351. Milton Keynes: Open University.

Open University (1977) *Education and the Urban Environment*, Course E361. Milton Keynes: Open University.

Open University (1981) *Society, Education and the State*, Course E353. Milton Keynes: Open University.

Open University (1982) *Ethnic Minorities and Community Relations*. Milton Keynes: Open University.

Pahl, R.E. (ed.) (1968) *Readings in Urban Sociology*. London: Pergamon.

Pahl, R.E. (1975) *Whose City?* Harmondsworth: Penguin.

Park, R., Burgess, E. and McKenzie, R. (eds) (1967) *The City*. Chicago: University of Chicago Press.

Parsons, C. (1978) *Schools in an Urban Community: A Study of Canbrook, 1870–1965*. London: Routledge & Kegan Paul.

Patrick, J. (1973) *A Glasgow Gang Observed*. London: Eyre Methuen.

Peach, C. (1968) *West Indian Migration to Britain*. London: OUP.

Peter, M. (1984) A hard act to follow, *Times Educational Supplement*, 3535, 30 March 1984, p. 25.

Pickvance, C.G. (ed.) (1976) *Urban Sociology: Critical Essays*. London: Tavistock.

Plowden Report (1967). See CACE (1967).

Potts, P. (1982) *The Professionals*. Milton Keynes. Open University.

Poulantzas, N. (1978) *Classes in Contemporary Capitalism*. London: Verso.

Pryce, K. (1979) *Endless Pressure*. Harmondsworth: Penguin.

Raban, J. (1975) *The Soft City*. Glasgow: Fontana.

Raggatt, P. and Evans, M. (eds) (1977) *The Political Context*. London: Ward Lock.

Raynor, J. and Harris, E. (eds) (1977a) *The City Experience*. London: Ward Lock.

Raynor, J. and Harris, E. (eds) (1977b) *Schooling in the City*. London: Ward Lock.

Reeder, D. (ed.) (1977) *Urban Education in the Nineteenth Century*. London: Taylor & Francis.

Reiss, A.J. (1964) *Louis Wirth on Cities and Social Life*. London: University of Chicago.

Rex, J. and Moore, R. (1967) *Race, Community and Conflict: A Study of Sparkbrook*. London: OUP.

Robins, D. and Cohen, P. (1978) *Knuckle Sandwich: Growing Up in the Working Class City*. Harmondsworth: Penguin.

Rose, D. (1983) Thatcher's secret unemployment plans, *Time Out*, 20–26 May, pp. 5–7.

Rothstein, A. (1966) *A House on Clerkenwell Green*. London: Lawrence & Wishart.

Runnymede Trust and Radical Statistics Group (1980) *Britain's Black Population*. London: Heinemann.

Rutter, M. *et al*. (1979) *Fifteen Thousand Hours*. London: Open Books.

Saunders, P. (1979) *Urban Politics: A Sociological Interpretation*. Harmondsworth: Penguin.

Saunders, P. (1981) *Social Theory and the Urban Question*. London: Hutchinson.

Select Committee on Race Relations and Immigration (1977) *Report with Minutes of Proceedings and Appendices to Report, Session 1976–7*. London: HMSO.

Sharp, R. and Green, A. (1975) *Education and Social Control: A Study in Progressive Primary Education*. London: Routledge & Kegan Paul.

Simon, B. (1960) *Studies in the History of Education, 1780–1870*. London: Lawrence & Wishart.

Simon, B. (1965) *Education and the Labour Movement 1870—1920*. London: Lawrence and Wishart.

Simon, B. (1971) *Intelligence, Psychology and Education: A Marxist Critique*. London: Lawrence and Wishart.

Smith, D. (1977) *Racial Disadvantage in Britain*. Harmondsworth: Penguin.

SSEG (Socialist Society's Education Group) (1983) *The Youth Training Scheme: A Strategy for the Labour Movement*. London: Socialist Society.

Stewart, M. (ed.) (1972) *The City: Problems of Planning*. Harmondsworth: Penguin.

Stone, M. (1981) *The Education of the Black Child in Britain: The Myth of Multicultural Education*. Glasgow: Fontana.

Street-Porter, R. (1977) Race, children and cities, Block V of Course E361 *Education and the Urban Environment*. Milton Keynes: Open University.

Sutton, A. (1981) The social role of educational psychology in the definition of educational subnormality, in Barton and Tomlinson (ed.) (1981).

Sutton, A. (1982) *The Powers that Be*. Milton Keynes: Open University.

Swann, W. (ed.) (1981) *The Practice of Special Education*. London: Basil Blackwell.

Swann, W. (1982) *A Special Curriculum?* Milton Keynes: Open University.

Swann, W. (1985) Is the integration of children with special needs happening? An analysis of recent statistics of pupils in special schools, *Oxford Review of Education*, **11**(1).

Tarrant, G. (1982) Method for problem readers, *ILEA Contact*, 25 June 1982.

Taylor, M. (1981) *Caught Between*. Windsor: NFER.

Tierney, J. (ed.) (1982) *Race, Migration and Schooling*. London: Holt, Rinehart and Winston.

Tizard, J. (1973) Maladjusted children and the Child Guidance Service, *London Educational Review*, summer 1973.

Tomlinson, S. (1981) *Educational Subnormality — A Study in Decision Making*. London: Routledge & Kegan Paul.

Tomlinson, S. (1982) *A Sociology of Special Education*. London: Routledge & Kegan Paul.

Tönnies, F. (1955) *Community and Association*. London: Routledge & Kegan Paul.

Townsend, H. and Brittan, E.M. (1972) *Organisation in Multiracial Schools*. Slough: NFER.

Tyack, D.B. (1974) *The One Best System*. London: Harvard University Press.

United Nations (1955) *Demographic Year Book, 1952*, New York: United Nations.

Van Den Berghe, P.L. (1967) Race and Racism. New York: John Wiley.

Waller, W. (1932) *The Sociology of Teaching*. New York: John Wiley.

Warnock, H.M. *et al.* (1978) *Special Educational Needs (The Warnock Report)*. London: HMSO .

Watts, A.G. (1983) *Education, Unemployment and Future of Work*. Milton Keynes: Open University.

Weber, M. (1958) *The City*. London: Macmillan.

Weinstock, A. (1976) I blame the teachers, *Times Educational Supplement*, 23 January 1976, p. 2.

White, R. and Brockington, D. (1983) *Tales Out of School: Consumers' Views of British Education*. London: Routledge & Kegan Paul.

Willis, P. (1977) *Learning to Labour*. Farnborough: Saxon House.

Willis, P. (1983) Cultural production and theories of reproduction, Barton and Walker (eds) (1983).

Wirth, L. (1938) Urbanism as a way of life, in Reiss (1964).

Wright, N. (1977) *Progress in Education*. London: Croom Helm.

Youth Task Group (1982) *Report*. London: MSC.

(YTS) Youth Training Scheme (1982) *A Handbook for Managing Agents*. London: MSC.

(YTS) Youth Training Scheme (1983) *Guide to Managing Agents*. London: MSC.

Index